PLARYERS

The Story of Sports and Money,
and the Visionaries Who Fought
to Create a Revolution

Matthew
Futterman

SIMON & SCHUSTER
New York Toronto London Sydney New Delhi

Simon & Schuster
1230 Avenue of the Americas
New York, NY 10020

First Simon & Schuster hardcover edition April 2016

SIMON & SCHUSTER and colophon are registered trademarks
of Simon & Schuster, Inc.

For information about special discounts for bulk purchases,
please contact Simon & Schuster Special Sales at 1-866-506-1949
or business@simonandschuster.com.

The Simon & Schuster Speakers Bureau can bring authors to
your live event. For more information or to book an event,
contact the Simon & Schuster Speakers Bureau at 1-866-248-3049
or visit our website at www.simonspeakers.com.

Interior design by Lewelin Polanco

Manufactured in the United States of America

1 3 5 7 9 10 8 6 4 2

Library of Congress Cataloging-in-Publication Data
Futterman, Matthew.
Players : the story of sports and money—and the visionaries who fought to
create a revolution / by Matthew Futterman.
pages cm
Includes bibliographical references and index.
1. Sports—Economic aspects. 2. Athletes—Salaries, etc.—United States. I. Title.
GV716.F87 2016
338.47796—dc23
2015025635

ISBN 978-1-4767-1695-4
ISBN 978-1-4767-1697-8 (ebook)

For Amy

You've got to get to the stage in life where going for it is more important than winning or losing.

—ARTHUR ASHE, Tennis Champion;

Civil Rights Activist

PLAYERS

Introduction

After graduating from the US Naval Academy at Annapolis, Maryland, where he won the Heisman Trophy, Roger Staubach served the four years in the Navy that came with a diploma from the academy. Then, in 1969, the man who had been college football's best player joined the Dallas Cowboys. He took over as the starting quarterback in 1971, but Staubach may have made his smartest move in 1970, when he began selling commercial real estate in the off-season for the firm of Henry S. Miller. He continued to spend his off-seasons hawking office space throughout his career. In 1977, two years before he retired, he launched his own commercial real estate firm.

Staubach didn't begin showing Dallas-area office and warehouse space in the early 1970s because he loved the business or planned eventually to become a property mogul and launch his own company. He did it because he had a young family and he needed the money. In 1971 his job as the starting quarterback of the Dallas

Cowboys paid him a whopping $25,000, about the same salary as a mid-level lawyer in the US Department of State at the time. I know this because my father was an assistant legal advisor in the State Department in 1971, and he was being paid slightly more than the starting quarterback for the Dallas Cowboys. Today the assistant legal counsel in the State Department makes about $80,000 a year. Tony Romo, the Dallas Cowboys' starting quarterback, is currently playing under a six-year contract worth $108 million.

Roger Staubach bears no bitterness. In 2008 he sold his eponymous real estate company for $613 million. Still, comparing his football existence and Tony Romo's leads to one very simple conclusion: in the span of a generation, everything about the sports business changed. And the changes touched even the people who connected with sports in the most innocent ways. This book is about the people behind the series of events—many of which began as happy accidents—that created the modern world of sports. In this world money determines everything from who plays for what teams, to how dynasties are created. It determines how the stars of tomorrow are made. It shapes the star-centric style of play that dominates many of the world's top sports leagues. It even determines how big a commitment children and their families are expected to give to their travel soccer team. This world is about the business of creating champions in societies conditioned to worship them, and to reward the most sought after of them with annual compensation of more than $100 million a year.

An essential shift occurred in the sports industry in 1960, before anyone would have ever thought to have called sports an "industry" or believed its biggest stars might one day be on equal footing with the people who ran it. No one, that is, besides Mark McCormack.

The story of professional sports in the United States for the first eight decades of the twentieth century is largely one of exploitation. It's a story of one-sided contracts and lopsided deals in which teams, leagues, national and international sports federations, and countless other moneyed interests who had put themselves into positions of power took advantage of athletes who were some combination of too young, too uninformed, or too uneducated to realize just how they were being used, and too unrepresented and unorganized to do anything about it. If there is a single turning point in the transformation of sports, then Mark McCormack's arrival on the scene is undoubtedly it. Before McCormack—who began a revolution when, in 1960, he convinced Arnold Palmer to hire him as his exclusive agent—the grand old men who ran pro sports believed the sports industry was about them. These were the blue blazers at the Royal and Ancient Golf Club of St. Andrews (known as the R&A), the green jackets at Augusta National, the bureaucrats at the International Olympic Committee (IOC), and the plutocrats who owned teams in the NFL or Major League Baseball. As far as they were concerned, the inefficiencies of sports were whatever prevented the maximum amount of money and power from flowing their way.

This was the way the world had always existed for them, no matter how they had come to their positions of power. Those paths were as different as the sports themselves. New York Giants owner Tim Mara, a well-known bookie, bought his franchise for $500 in 1925 when the NFL was first taking shape. The team has been the lone source of income for his family ever since. For William Wrigley Jr., the chewing gum and real estate industrialist, acquiring the Chicago Cubs baseball team in 1921 was like picking up a toy, as it was for so many owners who would come after him. Avery Brundage, who ran the IOC from 1952 to 1972, was an amateur athlete who competed with Jim Thorpe in the 1912 Summer Olympics, then climbed the ladder of the sports federations for the next forty years before becoming the supreme leader of the modern Olympic Games. Yet no matter how these men—almost all of them were male—rose to power, invariably they and their peers shared that fundamental misunderstanding of the sports industry and its purpose. Mark McCormack, a Cleveland lawyer who cultivated a very good golfer named Arnold Palmer as his star client and essentially created the modern sports business, taught them and a generation of athletes otherwise.

At the heart of McCormack's ideas was a simple theory: sports were about the athletes, and especially the stars. The stars were the gasoline that made the engine of any sport go. People wanted to connect with them, however they could. They were a salable commodity that was being undervalued, and by undervaluing the athletes, the industry was preventing these athletes and the sports themselves from being as good as they could be.

McCormack didn't stop there. His philosophy wasn't just about demanding higher salaries and finding ways to enrich the clients he represented. It was about creating an environment where television networks could give fans the convenience of watching competitions from all over the world in the comfort of their homes; where sporting events offered those fans an opportunity to get a decent meal instead of a greasy hot dog and a flat beer or soda; where a company could delight in associating with a superstar athlete or the world's grandest competitions. McCormack understood that sport was far more complicated than a zero-sum power struggle between labor and management. Yes, the more control and freedom the athletes had, the better off they would be, but he preached that everyone else would be better off, too. With more money and freedom, the athletes could train more, which would improve the quality of the competition, which in turn would make sports more valuable as a form of live and televised entertainment. That would provide more money for leagues and event organizers to invest in the experience for fans at stadiums, arenas, golf courses, and ballparks. Then they could charge higher prices, with some portion of the money flowing back to the players, which would make their jobs even more desirable, stoking competition and raising the quality of play all the way down to the youth level, allowing the whole process to snowball. McCormack was determined to make life better for the athletes, but in doing so he could make it better for everyone—leagues, team owners, athletic federations, and fans. That was his plan.

Few of those who were in power wanted to listen to that message at first, whether it was coming from McCormack, or, later, a union organizer like Marvin Miller, or a star pitcher like Catfish Hunter, or an Olympic gold medalist like Edwin Moses, or Wimbledon champion Stan Smith, or any of the other stalwarts of the sports revolution this book explores. The powers that be liked things just the way they were, with their athletes scrounging for crumbs at the bottom of the pyramid. The battles the men in charge waged against the athletes, the fallout from those battles, and how that revolution created the behemoth that sports have become is the arc of this story. It's an attempt to understand how we got to a place where sport is simultaneously a highly produced, often overcommercialized extravaganza but also a thrilling Darwinian narrative filled with surprise and intrigue.

It's particularly telling that two of the most important events in this revolution, Arnold Palmer's termination of his exploitative relationship with Wilson Sporting Goods and Catfish Hunter's happenstance journey to becoming baseball's first free agent, turned on their employers' refusal to follow through on promises to buy the athletes cheap life insurance policies. Today a superstar can earn enough in a season to ensure that his grandchildren won't have to work a day in their lives. Forty and fifty years ago, a life insurance policy that might cost $1,000 a year played such an essential role for an athlete who wanted to guarantee the security of his family that it had enough power to transform jocks into sophisticated businessmen and businesswomen. Of course, for most women who play professional sports—other than those fortunate few stars of individual sports—there is still much progress to be made. That battle continues to unfold, and its story will eventually deserve its own book.

Nostalgia is an inevitable emotion for sports fans. Each generation yearns for sports to remain just as they were when they fell in love with games and their heroes. A corollary of such nostalgia is the sense that sports were better when there was less money involved—that not very long ago they were simpler and somehow more pure. As inevitable as these emotions might be, they are worth resisting. There isn't much purity in a system as exploitative toward its labor force as professional sports was, or in the best athletes in the world being forced to hold down jobs that deprive them from training to be the best that they can be. Despite the inevitable pitfalls and crassness money has wrought, money has also made athletes and the sports they play immeasurably better. An upside-down business needed to be turned right-side up, for better or for worse.

The worse side has tested the devotion of even the most devout sports fanatics. In 2012, in the midst of Lance Armstrong's doping scandal psychodrama and downfall and the constant hype surrounding the LeBron James–led Miami Heat, a still-rabid sports fan who had become increasingly frustrated with the crassness, the commercialism, the lying and the cheating, and the soaring prices that come with sports these days, shook his head and said, "I just want to know how we got here."

This is my attempt at an explanation.

1

The Man Who
Invented Sports

During the first week of November in 1958, Mark Hume McCormack traveled to Atlanta, Georgia, and checked into the Heart of Atlanta Motel for a forgettable golf tournament known as the Carling Open. It was held that year at the Cherokee Town and Country Club. McCormack didn't go to the tournament to play golf, although he was good enough to have qualified for the US Open earlier that year. He didn't go there to watch much golf, either. McCormack went to act on a dream.

For nearly three years he'd been practicing law at the estimable Cleveland law firm of Arter, Hadden, Wykoff & Van Duzer. He was billing $15 an hour and collecting a modest associate's salary, but he had an infant child at home and a wife who wanted to buy a bigger house. He'd already realized the life of an attorney wasn't going to do it for him. He had no appetite for endless hours of managing cases and babysitting corporate matters and loan closings.

He needed and wanted more, and he hoped he was going to find it at the Heart of Atlanta Motel.

With its two swimming pools, three diving boards—one of them thirty feet high—and sprawling sun patios, the two-story, 216-room motel was the essence of faux swank in 1958. Six years later it would come to symbolize something else entirely when its owner, a committed segregationist named Moreton Rolleston Jr., sued the US government over the Civil Rights Act of 1964 to assert what he mistakenly viewed as his right not to serve blacks if he didn't want to. But, in 1958, McCormack saw the Heart of Atlanta as the ideal locale to convince the best golfers in the world that he was just the right person to book their exhibition appearances.

McCormack had run the idea past a golfing buddy of his named Richard Taylor, who headed up public relations for the Carling Brewing Company. McCormack had spent time rubbing elbows with the country's top golfers at the US Open and at a few other tournaments, and he had picked up on something he thought was a little strange for a collection of people who were so much better at what they did than 99.9 percent of the population: they didn't make very much money. Tournament purses were worth a couple thousand dollars. McCormack didn't think he could do much about that. But the low pay forced the best golfers to hunt for money off the course. The really good ones had deals with equipment manufacturers, which helped cover their travel expenses. Yet even the best golfers still scrounged for extra work, endorsing a product or appearing at an exhibition at a country club for a couple hundred dollars, plus a steak dinner and drinks with the membership or the executives at whatever company might be sponsoring the outing. There also didn't seem to be any mechanism for how they could secure these opportunities. Winged Foot or The Country Club in Brookline or Atlanta Athletic or Chase Manhattan Bank either called a pro, usually one they had some personal connection to, and offered him the chance to play in an exhibition, or they didn't.

The money—sometimes it was $100, sometimes it was $500—was the money.

McCormack told Taylor he thought together they might be able to build a little business out of this inefficiency. McCormack knew a handful of players from the various tournaments he'd played in, and he had the legal background that would help with the inevitable contract work and negotiations the venture would require. Taylor, as director of public relations for Carling, had been in charge of two professional tournaments his company sponsored. He knew how to sell an event. Together, McCormack figured, they could recruit a stable of top golfers and set about selling their services for exhibitions throughout the country.

Taylor liked the idea and together they hatched a plan to launch it. The Carling Open would be the place, they decided. Since Taylor worked for Carling, they'd have access to any golfer they wanted during the day. Each night, after play ended, they met with any players willing to take the twenty-mile drive south from Cherokee near the Chattahoochee River in Sandy Springs to visit them at the Heart of Atlanta Motel downtown. There, McCormack and Taylor sat, offering drinks and explaining their half-baked vision of how they might put some extra dollars in a top golfer's pockets—and along the way turn themselves into something more than white-collar working stiffs.

They talked to Bob Toski and Mike Fetchick, and Gene Littler, and Julius Boros, who ended up winning that weekend at Cherokee, and Billy Casper, and Dow Finsterwald, and Art Wall, Jay Hebert, Ernie Vossler, Jim Ferree, and Doug Ford. Each one listened to the plan for a company called National Sports Management, which they were told would put the golfers' needs first. It was what every golfer ultimately wanted, McCormack knew, especially a rising star he pitched one night named Arnold Palmer, the reigning Masters champion whom McCormack had first met during college golf tournaments.

The exhibition engagements would happen on the players' days off before a tournament began, in areas where they would be preparing to compete anyway, McCormack said. He promised not to inconvenience them. He knew the last thing a top athlete getting ready for a tournament wants is some kind of hassle, no matter how much it might pay. He was ready to begin soliciting country clubs and corporations in the new year. He would suggest a rate for each pro. Palmer, Toski, and the other top players could get $500 for a weekday and $750 for a weekend or holiday. Lesser names might get $400 for weekdays and $600 for weekends and holidays. McCormack promised not to rope them in against their will. These would be nonexclusive contracts that gave the athletes the opportunity to suggest their own rates or end the deals after a year. They just had to show up if McCormack found them a gig at their agreed-upon rates and they didn't have any scheduling conflicts or injuries. For their work, McCormack and Taylor asked for 20 percent for new exhibition engagements and 15 percent for negotiating a new deal with a corporation or club where the player had played before signing on with the new venture. *Just give it some thought*, McCormack and Taylor told them. A proposed contract would arrive in a few weeks.

A month later, on December 13, McCormack began to fire off a series of letters and contract proposals to everyone who had raised his hand in Atlanta. That included Toski and Fetchick, and Littler and Boros, and Casper and Finsterwald and Wall, and Jay Hebert, Ernie Vossler, Jim Ferree, and Doug Ford, and, of course, Arnold Palmer.

"I assume you escaped Atlanta unscathed since I have had no requests to defend any lawsuits in the Georgia courts so for that I am very pleased," McCormack began his letter of solicitation to Palmer.

Confronted with actual contracts that empowered them with flexibility and autonomy and the chance to make a few extra bucks, the golfers proved just as enthusiastic as they had said they were during the Carling Open. Some of them even seemed open to having McCormack and Taylor represent them for all of their marketing efforts. To those who did, McCormack sent a Chinese menu of services he could provide in addition to exhibition work: everything from tax preparation to real estate advice. If an athlete allowed National Sports Management to represent him for product endorsements, even on a nonexclusive basis, they would pay a 12.5 percent commission on exhibitions and 15 percent for all product endorsements.

For a group of players who either didn't have anyone working on their behalf or were used to having equipment contracts put in front of their faces and told that the terms were nonnegotiable, McCormack's offers were a revelation. Under McCormack's contracts, the players had a say in what they would be paid, and they could ditch the whole thing after a year if they wanted to. The players merely had to agree to send all solicitations they received McCormack's way. He explained that this would spare them the awkwardness of saying no when friends asked for favors or discounted deals. The players agreed that any money they earned would get paid first to NSM, and then NSM would distribute the money to them. It would make it easier for McCormack to keep track of their payments for tax purposes, McCormack explained. He also insisted they send him copies of all the current deals they had with clubs, corporations, or equipment manufacturers. This would allow him to understand how and where he could boost their incomes. There was a side benefit in this for McCormack, of course: he was about to gain an overnight education in the market for the services of the best golfers in the world. Within weeks he was going to be the only one on the sell side of the business to know the going rate for Spalding's name on a golf bag or for Julius Boros to show up and play Merion with the executives of Philadelphia's top utility company.

Littler, Toski, Ferree, and Vossler all signed their contracts by December 17, just four days after McCormack sent them. By early

February, Wall, Ford, Hebert, Boros, Finsterwald, and Casper had signed theirs, and by early March, National Sports Management was representing seven of the top ten money winners on the 1958 PGA Tour. Palmer, who, according to the legend, never had anything but a handshake deal with McCormack, actually signed a contract, too. The greenskeeper's son from Latrobe, Pennsylvania, who'd sneaked off with the 1958 Masters by a stroke, entered McCormack's stable on January 15, 1959. The concept of International Management Group, the industry behemoth that would eventually influence nearly every corner of the modern sports industry, still wasn't even a germ of an idea in McCormack's mind. But maybe, just maybe, this frustrating and fascinating game McCormack had started playing as a grade-schooler would start to pay him back in some small way. That was the dream.

The defining event of Mark McCormack's childhood occurred when he was just six years old. McCormack was playing in the street near his Chicago home when he was struck by a car. The accident fractured his skull. He would eventually make a full recovery, but doctors recommended that he not play contact sports. Even at six years old, McCormack already loved playing football with his friends. A prohibition on contact sports was a prison sentence.

From his earliest years, Mark McCormack had a broad athletic frame. He wasn't a massive kid, but the earliest pictures of him, taken when he was just a toddler, show a young boy with long legs and the sort of chest and torso that look like they've been puffed up with a few shots of air from a bicycle pump. His hair is a light strawberry blond, his eyes narrow but deep and contemplative, windows into a mind that even then appears always in motion. His brow is often furrowed. There is a degree of dissatisfaction with the current state of affairs and an almost palpable belief that he can change them for the better.

Yet there were two things McCormack knew he couldn't change: his inability to play contact sports and his existence as an only child. He never complained about it, but the inherent loneliness drove an almost obsessive need for structure and activity. As a young boy, sitting around the house and letting activities evolve organically wasn't an option, so he incessantly sought out friends on the block to take part in sports and other games that he would organize and whose results he began to track. Even when just a couple of friends were playing cards, or if McCormack was alone on his porch throwing a ball in the air all afternoon, he was always keeping score, even when the games were ones he imagined in his head. A statistics nut, he played out an entire Major League Baseball season on his front porch while bouncing a ball against a wall and keeping batting averages of imaginary players. He drew chalk lines across a wall and played a tennis match against an imaginary avatar of the best player in the world at the time. Every time he swung a golf club, even if he was just swatting grass in a yard, he was teeing off against Sam Snead or Cary Middlecoff or somebody else from those days and keeping scores and records in his head. When childhood friends weren't available or the weather wouldn't cooperate, McCormack would take out his toy soldiers and stage elaborate battles. He tracked those outcomes, too. Sitting at a table, he would stage a football game between his left hand and his right, with each finger representing a different player. The drama would unfold as he slammed one hand into the other.

As Mark's father, Ned McCormack, looked around his Chicago neighborhood, he saw a lot of kids who were pretty good at basketball, pretty good at baseball, pretty good at football, and played a nice game of tennis. But he decided his little boy with the damaged skull would be more fulfilled if he could do one thing and look at everyone around him and say, *You may be stronger than I am and taller than I am and faster than I am and a better football player than I am but I can beat you in golf.* The self-confidence would flow from there and more than make up for any lingering inhibitions from an unfortunate collision with an automobile.

From Ned's vantage point, there weren't many kids playing golf. If you had some coordination and started early enough, having some success at the local and regional levels wouldn't be very hard. Beyond that, Ned, the publisher of a farm journal, believed in the value of concentrating your talents in a single pursuit and being very good at it rather than playing a lot of different sports and having moderate success with any one of them.

It was Mark McCormack's first lesson in the value of an obsessive pursuit of excellence in a single field. Choosing golf was convenient, too. The family of Grace McCormack, Mark's mother, owned a home in the country idyll of Sawyer, Michigan, just eighty miles around the bottom of Lake Michigan from downtown Chicago. The home, built atop a 280-foot dune, with a stairway that offered a 180-step trip down to Lake Michigan, was just five miles from Chikaming Country Club, a 6,400-yard, par-71 track. McCormack's grandfather, Richard W. Wolfe, a Chicago commissioner of public works, was a member. Chikaming became a daily haunt for young Mark, a place to swing a club every day and grow comfortable in the world of a sport that was foreign to most of society.

On summer mornings McCormack would grab his buddy Fred Adams, whose parents had a house near the McCormacks' home on Lake Michigan, and drag him out to Chikaming. McCormack was a far better golfer than Adams. No matter: McCormack would just invent a new set of rules, giving Adams extra strokes or letting him tee off close to the green—anything to make the contests as competitive as they could possibly be. When golf was finished, McCormack would gather up the rest of the neighborhood for his "McCormack Olympics," a series of competitions in swimming, tennis, table tennis, whatever he could come up with where he could develop written rules and a means to victory that, at his urging, he and his friends would assiduously follow. Then the next morning he would return to the golf course, where all those rounds eventually led to a Chicago prep school championship and a spot on the golf team at the College of William & Mary in Virginia.

While Ned McCormack focused on his son's physical talents, Grace McCormack, a woman obsessed with planning, structure, punctuality, and money, went to work on his mind. Grace never missed an opportunity to tell her son how important money would be in his life. He shouldn't obsess over it, but it was important—something that could open doors and provide a level of comfort.

After church on Sundays, Grace and Ned would drop their son off at his grandparents' house for lunch. Grace would give Mark, who was eight years old then, a quarter. He was supposed to use it for a cab ride home. Twenty cents would cover the fare, and a nickel was to be given to the driver for a tip. After a few weeks Mark noticed that the fee for the cab ride increased from fifteen cents to twenty cents about five hundred yards from his home. The next week he began asking the driver to drop him off at a distance that would allow him to pocket an extra nickel. He could walk the rest of the way. The tip ended soon after that, too. By nightfall most Sundays, Mark was a dime richer than he had been when the day began.

Grace McCormack also fixated on organization and punctuality. She set the family breakfast table before she went to sleep at night. After Mark went away to college, his mother would write to tell him she would phone at three o'clock on Sunday afternoon, and that is precisely when the phone in his dormitory would ring.

The lessons paid off. Howard Katz, who helped run McCormack's television company, TWI—the event and production company of International Management Group (IMG)—from 1974 to 1983, said his boss once scheduled a breakfast for the two of them at the Beverly Hills Hotel for 7:25 a.m. Katz arrived at 7:20. McCormack was waiting in the hotel lobby, reading the newspaper. He looked up at Katz and told him he was five minutes early. Katz told him he wanted to make sure not to be late. McCormack said he'd planned to read the newspaper for another five minutes. And that's exactly what he did: he read the newspaper until 7:25, and then it was time for him and Katz to begin their breakfast.

"Time is supposed to be the great, unconquerable enemy," says Katz, now a senior executive with the National Football League. "Mark conquered time, and he did it with yellow legal pads and three-by-five cards."

On those pads and cards were lists of how he would spend every minute of every day, from the moment he woke up until the moment he went to sleep, sometimes three and six months in advance, just as his mother had planned out vacation meals in London and Paris ahead of time. "Every second of his life was preplanned," said Peter Smith, a Brit who ran IMG's Asian operations, among other postings. "Wherever you were in the world he would tell you, 'I will call you at 4:00 p.m. your time,' which might very well have been 4:00 a.m. wherever he was. Sure enough, a minute or two before 4:00 a.m. your phone would ring, and you would have to have your list ready because you very well knew that he would have his list. There was never any small talk. He'd say 'What's new?' and that was your signal to move right into 'Here's where we are with this and that.' The level of efficiency was frightening. No general could run an army like it."

It helped that McCormack had the look of a general, too. He stood six feet three inches tall, with deep, light eyes and, once he grew out the buzz cut of his twenties and thirties, a mane of thick strawberry-blond hair that stayed that way into the final years of his life. He spoke in deep, serious tones and wore suits from Savile Row. Yet he also managed to affect a kind of midwestern humility that allowed him to move almost seamlessly among New York bankers, West Coast television producers, European royalty, and raw sports stars from either the American heartland or the French Alps.

For corporate events, IMG would fly its executives down to

Bay Hill, the Orlando country club where Arnold Palmer lived. By the time the executives arrived, the golf and tennis outings were already arranged in a "US versus the world" format. McCormack had set up the teams so that he was always playing with the very best player. He organized strawberries and cream to be served, just like it was at Wimbledon. He set up dinner for twenty people, table cards at every place setting, all arranged by Grace McCormack's son. If his friends or colleagues or his family did something two years in a row with him, it automatically became a tradition that needed to be followed for a decade. Christmas in the McCormack household followed the set schedule of gift giving, lunch, and an afternoon movie. Suggest an alternative at your own peril.

In the spring of 1950, when McCormack was a college student, he drove from Annapolis, Maryland, to Raleigh, North Carolina, for a golf match that pitted his team from the College of William & Mary against Wake Forest University. McCormack headed out to the course early in the morning to warm up. In the distance he saw a kid named Arnold Palmer whacking irons across the driving range. He'd never seen anything like it before. Once the match got under way, Palmer wrecked one of McCormack's teammates. McCormack didn't see it. He was busy with his own match. But the image of Palmer blistering his irons remained etched in his mind.

Five years passed before McCormack saw Palmer again. This time it was at the Masters in Augusta, Georgia. McCormack, who had joined the Army's Judge Advocate division in 1955, was stationed at Fort Gordon, on the other side of town. He attended as a spectator, tracked down Palmer on the putting green, and made small talk about their days as collegiate opponents. Palmer, playing in his second Masters, shot 13 over par, finished tied for tenth, and took home $696 for his efforts. McCormack met Arnold's wife,

Winnie, took in the golf from the gallery, and returned to Fort Gordon to finish out his military commitment.

After his discharge, McCormack and his wife, Nancy, settled in Cleveland, where McCormack had landed his job at Arter, Hadden and began what was supposed to be the rest of his life. Golf remained a passion, even an outlet for McCormack's competitive drive. In the spring of 1958, McCormack qualified for the US Open in Tulsa and finished fifth among the amateurs. Later that summer, he shot 149 over thirty-six holes to qualify for the US Amateur Championship, a tournament he would qualify for multiple times. At the 1958 Amateur, he lost in the third round to the runner-up in the Canadian Amateur Championship. The guy had played poorly but had a hot putter and one-putted ten greens, making all ten putts from beyond five feet.

McCormack knew he wasn't good enough to make a living on the golf course. By the 1950s, professional golfers had finally surpassed for good the gentlemen bankers and lawyers who competed as amateurs. Those amateurs had been good enough during the first half of the twentieth century to win the biggest tournaments, but not anymore. That was fine with McCormack. There wasn't much money in golf anyway. Plus he'd come upon another idea that was starting to hit: laundry. Yes, in the spring of 1958, as Arnold Palmer was on the cusp of winning his first major golf tournament, Mark McCormack was betting the string of "washaterias" he was opening in the Atlanta area would provide the path to salvation. "Washaterias" made these operations sound like something more than what they actually were: self-service Laundromats.

McCormack opened his first washateria in March of 1958. The barriers to entry were almost nonexistent. A mere $5,000 investment and he was up and running. Then he bought a half ownership in another operation two months later, becoming a 50 percent partner in two ventures managed by one of his buddies from the Army, a lawyer named William Bonham. All it took was a down payment on the equipment—twenty washers, six dryers, one water heater, a prefabricated plumbing unit, meters—in addition to utility deposits, a business license, installation, the first month's rent, initial advertising, and some minor insurance. Crunch the numbers and it produced a monthly break-even point of $600 to $650, with a monthly pretax profit of $150 usually starting around the second or third month and growing exponentially from there.

Then McCormack and his partners figured out the real magic of the venture: a tax trick known as the double declining balance depreciation. He gushed about it to another Army buddy, Al Mulberry, as though he had struck oil and liquid gold was streaming fifty feet into the air. By depreciating the value of the laundry machines, for accounting purposes, the washaterias were actually operating at a loss. That gave them a tax break that was huge relative to the size of their incomes. The financial acrobatics made the young Mark McCormack feel triumphant.

Yet as 1958 wore on, for all the thrills that the laundry business provided, McCormack started to think that there had to be more to life than practicing law and running washaterias. He had two loves: golf and making money. He needed to find some way to combine them. Perhaps, he thought, he could represent a professional golfer the way he represented his other clients.

The idea that someone might be able to make a living representing an athlete was a pretty silly notion in the pre-McCormack era. Babe Ruth used a Boston druggist to represent him in salary talks. For years, lawyer Morris Engelberg represented Joe DiMaggio, but the Yankee Clipper's riches mostly came long after he retired from baseball. Boxers had agents, but their sport necessitated it. They had no organized league or federation setting competition schedules. Two fighters needed managers to set up a fight. The agents needed to work with the promoters who would put up the prize money and set up the event like the producer of a show. Professional basketball had only started a decade before. Pro hockey had six teams. Pro tennis barely existed at all; it was little more than a couple dozen players barnstorming around and playing wherever they thought they might be able to sell tickets; the so-called Open era, when professionals were finally allowed to play in the grand slams, was still a decade away. If athletes were barely scraping by, then a profession built on taking a small percentage of their earnings wasn't going to be particularly lucrative, either.

The more McCormack thought about the situation, the more puzzled he became. Pro athletes were adored and had a unique skill set. Why didn't they make more money? Pro golf was a bunch of guys spending months on the road in beat-up cars and competing for a couple thousand dollars a week. The prize money was paltry, barely enough to cover the expenses of most pros. The occasional product endorsement—a cigarette ad, for instance—might garner a couple hundred dollars and a few cartons of cigarettes. Shouldn't they get more than that? he wondered. Yes, of course they should, and he was pretty sure why they weren't: most pro golfers didn't have any kind of lawyer or manager or agent. There was an opening, and it was a lot bigger than some of the cracks of daylight he had seen Arnold Palmer smash some miracle shots through the past couple of years.

Supposedly, it all began with a simple handshake. The legend holds that Mark McCormack and his first star client, Arnold Palmer, shook hands on a deal for representation and everything fell into place from there. Not exactly.

On January 31, 1959, McCormack filed articles of incorporation for National Sports Management with the state of Ohio. The stated purposes of the company included just about every sort of commerce imaginable. That included representing sports figures and buying, selling, and renting all forms of real estate and property of every class and description. The board of directors had four members: McCormack, Taylor, and their wives. The company had twenty-eight shares, each valued at $50 each. Taylor and McCormack would split the shares equally, with each of them kicking in $700 to get the business off the ground. That was the easy part.

By mid-March, McCormack was practically begging an IBM executive from Philadelphia named Dick Sayford to sponsor an exhibition or pay a leading pro to endorse a new IBM machine. A month later he offered Sayford a cut of the gate at any exhibition the company sponsored. He went after his old Army buddy Al Mulberry, who was still serving and had little money or reason to sponsor a golf exhibition. He told Mulberry he could charge $2 to $3 for tickets and act as a kind of bookie during the event. He cut the rates on clinics with his stable of pros to $200 to $400 for 90 to 180 minutes. He told prospective customers he had top female players to offer, too: Louise Suggs, Barbara Romack, and Beverly Hanson could all be hired for $300 for a weekday or $500 on a weekend. He never bothered to explain how a club or a customer might benefit from having a professional golfer stage an exhibition, or give lessons, or endorse a product or a business that had nothing to do with golf or golf equipment.

By September, players were starting to wonder what they were paying McCormack for. Barbara Romack and Doug Ford wanted out. After beginning the year with $1,400 in the bank, National Sports Management concluded it with a cash balance of $1,646.24. The company had also tallied $1,650 in legal fees—essentially, money McCormack would have demanded a company pay him for his time had he not been both the client and the lawyer. Had Arter, Hadden demanded McCormack pay the firm for the time he spent on his own business ventures, National Sports Management would have burned through its original investments. The business was proving to be a significant money loser.

Even Arnold Palmer was getting turned off. Palmer had signed on with McCormack reluctantly. "I wasn't looking for an agent. I had my wife. She was handling everything," Palmer says. In reality, Winnie Palmer was doing a pretty terrible job representing the best interests of her husband, but all Palmer knew in 1959 was that this gentleman McCormack, whom he kind of remembered playing against in college, had promised to make him a healthy amount of additional income by placing him in exhibitions, and that wasn't happening. Still, after convincing Palmer to sign on for the exhibitions, McCormack continually pressed him to allow him to represent all his marketing and endorsements and to serve as his business manager.

"We kept talking all through 1958 and 1959," Palmer says. "He would tell me about all the business he was creating for all the golfers he had signed up. It was him and this public relations guy from Carling, the beer company. They had Littler and Ford and eight or nine or ten other players. He asked me again and again, and I kept saying no. I had my wife. She was running my office. I wasn't looking for anyone. I was fine doing my own thing."

Palmer toiled away in his home workshop in Latrobe, grinding clubs so they were the exact specifications he wanted. Winnie Palmer sat inside the house, opening the mail and answering the phone, which was beginning to ring incessantly. Palmer understood he was already the most popular golfer on the tour. He sensed he was on the cusp of becoming the best one, too, and he felt there was an inherent flaw in McCormack's business plan. On the golf course, Palmer's game was following a steady upward arc. In 1957 he'd won four tournaments and $29,511, finishing in the top ten fifteen times. In 1958 he'd won his first Masters and a total of $44,531 in prize money and had finished in the top ten sixteen times. He slipped slightly in 1959, with just three tour wins and $35,211 in prize money, but he still had seventeen top-ten finishes, and the drop in prize money was largely the result of not collecting the Masters purse of $11,250, since he failed to repeat as champion. He also played in front of the biggest galleries, leading a screaming throng known as "Arnie's Army" that loved his grip-it-and-rip-it approach to the game. Palmer rarely saw a shot he didn't think he could hit, no matter how many trees he needed to bend the ball around or how much water might stand between him and the green. He'd take a long draw on his cigarette, toss it down on the grass, and take dead aim. He could hit the ball a mile, split the fairway seemingly every time, and always appeared fearless as he charged up to the green to confront his putts.

Palmer knew he could probably charge more for his time than anyone else on the tour. If McCormack was simultaneously representing him and a stable of less popular golfers, Palmer was bound to get undersold. "I wanted someone to represent me alone," Palmer says. "I didn't want to be compared with and bargained for against two or three or ten other guys." Despite his quoted prices of $750 for a weekday and $1,000 for a weekend or holiday exhibition, Palmer was only fetching $350 to $500. Worse, McCormack had only booked him for a few exhibitions all year.

In the fall of 1959, McCormack once again suggested he take a more active role in representing all of Palmer's affairs. "I said if you want to do this, then you go and get rid of all those other players and represent me exclusively," Palmer recalls. "He said he would think about it and get back to me."

For McCormack the decision was something of a no-brainer. If there was one player to bet on becoming a megastar, it was Palmer. But there was also a dashing South African named Gary Player he'd met during the 1958 US Open. Despite his early frustrations, McCormack was already thinking internationally, figuring golf was going to become a true worldwide game, and Player was a known quantity nearly everywhere on the planet where golf was played. His opportunities appeared almost limitless, too.

McCormack's partnership agreement with Richard Taylor became another problem. It didn't foresee the top player in the world, the one who presented the most upside in marketing and just about every other endeavor, wanting to work with one National Sports Management partner and not the other. Some sort of split would have to be worked out, and Mark McCormack was going to come out of it looking like the bad guy.

Then McCormack caught a break. Just as he was figuring out what to tell Palmer, Taylor got an offer to become the tournament supervisor for the Ladies Professional Golf Association (LPGA). He wanted to take it. McCormack gave him his blessing and crafted a breakup agreement. Taylor continued to have a limited association with the company, booking players. McCormack represented the athletes "for taxes, investments, business decisions, estate-planning and contract negotiations." Since Palmer wanted out of his previous contract with National Sports Management and wanted McCormack to represent him for all business affairs, Mc-Cormack allowed Taylor to continue to book Palmer for exhibitions through 1961.

As he negotiated with Taylor, McCormack kept an open line with Palmer, making it clear he wanted to find a way to pursue the relationship. Then, near the end of the year, McCormack called Palmer and told him he'd made a decision. "He said he had given everyone else up and was ready to go with just me," Palmer says. (In fact, this was only partly true.) "I said that was terrific. He said he would draw up a contract. I said, 'No you won't.' He said, 'I'm a lawyer, that's what I do. My business is doing contracts.' I said, 'I don't really care what you do as a lawyer. What you're going to do is you're going to tell me what you're going to do for me, and I'll tell you what I'm going to do for you, and then we'll shake hands and go ahead and do what we said.' "

And thus the legend of the Palmer-McCormack handshake deal was born. It's a sweet story, but largely an apocryphal one. Eventually there would be thousands of pages of legal agreements that certified the business relationship between McCormack and Palmer, including the one that gave Palmer a significant stake in IMG. But

McCormack made sure the legend of the handshake endured. An impresario like McCormack knew it would reveal exactly what he wanted to about the instincts and personalities of its two characters, the down-home golfer who played the game like a fighter jock and the trailblazing entrepreneur who valued quality over quantity, the biggest single name rather than a series of smaller ones, the intrinsic worth of the best and most enduring people and institutions. He was drawn to Palmer the same way he would be drawn toward Wimbledon or the R&A or the IOC or the World Cup. He knew that quality would serve as an entrée to more quality.

By the spring of 1960, Mark McCormack had every reason to believe his career had just taken a sharp turn for the better. He had just signed the client of his dreams, a singular talent in the prime of his career with unmatched skills, innate charisma, and unlimited potential. No sports agent or manager had made any real money in the business, and it didn't take long to see why. McCormack came across one deal with Heinz, the ubiquitous ketchup company, that paid Arnold Palmer, the Masters champion, $500 to be able to use Palmer's name endorsing their brand basically wherever and whenever they wanted. One print ad in *Life* magazine had Arnold explaining, "I guess I eat several hundred meals away from home every year, so naturally I've learned to size up eating places. One of the signs I go by is Heinz catsup. When I spot that familiar Heinz bottle on the table, I feel sure the food, the service and everything else will be good." When McCormack asked Palmer about the deal, he had almost no recollection of when he signed it, how long it lasted, or if it had any limits.

Yet the relationship with Palmer was going to allow McCormack to make money in a multitude of ways. He would collect a 10 percent commission on Palmer's contracts. He could set himself up as an investor and executive in whatever businesses Palmer might ultimately create, and his mind and yellow legal pads were already filling up with ideas: instructional films, sportswear, a chain of dry cleaners.

He even inquired about copyrighting Palmer's swing. Dancers could copyright what they choreographed; why shouldn't Palmer be able to copyright one of the world's most famous athletic motions?

The new decade started off rocky for Palmer. During the first four tournaments of the season, he finished no better than seventh. A month's work produced a whopping $2,500 in prize money. Not awful, but not what Palmer was looking for, with a wife and two young daughters to support at home in Latrobe, or what McCormack was hoping for from his star client. But Palmer didn't play the game to get rich. He played it because he loved it, because it was just about the only thing he knew how to do really well, and because it seemed like the surest way to build a secure life for his family, which was what he cared about most. Palmer had a picture of President Dwight Eisenhower hanging in his family room at home. He aspired to Ike's conservative simplicity and heroic dedication. Palmer's battlefield was the golf course. If he could live up to Ike's ideal, he would be happy.

After that bumpy first month, Palmer rolled into Palm Springs for the first playing of that city's Desert Classic. (The event would eventually become the Bob Hope Desert Classic.) It was a five-round tournament, to be played on the resort city's poshest courses. The format favored a young buck like Palmer, who *Sports Illustrated* described that week as "a broad backed boy from Latrobe, Pa., who probably could play five rounds in a day if the price was right." Palmer opened with a 67, then stumbled to a 73 in the second round; but he followed that with a 67 and a 66 to begin the final round a stroke behind a tour veteran named Johnny Palmer. The "broad backed boy" birdied the second, seventh, and ninth holes, then made three more birdies on the back nine and won the inaugural Classic by three strokes. That win brought a $12,000 payday and the sixteenth win of his career.

Next, Palmer went to Arizona and finished twelfth and fifth in two tournaments, but shot just a single round over par in the Grand Canyon state. He had played well but had to tip his cap to the guys who had played better and move on. Next came one of those rolls that golfers dream about. At Fort Sam Houston Golf Club in San Antonio, Texas, Palmer shot 69-65-67 in the first three rounds and won by two strokes despite a 75 on Sunday. The obliteration continued a week later when he won at Baton Rouge by seven strokes, closing with 69-68. Next up was Pensacola. There he birdied six of the last ten holes, including the seventy-second, to beat Doug Sanders by a stroke. No golfer had won three straight tournaments since 1952. Two more top-five finishes in St. Petersburg and the Desoto Open sent Palmer to the Masters as the tour's hottest golfer and the odds-on favorite.

He did not disappoint. The 1960 Masters would mark the turning point for both Palmer and the tournament—a televised drama that captivated the country, even if most sports fans caught it only on a replay. A stroke ahead of Ken Venturi entering the final round, Palmer found himself down a shot with three holes to play. Already in the clubhouse, Venturi could do nothing but watch and wait. On sixteen, Palmer's birdie putt knocked off the flagstick. (This was before flags had to be removed before putting.) On seventeen, Palmer landed his approach shot twenty feet from the cup. His birdie putt slowed as it approached the hole. Then somehow it found the strength to roll in, sending Palmer dancing across the green and his Army into a frenzy. He'd tied Venturi. On eighteen, Palmer stuck his approach four feet from the hole. The Army followed him up the fairway and exploded when he sank the putt for a comeback win and his second green jacket. When it happens for the second time, it is no longer luck.

McCormack watched it all and couldn't quite believe his good fortune. The charismatic golfer who was already the crowd favorite was evolving into a superhero just as he'd agreed to let McCormack take over his business. McCormack had rolled the dice. He'd largely agreed to give up pursuing other golfers to work only with Palmer, who could have just as easily thrown out his back and missed the rest of the year. Instead, it felt like the sports equivalent of emptying your life savings to splurge for the impressive four-bedroom on the lovely block, then discovering it was sitting on top of an oil well.

With their partnership solidified, working for Palmer quickly became the central obsession of McCormack's professional life. Every other day he would call Palmer with another proposition. The phones didn't stop ringing. The offers kept rolling in. There seemed to be no limits to the empire that Palmer might be able to build.

And then McCormack read Arnold Palmer's contract with the Wilson Sporting Goods Company of Chicago.

2

Liberation

August 28, 1954, the day of the final of the US Amateur, began very badly for Arnold Palmer. It was a Saturday, and Palmer was seven months removed from his three-year stint in the US Coast Guard.

His golf game since his discharge had been good but inconsistent, nowhere near the level where he could seriously consider trying to make a living playing on the professional tour. Instead, at the age of twenty-four, he was selling paint and feeling about as far from the world of professional golf as he could be.

In midsummer, though, Palmer's game began to click. At the All-American Open at Tam O'Shanter Country Club near Chicago, Palmer was the low amateur. It was the most success he'd had since Wake Forest. The win put an extra bounce in his step as he traveled in late August to the Country Club of Detroit for the US Amateur, the tournament in which golf's greats, including Jack Nicklaus and Tiger Woods, have long announced themselves to the world.

Palmer survived the first five rounds of the match play event without much trouble. Then, in the quarterfinals, he was two holes down to reigning Canadian Amateur champion Don Cherry at the halfway mark before storming back to win. His parents drove eight hours from Latrobe for the semifinal match with Ed Meister, a former captain of the Yale golf team. Palmer and Meister were all square after the first thirty-six holes. The match went to sudden death. On the thirty-seventh hole, Meister missed a five-foot putt to win. Then he missed a sixteen-footer for the victory on the thirty-eighth. On the thirty-ninth, a 510-yard par 5, Meister found the trees off the tee while Palmer split the fairway and landed his second shot on the green.

The victory set up a finals showdown on Saturday, August 28, with Bob Sweeny, a forty-three-year-old American socialite and former British Amateur champion, who was everything Palmer was not. Sweeny was an aristocrat with a well-earned reputation as an international playboy. Sweeny had won the British Amateur in 1937. Winning the US championship was going to do little to alter the trajectory of his life. He had the luxury of playing without a care in the world, and that is exactly what he did. Sweeny birdied the first three holes and was three up when a woman as beautiful and elegant as anyone Palmer had ever seen waltzed onto the fairway and planted a kiss on Sweeny's lips. This was not the way Palmer wanted the day to begin. He wasn't just losing; he was lost. In match play, it doesn't get any worse than three down after three holes.

Then Palmer made a mental adjustment. He decided to ignore his opponent, a man he felt he was no match for in so many ways. Instead he focused on the golf course. He'd beaten golf courses before. He could beat this one, too. Sure, this was match play, but as is always the case in golf, the real opponent was the course itself, not Sweeny. He didn't need to beat Sweeny as much as he needed to play a good round of golf—well, two good rounds, since the final consisted of a thirty-six-hole match.

By the tenth hole he and Sweeny were all square. Finally, Palmer took a decisive lead on the thirty-second hole. Then he went two up on the thirty-third. By the final hole, though, the lead had shrunk back to one. Palmer blasted his drive into the center of the fairway. Sweeny faded his ball into the fescue. As the rivals walked to their next shots, Sweeny sidled up to Palmer and said simply, "Congratulations. You win." Arnold Palmer was the US Amateur champion.

Within the course of a week, Palmer's life had changed completely. No longer was he just a free-swinging, risk-taking paint salesman with a dream. Arnold Palmer was real. The US Amateur was prime scouting territory for the country's top equipment makers, and "Plug" Osborne, a leading representative for Wilson who had his eye on Palmer all week, went to work convincing Wilson president Fred Bowman that Arnold Palmer was going to be something special. Within two weeks Palmer had an actual contract in front of him and Osborne hanging over his shoulder, telling him where to sign. In the third week of September 1954, he did. Arnold Palmer was finally a professional golfer. Palmer loved the deal as much as he had loved anything. It allowed him to go out on the tour and do what he had always wanted to do.

*For Palmer and every other top golfer, the equipment deal has al*ways represented one of the first crowning moments of the outside-the-ropes career. For obvious reasons, no connection is more important than the one between a golfer and the clubs he plays with. To Palmer, the Wilson deal wasn't just about being able to call up a player rep like Osborne and ask for another wedge, a few dozen boxes of balls, or a new bag. Rather, it was a symbol of achievement. Wilson had guaranteed (well, sort of) Palmer $5,000, which was money he needed to go on tour and cover his expenses. The company was serving as a sort of angel funder. It was filled with salt-of-the-earth golf guys like Osborne, the director of its professional golf division, who made his living staking twenty-four-year-old country boys like Palmer to the life they dreamed of.

Even in this context, the original contract Arnold Palmer signed with Wilson was undoubtedly among the worst deals any athlete of Palmer's caliber has ever signed. Palmer's love for the deal ran so deep that when, in the spring of 1960, McCormack began to explain the level of exploitation within it, Palmer looked at him as though he were speaking Chinese. These were good and important men at Wilson, Palmer explained. Wilson was one of the biggest names in sports. They had been there for him right after that first amateur championship, then at the first Masters win in 1958 and the second one in 1960, and they would be there for him always. They had promised to do right by Arnold Palmer and they would, no matter what crazy ideas McCormack had about how they might be taking advantage of the boy from Latrobe.

At its roots, Wilson wasn't actually a sporting goods company. It was a failing New York–based meatpacking operation called Sulzberger & Sons that Thomas E. Wilson, a veteran meat industry executive, took over in 1916 at the behest of bankers looking to turn around the foundering company. Wilson moved the company's headquarters to Chicago. He turned it into a leader in the growing business of processed meats and deli products. Looking for something to do with the innards and intestines that were left after the rest of an animal had been turned into something edible, he pushed the company to expand the division that used the hides of the livestock to make sporting goods. Soon Wilson was one of the leading producers of footballs, basketballs, and baseball gloves. Pads and other protective equipment would eventually follow. So would tennis rackets and golf clubs. Then came the realization that selling golf clubs became a lot easier if the clubs had a pro golfer's name on them, especially since the partnerships with the golfers could be had on the cheap. By the 1950s, Wilson had cultivated a series of relationships with top golfers that it counted as members of its "professional staff."

How cheap were the deals? Here are the main terms of Palmer's original three-year deal with Wilson, signed before his rookie year in 1954:

Palmer would receive $2,000 per year in travel expenses and a $5,000 salary, but that payment was really an advance against royalties on club sales. Palmer would receive 2.5 percent on the first $200,000 worth of merchandise sold and 1.5 percent for all sales after that. If the royalties didn't reach $5,000, the shortfall would be applied against his advance the following year. If Palmer won the US Open, he would receive a $2,000 bonus. A win in the PGA Championship carried a $1,500 bonus. Wins in the British Open, the Masters, or the Western Open would bring a $1,000 bonus. Needless to say, the amount of sales that victories in those tournaments would produce for Wilson would far surpass the amount promised to Palmer in bonus money. Palmer was earning about $10,000 a year from Wilson.

Arnold and Winnie Palmer didn't sweat the details of the deal. They barely bothered to read them. Palmer signed where Osborne told him to sign, then he won the Canadian Open as a rookie in 1955, when he finished in the top ten in nine tournaments to win $8,974 in prize money. In 1956 he won four tournaments and finished in the top ten eleven times, collecting $21,490. The next year, 1957, brought four more wins and fifteen top tens, generating $29,511 and vaulting Palmer into the top five money winners on the PGA Tour. Realizing they had a rising star on their hands, Wilson sent Palmer a letter on September 25, 1957, informing him the company would exercise its option to renew his contract for three additional years. To sweeten the deal, they raised his guarantee to $6,500, which wasn't much of a risk, since it was an advance against royalties anyway.

To Palmer, life couldn't have been better, and he played like it, too. The next year would bring his first Masters title and $44,531 in prize money, putting him at the top of the money list. Without a major title in 1959, his earnings slipped to $35,211, but he had three wins and seventeen top-ten finishes, good for fifth on the money list. Then came the magical spring of 1960, the three straight Tour wins, and the captivating second triumph at the Masters. In a matter of weeks, Palmer had become one of the hottest commodities in sports. Everyone wanted a piece of him, and now he had this aggressive lawyer from Cleveland taking care of his business ventures.

Among the suitors was a gentleman named Jack Harkins from Tennessee. Harkins owned a golf equipment company and decided to approach Palmer about launching a new venture with him. Harkins had heard Palmer's deal with Wilson might be expiring the following year. Palmer was intrigued enough to reach out to McCormack, and the three decided to get together during the Tour stop in Houston in late April.

Harkins had a reputation on the Tour as something of a blowhard. He was one of those characters that professional sports has always been lousy with: the moderately successful businessman who inserts himself into the lives of professional athletes, using his money and connections and bravado as entrées even though no one quite knows where his money comes from. McCormack once described Harkins as the sort who "had a reputation for being a fast player, a big talker, a dubious promoter . . . monopolizing all six hands at a Las Vegas blackjack table, wagering maybe $50,000 in the process, and dominating the crap games, and blowing off steam, and, in general, acting like a big shot. Nobody ever said as much but the general impression was that you had better leave your wallet at home when you went into a meeting with Harkins."

Nevertheless, McCormack liked him—a lot. So did Palmer, in part because Harkins knew the dirty secret about Wilson's line of Palmer clubs that always stuck in Palmer's craw: the clubs were crap, a down-market product that were meant to be sold on a mass scale as opposed to a premium line that could command a much higher-level customer and price. Harkins wanted Palmer to design a line of clubs himself, giving him the power to make a club that met his own exacting standards of excellence.

Palmer liked the idea and directed McCormack and Harkins to get to work on a deal. Within a couple of weeks they'd hammered out the framework of a contract that would guarantee Palmer $150,000 a year and make him a director of First Flight Golf Equipment, with stock options in the company. Harkins also agreed to a $5,000 bonus for winning the Masters and a $2,000 bonus for winning the US Open. Compared with the Wilson deal, Harkins's offer represented roughly a tenfold increase, depending on royalties. This wasn't so much about McCormack being a great negotiator as both men understanding what Palmer was worth and how much revenue his personal brand of clubs could produce.

As he negotiated with Harkins, McCormack was badgering Wilson to send him a copy of the company's contract renewal that Palmer had agreed to in 1957 so he could inspect it. (Not surprisingly, Palmer didn't have one.) On May 12, Wilson finally sent it along, and McCormack would spend the next ten days holed up in his Cleveland office puzzling over the document, because as soon as he read the cover letter that accompanied it his eyes popped out. "It is also understood," the cover letter stated, "that we have the right to renew at the expiration of this renewal for a period of one, two or three years, as outlined in the contract."

Palmer was twenty-eight when he signed that first renewal, the age when most golfers reach their peak and begin to play at a level they will maintain roughly through their midthirties, when their performance begins to tail off. The deal Palmer had agreed to with Wilson in 1957, which included all the deal terms in the first contract, would likely carry through to the end of 1963, just after his thirty-fourth birthday.

Before getting down to the business of writing up a review of the Wilson deal, McCormack had a simple question for Palmer: had he asked a lawyer to look over the Wilson deal before he signed it in 1954 or agreed to renew it in 1957? No, he hadn't, Palmer told him. No shock there, but Palmer assured McCormack this wouldn't be an issue and that he shouldn't worry about it. The good folks over at Wilson had told him that if at any point there was something he didn't like about the deal or was unhappy with, he should just go talk to them about it and it would get taken care of. It wouldn't be any problem at all.

McCormack knew better, however. The job of transforming Arnold Palmer into a bankable superstar had just gotten a lot harder. The equipment deal was the backbone of his portfolio. He needed a good one, not just because the world's best golfer deserved it, and not just because McCormack had staked his reputation on his ability to turn Palmer into a kind of sports celebrity that had never existed. He needed Palmer to have the best possible equipment deal from his primary sponsor to establish his true value and show every other top athlete how different life could be. In terms of pure dollars and cents, the highest salary in any industry sets the market. Major League Baseball players would learn this lesson firsthand in the 1970s with the advent of free agency. Not only did the game's best players earn a windfall, but the salaries for the very good and even the mediocre players improved dramatically, too. If Palmer could get a deal that paid him what he was worth, then the price for Gary Player or Jack Nicklaus would rise, too. Beyond that, there was the message that would go out if McCormack couldn't secure a fair deal for Palmer. If the world's top golfer, a champion as charismatic and beloved as Palmer, couldn't get a deal from his main sponsor that paid him like someone who is better at what he does than anyone else on the planet, then no one would be able to.

McCormack and Palmer had told Wilson about the approach from Harkins. Now McCormack had to craft a letter on Palmer's behalf explaining to Harkins that a venture with First Flight couldn't happen until 1964. Still, he might be able to salvage something. On May 25 he sent Palmer a letter explaining that even though Wilson could renew the deal as is, they should take the opportunity to try to keep the people at the company true to their word and suggest a number of changes they should make for their star client, especially if they had any hope of re-signing him when this next deal ended. It was the only leverage he had. Clearly, Wilson had Palmer wrapped up for the next three years, but now that he was actually having a lawyer review his contracts, the company faced the prospect that this might be its last renewal.

McCormack demanded that Palmer's royalties accrue on top of the salary, so the payments he received at the start of each year weren't just an advance against sales. If, for some reason, sales collapsed one year, Palmer shouldn't have to take the hit for it. McCormack wanted Wilson to produce three lines of clubs so that Palmer could have his name on a premium product but not give up his appeal to the mass market. He wanted a portion of the income deferred, especially in years when Palmer cleaned up on the Tour. That way he could avoid the substantial tax hit from having a high income but would still have a substantial salary down the road when he wasn't winning as many tournaments. Bonuses for tournament wins should be paid the following year—again, to minimize his tax hit. If Wilson had an annual opt-out clause in the contract, then Palmer should have one, too. Palmer should also be able to endorse another product without mentioning Wilson. Having to say "I'm Arnold Palmer and I play with Wilson and I like Penzoil" didn't make a lot of sense. Also, McCormack wanted Palmer to have the right to sell clubs in places like Australia, where

Wilson didn't even have a business. Finally, McCormack asked that if Palmer died, Wilson should continue to pay to his estate through the life of the contract. And McCormack wanted Palmer to be able to keep his damn balls and clubs after he used them. It wasn't exactly Thomas Jefferson declaring independence from the British crown, but it was a start.

This all seemed perfectly reasonable to Palmer, who let McCormack arrange a meeting with his contacts at Wilson. Palmer was sure everything would get straightened out there. These were men who'd given him their word.

In May, Palmer played the Tournament of Champions at the Desert Inn Country Club in Las Vegas and finished fifth, collecting $1,650 for his efforts. Then McCormack, Arnold, and Winnie Palmer traveled to Wilson headquarters in River Grove, Illinois, for a meeting with Wilson's president, Bill Holmes. McCormack and Palmer went into Holmes's office. Winnie Palmer was told to remain in another room. Also at the meeting were Wilson vice president Harry Colburn and Joe Wolfe, who worked in the professional players division and was Palmer's main contact with the company. Fred Bowman and Plug Osborne, the duo who had originally signed Palmer and given him their word, had long since left the company.

As the group sat down, the conversation quickly grew awkward. Holmes produced a letter McCormack had written to Dunlop about Palmer using one of their balls in the British Open. It was an attempt to show Palmer how McCormack was going behind everyone's back and screwing up this terrific long-standing relationship Palmer had with the good folks at Wilson. Palmer laughed and said he knew about the letter. They'd contacted Dunlop at the suggestion of a Wilson executive. Then Joe Wolfe began a lecture about how much better Wilson's line of clubs were than Jack Harkins's First Flight sticks. The lecture was both absurd and irrelevant.

Palmer ground his own clubs in his shop at his house in Latrobe. Few people on the planet knew more about golf club construction than Palmer. In addition, Arnold was going to design his own line of premium clubs for Harkins that were nothing like what First Flight had been making before.

McCormack listened to all this for nearly two hours. Then he cut to the chase. He asked if Wilson might consider releasing Palmer from his contract. The answer was no, of course. Palmer had collected nearly $11,000 in royalties in 1959, which translated into nearly $560,000 in sales on equipment with Palmer's name on it. Sales for 1960 were up 35 percent. Palmer was going to clear about $13,000. He was going to enter 1961 as one of the world's biggest sports stars. Wilson was going to collect $1.26 million from selling Arnold Palmer golf equipment, including some fifty thousand dozen golf balls, the product with the largest profit margin. Palmer's share would be $21,500. Only a fool would let Palmer out of a contract like that.

Shortly after that, the meeting broke for lunch. Winnie was invited to join the men at a nearby restaurant and the conversation turned friendly. Then it was back to Wilson's offices for more discussions. Finally, midway through the afternoon, Bill Holmes realized the earth was beginning to move under his feet. He could tie up Palmer under the current deal for three more years, but if he did that, Palmer would undoubtedly leave in 1964. By then Palmer would likely be far more famous and valuable than he was now. In a moment of enlightenment, Holmes suggested they rip up the current contract and get to work on a long-term deal that would last a decade and carry Palmer into his forties. McCormack's demands could be met. Palmer could design some clubs. Wilson could go on making a mint off the world's top golfer. Everyone would be happy, especially Arnold Palmer.

As the meeting broke off at the end of the day, Palmer, for one fleeting moment, felt like he was going to get the security he'd always sought. Even better, he was going to prove McCormack wrong. He'd told McCormack that Wilson would address any of his complaints, now and always. McCormack had doubted him. Yet right there at the company headquarters, they'd followed through in just the way they had promised.

There were smiles and handshakes all around. McCormack and Palmer went off to fulfill their professional duties. Palmer began his final tune-ups for the US Open at Cherry Hills, near Denver. McCormack went to work crafting a new deal with Wilson. In the process he would receive an invaluable first lesson on the strange upside-down business that he had entered.

Just as he had done at the Masters, Palmer triumphed in the most dramatic fashion at Cherry Hills. It didn't start out pretty. He shot a one over 72 in the first round and even par 71 in the second. This was still the era when the US Open concluded with a single day of play for the third and fourth rounds. Palmer began that Saturday eight shots behind leader Mike Souchak, who had opened with a 68-67 on a typically tough US Open course. Eighteen holes later Palmer had made up just a single stroke. He began the final round tied for fifteenth place. He knew he'd have to go uncommonly low to have a shot at winning.

Palmer opened his final round with one of the great charges in major golf history. He birdied six of the first seven holes, including a chip-in from ninety feet on the second. While the birdie festival ended after the seventh, Palmer remained steady enough to hold off back-nine charges from a forty-seven-year-old Ben Hogan and a twenty-year-old US Amateur champion named Jack Nicklaus. Palmer was halfway to the Grand Slam and the toast of the sports world, as close to unbeatable as it gets in a game where everyone is eminently beatable. Before the tournament, Palmer had appeared on the cover of *Sports Illustrated* with Ken Venturi and Dow Finsterwald under the headline "Golf's Young Lions." Within months he would appear on the cover alone under a different headline: "Sportsman of the Year."

To Mark McCormack's great relief, the victory and Palmer's rise to the next level of superstardom convinced Bill Holmes and his minions that they really ought to follow through with their pledge at the end of their recent meeting in River Grove and try to tie Palmer up as long as they could. Through the summer of 1960 there was a marked difference in the tone of the interchanges between McCormack and the Wilson higher-ups. The parties passed drafts of contracts that actually look reasonable, even in hindsight.

Those contracts began with a several-page-long preamble that noted how "the special skills and particular talent of Palmer make him invaluable and irreplaceable to the company." The document proposed a ten-year deal that included a plan for Wilson to defer income for Palmer and use a portion of the money to purchase a $300,000 life insurance policy on his behalf. In the case of Palmer's death, the company would get the cash value of the policy and Palmer's beneficiaries would get the rest. Palmer would have the right to terminate the deal after five years. He would receive a guaranteed $6,500 salary plus royalties of 2 percent on all products, with additional income deferred until 1980.

Over the next several months, the deal actually got sweeter. There were negotiations about the size of the life insurance policy, which fluctuated between $350,000 and $750,000. A win in the US Open would garner a bonus of $6,500. Victories in the other three majors would produce bonuses of $3,500. He'd get $500 for each first-place finish, $500 for winning the Vardon Trophy (awarded to the PGA Tour player with the best scoring average), and $500 for making the US Ryder Cup team. Royalties above $25,000 would be deferred and converted into shares of Wilson stock. Palmer would also be free to endorse other products without any mention of Wilson. There were even discussions about guaranteeing that Palmer would remain the highest-paid member of the Wilson staff.

The only sticking point appeared to be the details of the life insurance plan. How much should Wilson pay? How much should Palmer pay? In both cases, the answer was not much. Over ten years the cost figured to be about $8,000 for Wilson and about $2,200 for Palmer. And yet some niggling detail about the deal kept arising, for reasons McCormack couldn't understand, since the sort of insurance plan they were discussing seemed to benefit both sides. The benefit for Palmer was obvious. He would be able to acquire an insurance policy tax-free, because the money would stay on Wilson's books as a guaranteed asset. If the benefit ever got paid out, that would be tax-free, too. While the premiums were not deductible for Wilson, the insurance plan represented a way to give Palmer something of great value at a relatively small cost.

In August the parties gathered for another meeting at the Prudential Building in Chicago. Judge James D. Cooney, the autocratic chairman of Wilson's parent company, attended this one. He brought more pledges of goodwill but little concrete progress. Cooney was noncommittal about buying a professional golfer a tax-free, deferred-income insurance plan when no one else in the company had one. McCormack suggested Cooney could make the insurance plan and deferred compensation available to all "qualifying employees," but the qualifications would include winning both the US Open and the Masters. Cooney didn't find that suggestion very useful, but he did promise to do whatever was needed to keep Palmer happy and maintain a relationship with the world's top player.

Arnold Palmer, like so many of his contemporaries in golf and every other sport, was about to learn the true value of such promises.

*Wilson sent the first signal that trouble might lie ahead in a Sep*tember 23 letter from Charles Hare, the Wilson vice president in charge of Palmer, to the golfer himself explaining that the company planned to pick up its option to renew the existing contract. The deal was set to expire in thirty-seven days, Hare explained. The company had to pick up the option while discussions on the new deal continued. "Mark said he understood the situation," Hare wrote. Hare added that he was hoping for a meeting in mid-October. Hare also dashed off a letter to McCormack stating that Wilson was exercising its option to renew the contract for three more years "under the terms and conditions now in effect."

In Cleveland, McCormack began to worry. At best Wilson was stalling. At worst he'd been had. After three weeks with little contact, a frustrated McCormack finally sent back to Hare a new set of revisions to the working proposal. He explained that the salary deferment plan was simple stuff that plenty of major companies used with top executives. Other than that, there wasn't much new in the contract. "Most of the things that Wilson is obligated to do they are already doing and most of the things that Palmer is obligated to do he is already doing," he wrote.

McCormack suggested they hash out the final details of the long-term contract over dinner in New York on October 17. Then they could finalize the contract at a meeting within days of that and finish their work. If he didn't finalize a new deal quickly, on November 1, the renewal of the previous three-year deal under the old terms was going to kick in. He'd promised his star client a new, secure long-term deal.

McCormack couldn't let that renewal kick in. This battle wasn't only about Palmer. It was about a young lawyer trying to establish himself as a new power in an industry where the power had always rested on the other side of the business—with management. McCormack was trying to build a business and develop a reputation so he could build something bigger than a venture with the golfer from Latrobe. McCormack's relationship with Palmer was his biggest calling card. Every agent knows there is no better magnet for additional clients than being able to claim that you represent the biggest client of all. But McCormack was going to have to show that he could do something important for Palmer, something new and different that would send a message about his own viability and his view about where athletes should stand in the pecking order of sport. He needed this Wilson deal in the worst way.

A week and a half after McCormack begged Charles Hare and his colleagues to stop dragging their feet, Louis Simpson, the Wilson general counsel, wrote to tell McCormack that he was going to need more time to review the deal and that scheduling a meeting to cross the *t*'s and dot the *i*'s around November 1 would not be possible. Simpson neglected to say how much time he would need or specify just what he needed to review. It was an amazingly dismissive tack to take with someone who was supposed to be the company's essential golf client. The next day he wrote to Palmer directly and blamed McCormack for the delays. Simpson told Palmer that McCormack had taken four and a half months to get a counterproposal back to Wilson, an accusation that was patently false, since they'd been exchanging ideas and concepts about the deal throughout the summer.

Then, on November 3, Wilson's Joe Wolfe sent Palmer a check for $3,250. It was the first installment on Palmer's new three-year contract, the one Wilson had told McCormack in September they'd planned to renew under the same terms as the old one. That contract had gone into effect on November 1. It called for Palmer to receive an advance against royalties of $6,500 a year in two installments. Since the check was sent directly to Palmer, it marked the latest in a series of attempts to cut McCormack out of the process. McCormack did not appreciate that.

It was a completely unethical move, but it was hard to blame the Wilson folks. Things had gone much more smoothly for them before Palmer had a lawyer representing him. Three years before, all it had taken to tie him up through 1963 was slipping an extra paragraph into a cover letter. Now they had to get a check into

Palmer's hands. Since Palmer hadn't ever signed a renewal agreement, getting him to deposit the first payment would serve as an
acknowledgment that he was a party to a contract for the next
three years. They didn't really need his acknowledgment, since
he'd signed over any right to have a say in the matter in 1957, but
accepting the check would certainly look a lot like an acceptance
of the three-year renewal.

Fortunately Palmer had listened when McCormack said to make
sure to include him in every communication he had with Wilson,
even if Palmer thought this was McCormack just acting like a para-
noid lawyer who didn't understand human relations and the meaning of things like promises and handshakes. Palmer didn't deposit
the check. He sent it to McCormack, and on November 22, McCormack sent the check back to Wilson with a shot across the bow.

Gentlemen:

*I am enclosing herewith check No. 17068 of the Wilson Sport-
ing Goods Company, payable to the order of Arnold Palmer in
the amount of $3,250.*

*Pursuant to Arnold Palmer's discussion with Judge
Cooney of Wilson in August of this year, it is our understanding that the contract you referred to in the letter you sent to
Arnold enclosing the above mentioned check is no longer in
existence pending the execution of a new agreement within the
next few weeks. In this regard I have advised Arnold Palmer
that the legal effect of accepting, cashing or retaining the en-
closed check would be to constitute ratification of the original
contract, ending October 31, 1963 and to reinstate it.*

Very truly yours,
Mark H. McCormack

That day, McCormack also sent a note to Charles Hare. Hare had
been going behind McCormack's back and meeting with Palmer on

his own in Arizona to relay the message about how badly Wilson wanted to wrap up a new deal. McCormack wanted to let Hare know he'd seen Palmer in Alabama and he knew all about the discussions. McCormack was drawing a line in the sand. In response, Hare accused McCormack of putting words in the mouth of Wilson's chief executive. "I was in Judge Cooney's office with Arnold at the meeting you refer to and I know nothing was said that in any way suggested the termination of the existing contract between the Company and Arnold," Hare wrote. "We should all understand that the present contract will continue in effect until changed by mutual agreement."

With the relationship worsening with each communication, McCormack decided to meet up with Palmer in early December in New York. The city was in the middle of a fierce cold snap. A snowstorm had closed the airports and blanketed the city. With the air frigid outside, the two settled into the bar at the Plaza Hotel's Oak Room, one of those cozy, dark haunts where important people met to discuss important matters.

Wilson had made its feelings about Palmer crystal clear. In the company's eyes, he was staff. McCormack told Palmer he would be well-compensated staff for the rest of his life with Wilson. But there was still an alternative to signing his life away for the next twenty years. A deal with Wilson would produce maybe $75,000 a year—undoubtedly a nice income—but if he could put off his yearning for a lifetime of security for three more years, he had a chance to make the kind of money that the game's greats, men like Snead and Hogan and Nelson, never could. He could allow Wilson to renew his contract one last time and then be free to sign on to the Jack Harkins venture. Wilson simply didn't need him the way a young company like Harkins's First Flight did, and that gave him the chance to be something so much bigger than "staff"—to be an owner. Sure, there was a risk. Harkins didn't offer the security of a twenty-year deal with a big conglomerate. There were risks worth taking, and this was one of them. He had in front of him an opportunity that few men get, and on this night he had to think hard about his commercial destiny. The men finished their drinks, bundled up, and headed across the street to the Savoy Plaza for dinner at Trader Vic's. The restaurant and tiki bar had become a hot spot on New York's social scene. Clamshell lights, war clubs, carved masks, and Japanese fishing floats hung from ceilings covered with wooden palm leaves. The menu offered imitation Chinese and South Pacific fare ("Chicken Cantonese," "Shrimp Crepe Bengal") and cocktails like the mai tai that were exotic at that time.

As they sat down, McCormack launched into a speech that he hoped would make Palmer understand an alternative vision of the future. Palmer didn't have to settle for being comfortable, for merely having the ability to fly his family on commercial aircraft wherever he wanted. One day he might be rich enough to own the plane he would be flying on, to make enough money so that his children and even his grandchildren would never have to work. He would never have to wonder why he didn't end up with more.

Palmer heard McCormack out. He understood the stakes. His playing and practice and endorsement schedule was so busy that on this rare quiet night he and McCormack finally had the chance to think things through, and he was giving it the time it deserved. If he decided to go Wilson's way, this chance wouldn't exist for another ten or twenty years, by which time there would be a whole new generation of golfers as successful and famous as he was. The chance to build an empire would have passed. Yet as enticing as the picture McCormack painted might be, Palmer still couldn't make the leap. "I'm basically a conservative person," he told McCormack. The Wilson folks were big and powerful and they had been good to him. He didn't need his own plane or his own empire. Like any golfer, he knew how fleeting all this success might be. He might throw his back out on his next drive and never be able to compete at the highest level again. The yips are always only a bad night of sleep away. Sitting there in Trader Vic's, surrounded by the faux Polynesian décor, Palmer gave McCormack his marching orders: go along with the Wilson folks and work out an agreement. They could put the whole ordeal behind them and he could go back to focusing on smacking drives and sinking putts.

If only it would be that simple.

*For the next two months the relations between Wilson and McCor-*mack blew hot and cold. Plug Osborne reappeared, waving extra money if Palmer would show up at a store in Georgia the week before the Masters, and at a few other select events—$300 to speak to the Macon Golf Association. "I'm trying to look after you the best I can," Osborne told him.

Then the relationship was on the rocks again. A story had hit Max Kase's New York sports column that Palmer had turned down a $350,000 deal with First Flight for a long-term deal with Wilson that would give him stock in the company. Hare hit the roof. He accused McCormack of leaking a story that would let other Wilson golfers know Palmer was getting stock and they weren't. McCormack denied that he was the source and said Palmer wasn't, either, although he added that he never promised to refrain from commenting about the terms of the contract. Then Wilson started to raise more questions about the insurance plan, which McCormack insisted remained very important to Palmer.

January brought a new year and one last shot. McCormack attempted simple logic with Simpson, the Wilson general counsel. All Palmer wanted to do was defer $5,000 a year after his first $10,000 in royalties and have Wilson take a portion of that money and buy a $300,000 insurance policy. It wasn't long ago that they were discussing a $750,000 policy. Wilson wouldn't lose a deduction, because the money was going to be deferred anyway, and the company would even earn a dividend on its investment in the policy. This wasn't that complicated.

Simpson wrote McCormack on January 17 that he didn't see anything in the latest drafts of what had become a twenty-year deal that would prevent the contract from being executed in the coming weeks. Since McCormack was going away on vacation, and Judge Cooney was still away, too, they should plan to settle everything on February 6, when everyone was back. Just one last wrinkle, Simpson added: after ten years, each party had the right to end the deal, but if Palmer did so, Wilson wanted all of Palmer's deferred income to be paid at once.

Just like that, they were back at square one, back in 1957. If Palmer received all his deferred income in a single year, he would be subject to an enormous tax hit. His option to end the contract would be meaningless, since it would be prohibitively expensive. Wilson could opt out essentially without a penalty. If Palmer opted out, he stood to lose tens of thousands of dollars that would go to Uncle Sam, when the whole point of deferring income and spreading out payments over decades was to avoid just such a loss. It would defeat the entire concept and philosophy of the deferred-income proposal. Seven months of negotiations, and McCormack had essentially gotten nowhere.

February 7, 1961, would become the worst and greatest day of Mark McCormack's professional life. That morning McCormack's phone rang in his Cleveland office. It was Louis Simpson. He had bad news, he told McCormack. As much as Simpson and Charles Hare and Joe Wolfe and everyone else at Wilson who so loved Palmer wanted to make this deal, Judge Cooney had said, in a word, no. Cooney had said no to deferred incomes and split-dollar insurance plans and any other special treatment that none of his hardworking employees received. If that meant losing Palmer, then he was fine with that. Cooney still had Snead and Middlecoff and plenty of other golfers proud to serve as part of the "professional staff" of Wilson Sporting Goods. If Palmer didn't want to be a part of that, then Wilson was finished with him—after they used Palmer to sell their golf clubs for another three years, of course.

McCormack later wrote that he didn't know whether to laugh or to cry. Arnold Palmer was going to have to build a multimillion-dollar empire on his own whether he liked it or not. McCormack scratched out a note to Charles Hare assuring him this would be the most foolish and expensive thing Wilson had ever done.

Now it was Mark McCormack's turn to revel in the satisfaction of being right about the true nature of the good folks at Wilson. They had given Palmer their word that they would do whatever was needed to make him happy. McCormack hadn't thought that word was worth much, and now he knew its exact value. He also knew there had to be an alternative to this sort of indentured servitude. McCormack could see what the future of sports looked like. If athletes like Palmer took control of their own destinies, it wouldn't look like a 2 percent royalty and a promise to return all the equipment when they were done with it. McCormack hadn't gotten the deal with Wilson he'd been seeking, the sort of ground-shifting agreement with a major company that would have reset the market for such transactions. But that possible deal paled in comparison to the opportunity that lay before him now. He now had a three-year runway to get the Arnold Palmer Golf Company off the ground. This was the future of his business, not being nickel-and-dimed by some autocrat.

McCormack had won by losing, even though he hadn't intended to. In the most roundabout way, they had got what they originally pursued—freedom—even if it was going to take three years to become official. What was three years in the lifetime of an all-time great? Palmer just had to keep that back healthy. McCormack let a few weeks pass before he broke the news to Palmer. The talks had collapsed, he told his star client. Palmer would be a

Wilson staff member until October 31, 1963, he explained—but not a day longer.

The Wilson-Palmer relationship deteriorated through the remainder of 1961. Wilson harassed Palmer about being slow to approve a ghostwritten essay one of its marketing executives had crafted for Palmer about his advice to young golfers for the Junior Chamber of Commerce golf handbook. ("Putt past the hole. It has a chance to go in twice, once on the way and once on the way back.") Wilson refused to sponsor a Palmer exhibition trip to Japan. Then the company ordered him to pose for a set of brochure photographs, but it refused to send McCormack copies of the photos when he asked for them. In April, McCormack received a report that Wilson was selling twice as many balls and clubs as it had in 1960; then, in July, Winnie Palmer received a bill for a set of clubs Palmer had requested.

As the 1962 PGA tour was getting under way, Palmer grew desperate to put an end to the cross fire. He wrote directly to Cooney, one gentleman trying to appeal to the good senses of another. He made a startling offer:

> *I stand ready at the present time to return to you every nickel of royalties and salaries and bonuses that the Wilson Sporting Goods Company has paid me. If you would prefer, I would purchase from you your entire inventory of Arnold Palmer clubs. I would also like to let Wilson continue to manufacture and sell clubs and balls bearing my name until the present contract expires and would like to pay you any amount by which you feel that the concurrent manufacture and sale of a pro-only line of clubs in 1963 would damage the sale of my Wilson clubs . . .*
>
> *I shall look forward to hearing from you.*
>
> *Very truly yours,*
> *Arnold Palmer*

McCormack estimated the offer might have cost Palmer about half a million dollars in a negotiated settlement. The response? Crickets. Once again, the reason was simple: sales of Palmer's merchandise had risen from $558,324 in 1959 to $1,395,872 in 1962. Palmer's share of that amounted to only $23,538. Palmer won the Masters and the British Open in 1962 and came in second at the US Open. The following year, 1963, was going to be Wilson's biggest year of sales for Palmer equipment, and Palmer would still receive 2.5 percent of the first $260,000 of sales, and 1.5 percent thereafter.

As Palmer kept winning, Joe Wolfe kept sending the $500 bonus checks, along with his regrets that he wouldn't be able to keep sending them forever, until finally, on Halloween 1963, Palmer's nine-year relationship with Wilson ended. By 1966 the Arnold Palmer Golf Company was churning out one hundred thousand quality clubs a year, all designed by their namesake and marked with his seal of approval.

The extrication of Arnold Palmer from Wilson and Palmer's ability to take control of his name, his value, and everything associated with it would stand as the template for every deal McCormack would try to make for every iconic athlete and property for the rest of his career. This wasn't simply about money. McCormack was playing a new game. The object was liberation. Freedom would lead to more money—not just for the athletes but for everyone involved. He just knew it would.

McCormack taught Arnold Palmer that he was more than a golfer and an athlete. Like so many athletes who would follow in his footsteps, Palmer had become a symbol of excellence, a brand that needed to be cared for and protected. "Dior means something," McCormack wrote. "Tiffany means something. Rolls-Royce means something. The name projects an image, and the image sells." Arnold Palmer's image would sell, too, and eventually, so would those of Gary Player and Jack Nicklaus, and Jackie Stewart and Jean-Claude Killy.

Sometimes the clients had to remind McCormack that they were the stars, not him. When McCormack was wooing Killy in 1967, he traveled to France to have lunch with the skiing legend who would sweep the Alpine gold medals at the 1968 Olympics. Killy ordered a bottle of wine with lunch. McCormack admonished him, asking how a world-class athlete could drink wine with lunch. Killy smirked at McCormack wisely, then asked, "Would you rather I drink milk and ski like an American?"

While McCormack and Palmer became ever closer, they endured a lifelong disagreement over who was more responsible for the other's success. As much as he admired Palmer's skill, McCormack believed that, were it not for him, Palmer would have gone down in history simply as the best golfer of his era, not as the ruler of an empire that included private airplanes, real estate developments, a golf course design business, and so much more. Palmer would also receive a 10 percent stake in a little company called IMG. That would cash out at $75 million in 2004, when McCormack's estate sold IMG to the leveraged-buyout titan Ted Forstmann. For his part, Palmer believed McCormack wouldn't have gotten anywhere had it not been for what he accomplished on the golf course and his embrace of the responsibilities that went with the life of a champion. They were both right, of course. Neither would have existed in the way they did without the other. One had the guts to believe there was no golf shot he couldn't make. The other had the boundless confidence to try to bend the world to meet his desires. And bend it he did.

3

The Superstars

In early July of 1965, Mark McCormack decided to make a stopover on his way to the Open Championship, better known in the United States as the British Open. Instead of traveling directly to Royal Birkdale in Southport on England's west coast, McCormack scheduled a stay in London so he could attend Wimbledon, the most hallowed of tennis's grand slam events, held each year at the All England Lawn Tennis and Croquet Club. McCormack was no stranger to posh clubs by now. He'd spent plenty of time at Augusta National, for example. And yet McCormack was entranced as soon as he entered the All England Club's gates.

The place was resplendent with green ivy and tennis whites and strawberries and cream. Gentlemen took in the action in sport coats and ties. Fans clapped politely but were perfectly silent during play. Centre Court offered its otherworldly coziness. McCormack, a sucker for tradition, was hooked. There was little doubt in his mind this was far and away the finest tennis event in the world, if not the finest sports event, period. He watched Roy Emerson beat Fred Stolle in straight sets in the final on July 2. Then he began his trek to Southport. Along the way, he tried to shift his focus to golf, to Arnold Palmer, and to his more recent signings, Jack Nicklaus and Gary Player, whom he had formally brought into the fold with Palmer's consent. But he kept thinking about Wimbledon.

At one of his first meetings in Southport, McCormack sat down with Reginald Edward Hawke "Buzzer" Hadingham, the chairman of the British sporting goods company Slazenger. McCormack had negotiated contracts for Player and Nicklaus with Hadingham. He knew he was supposed to talk about golf and the golf business with him. Instead, McCormack couldn't help himself. He launched into a series of questions about Wimbledon: its history, how it operated, who controlled it. Finally, Hadingham grew tired of the questions. *If you're so curious about the place,* he told McCormack, *then you ought to meet my friend Herman David, the chairman of the All England Club.* That was exactly what McCormack wanted. Hadingham promised to help facilitate a meeting—a good thing, since McCormack knew he was going to need all the help he could get to infiltrate a place as steeped in British tradition as the All England Club.

McCormack was already well-known in sports circles as the brash American lawyer from Cleveland who was commercializing golf. Ventures like, say, Arnold Palmer Dry Cleaners could appear crass. He wasn't the sort of character who could break into the inner sanctum of one of England's most hallowed institutions without a connection. Buzzer Hadingham provided it.

Even with Hadingham's help McCormack still had to wait some eighteen months for his meeting. Then, in the winter of 1967, Mc-Cormack finally got his audience with both Herman David and Major David Mills, the club secretary. The delay actually ended up working to McCormack's benefit. It gave him another eighteen months to build up the fledgling film and television business he'd launched with his "Big Three" golf shows, featuring Palmer, Nicklaus, and Player dueling their way through rounds at a picturesque course. Making those shows wasn't easy. The equipment was heavy, expensive, and clunky. Filming a round of golf and making a television program out of it meant forcing players to spend six or eight hours playing eighteen holes. Then it would take weeks, even months, to edit the film into a two-hour show. But when the process was complete, McCormack had a product he could sell in the US and England and throughout Europe, and in Japan and Australia and everywhere else fans idolized his clients, who were partners in the venture and could share in the profits of a syndicated sale.

When McCormack sat down for his meeting with David and Mills, Wimbledon had only the most bare-bones television coverage. The blue blazers who ran the club hadn't really thought about how to broaden the event beyond Great Britain's borders. Trained as a lawyer to never ask a question to which he didn't know the answer, McCormack found his opening.

"Do you have a film of Wimbledon, of what happened this year?" McCormack asked.

They didn't, of course. *Well, you really should,* McCormack suggested, *because the grandest tennis tournament on the planet should have a film documenting the highlights.* David and Mills agreed that would be a good idea, but there was a problem. Making such a film was expensive. Who would pay for it? McCormack had an answer for this, too. He had just launched TWI, his event and television production company, and he said he would be happy to handle filming the tournament if he could then recoup his costs by selling it around the world. David thought that would be a fine arrangement. Then the conversation shifted to the international media rights to the tournament. At the time, Wimbledon had international television highlight contracts worth about $75,000. That was a pittance, McCormack told them. He suggested he could sell them for a lot more. David and Mills didn't necessarily disagree. They offered him the opportunity to prove it, but on one condition: he wouldn't get any credit for the first $75,000 in sales. That was just fine with McCormack. This deal was about a lot more than $75,000. It was like being tapped for a secret society.

On May 20, 1968, McCormack signed his first deal with the All England Club for the film rights to Wimbledon, and IMG's longtime representation of the All England Club was born. It gave TWI and its subsidiary 15 percent of the first $50,000 in sales, 20 percent of the next $50,000, and 25 percent of anything above that. TWI would make the film, with production costs estimated at $16,000. The venture didn't become profitable until 1971, when McCormack secured a $50,000 advertising deal with the Wilkinson Sword company. Then, in 1976, McCormack got the deal he really wanted: to represent Wimbledon for its worldwide television rights. That deal got TWI 10 percent of the first $300,000 in sales, 15 percent of the next $300,000, and 20 percent of everything beyond $600,000. The windfall came a year later, when McCormack helped engineer a new six-year, $5.2 million deal with NBC, which by then was also paying $150,000 for the one-hour highlight film. Wimbledon and TWI were on their way.

McCormack's deal with Wimbledon had dual purposes. By the mid-1960s he realized that to succeed on the level he wanted to, he was going to have to do a lot more than find a bunch of companies that wanted to attach themselves to his clients. He was going to have to create a new world, or at the very least a new industry and an environment in which those athletes and personalities could achieve success on their terms, and where he could achieve success on his terms. Golfers and tennis players needed more showcase tournaments in the biggest cities, so McCormack created them. They needed larger purses and higher attendance at the biggest tournaments to drive the growth. They needed an official ranking system that allowed everyday fans or a company that might pay an athlete to understand who the best of the best actually was. They needed head-to-head matches against each other to supplement the existing schedule. Most of all, they needed to be on television shows that featured their specific talents. McCormack was going to generate all this and much more. As McCormack saw it, he had no other choice.

By the time McCormack began pursuing the All England Club, he'd launched the Arnold Palmer Golf Company and become something of a new model in his industry, if it could even be called that. But McCormack had his eye on the career of someone who had nothing to do with sports—another Cleveland guy named Lew Wasserman.

Wasserman had started out like McCormack had, representing the biggest stars, including Ronald Reagan, Jimmy Stewart, and Bette Davis. He led them through their fight for liberation from the entrenched Hollywood studios. The battle had installed the talent at the top of the pyramid in Hollywood. But in 1962, when he was forty-nine years old, Wasserman had been around Hollywood long enough to realize the producers lived in the nicest houses in Southern California. So he completed a plan he had been working on for four years, buying Universal Studios and merging it with his own company, MCA. Suddenly, Wasserman was on every side of the business. He controlled the chessboard. He could place his clients in the most advantageous jobs and roles, take his commission out of their salaries, and also own the productions themselves. Wasserman became Hollywood royalty. His plan worked because Wasserman understood that the actors were the most important people in any film. Any other job could change and no one in the audience would notice. Change the actors and everyone notices. He might have been relatively new to the producing game, but he understood the modern structure of it before anyone else did.

McCormack was trying to adapt the Wasserman model to sports. He couldn't go out and buy Wimbledon or Major League

Baseball. However, he understood sports was going to be about putting the best athletes in the most important and entertaining events, then making those events as big and profitable as they could be. To do that, he needed to use television to make the whole thing come off like some grand Hollywood movie. The people who ran sports believed the games existed for their benefit. To McCormack, the sports industry existed primarily as a form of livelihood for a group of athletes with a set of extraordinary skills, men (and a few women) who were envied and admired by hundreds of millions of fans around the world. They were the heart of a business whose inefficiencies were whatever got in the way of the maximum amount of money flowing to them, whether it was the cranky chairman of a sporting goods conglomerate, a stuffy chairman of a tennis club who couldn't figure out how to make a highlight film, or a general secretary of a golf club who didn't like newfangled talk of international broadcast deals. If anyone didn't believe him or didn't see the pyramid flipping the way he did, McCormack was damn well going to figure out how to prove him wrong.

The problem was McCormack couldn't pull this off as "Arnold Palmer's guy," just another hustler on the 10 or 15 or 25 percent side of the business. He was going to have to find a way onto the 75 percent side of the business. To do that, he needed to become enmeshed in the fabric of prestigious events like Wimbledon and maybe even own some events that might not carry Wimbledon's prestige, but could do a better job of putting money into his clients' pockets and his own. This wasn't just about money, though. It was about protecting himself against the luck he had with choosing to represent Arnold Palmer, Jack Nicklaus, and Gary Player running out. Those three players would win fifteen of the twenty-eight major tournaments (the Masters, the US Open, the British Open, and the PGA Championship) during one seven-year stretch. Somehow, no one threw out a back or tore up a knee or got the yips. "Owning" the so-called Big Three or even tennis star Rod

Laver was one thing. Owning the events they played in, or at least owning their telecasts, was something else entirely. "Wimbledon," McCormack often said to anyone who would listen, "doesn't break a leg, sprain an ankle, fail a drug test, or lose six-love, six-love."

The shift began with a quick study of a dusty PGA Tour schedule, with its stops in what were then backwater towns like Phoenix, San Antonio, and Pensacola. Why not London? McCormack thought. In 1964 he decided to create the World Match Play Championship, where he introduced the US sporting public to the upper crust of London society at the tony Wentworth Club. Only the best of the best qualified for the Match Play Championship. Its head-to-head format held the potential for duels between the great players of the day: Palmer taking on Nicklaus, Nicklaus taking on Casper, Casper taking on Player. Then, believing that his clients needed and sports fans wanted more spectacles like this, he created "Big Three Golf." He brought the Big Three and their made-for-TV competitions to Africa and the Far East, proving to skeptical friends and colleagues that sports could become a global enterprise and cross borders like few other businesses.

After he convinced Wimbledon to hire him, McCormack set his sights on the Royal and Ancient Golf Club of St. Andrews, Scotland, to give the Open Championship similar treatment. The biggest obstacle was a longtime club secretary named Keith Mackenzie. Mackenzie had spent twenty years as an executive with Shell. He took over as secretary of the R&A in 1968, just when McCormack began working with Wimbledon. Mackenzie was the prickly sort, a typical ex–British Army snob who didn't take well to cavalier Americans invading his turf. Mackenzie could feel the pressure, though. The winner of the US Open Championship in 1968 received a check for $30,000, or about $200,000 in today's dollars. The winner of the Open Championship received a check for £3,000, or about $76,000 in today's dollars. The disparity was a direct reflection of the limited revenues the Open Championship produced. The event attracted just thirty-two thousand spectators, or less than the US Open might attract on a single day. The R&A grudgingly understood that they couldn't just keep this event to themselves and the dusty crowd of dandruff-speckled blue blazers. The organization desperately needed help.

The R&A went to school on the effect that IMG's television efforts were having at Wimbledon. In 1968, Wimbledon offered about £26,000 in total prize money. In 1972 it reached £50,000. By 1975 it hit £114,000. Three years later it was £279,000. And at the All England Club, television was just the tip of the iceberg. McCormack was in the process of persuading the club to add everything that is taken for granted today at a major sports event but didn't exist at the time. Borrowing from PGA Tour golf, where sponsorships were more common, he brought in advertising, including the iconic Rolex sign on the Centre Court scoreboard. Like plenty of wealthy sports fans, he stayed in fine hotels when he traveled, and he didn't much care for the low-grade, one-size-fits-all fan experience once he entered an arena. So he introduced corporate hospitality tents and other luxury entertainment dining options at the event. Realizing that a prized property like Wimbledon was no different from other great brands, from Tiffany to Arnold Palmer, that benefited from a single, recognizable symbol, he persuaded the All England Club to create its purple-and-green crossed rackets emblem and to build a licensing program that would include printed patterns on tennis strings, plates, rackets, shoes, bags, balls, sweatbands, socks, even fragrances. He mixed it all with Pimm's cocktails and strawberries and cream and sold the whole production not so much as a tennis tournament but as a symbol of tradition and excellence.

Slowly, Mackenzie began to submit to McCormack's ideas, first allowing him to make a film for the tournament that they could sell to the world. Finally, in 1975, IMG became the R&A's world-wide television representative. For McCormack, working for the All England Club and the R&A and a growing portfolio of leagues and federations represented true progress. It gave him prestige he couldn't buy, as well as a healthy commission. The windfall to those organizations also invariably boosted the purses that tournament organizers would make available to the participating players, many of whom were his clients. The more an athlete won on the field of play, the more he could ask for off it. And as the payouts to the athletes grew, so, too, would the size of McCormack's 10 percent share of his clients' winnings and his 20 percent share of their marketing deals. But all this still had McCormack on the short side when it came to his cut of the profits. Whether his client was Arnold Palmer or the All England Club, he was still working for a commission. He knew he couldn't end up atop the pyramid. That space was reserved for the athletes. But maybe he could end up owning the pyramid, or at least a part of it. In the oil business, if you can't own the oil, owning the pipeline is the next best thing, and in sports the pipeline was television.

One afternoon in 1969, a young sports producer at ABC named Barry Frank was kibitzing the day away with his friend and colleague Dick Button. Frank and Button made an unlikely pair.

Small, paunchy, and red-faced, Frank had come out of an Ivy League graduate business program in the 1950s and taken a job on the Ford account for the advertising firm J. Walter Thompson. Ford was one of the biggest advertisers in sports, a one-quarter sponsor of the CBS NFL Game of the Week and of McCormack's "Big Three" golf shows. In 1963, Frank suggested putting NFL games on Friday nights for four weeks in October, when Ford would announce its new models, an event that in its day was met with the same anticipation as the release of a new Apple product today. The idea caught the fancy of Roone Arledge, the innovative producer of ABC Sports. Pete Rozelle, the young and ambitious marketing whiz who'd taken over the NFL as commissioner, loved it, too. Then Walter Byers, the executive director of the National Collegiate Athletic Association, caught wind of it. Byers could see where this was going. The NFL would end up being a hit on Friday night, and soon their special October offering of five games would expand into thirteen games, and then the NFL would try to launch another series of games on Saturday nights. Byers got in touch with the leaders of every major high school sports league in the country and told them to call their congressman and push for legislation that would protect high school football by prohibiting a professional game from being played within fifteen miles of any high school game on a Friday night. Within days the NFL's Friday night plan was dead, but it got Frank a job at ABC in 1965.

Button, meanwhile, was a former Olympic figure skating champion who had become a wildly popular and outspoken analyst of the sport during Olympic and world championship broadcasts. He also acted and produced ice shows in his spare time.

On Frank's desk, *Life* magazine lay open to a story on the ballet dancer Edward Villella. The headline read: THE BEST ATHLETE IN THE LAND: EDWARD VILLELLA IS A DANCER, BUT YOU HAVE TO RANK HIM WITH THE YASTRZEMSKIS, THE NAMATHS AND THE MUHAMMAD ALIS.

Button pushed the magazine across Frank's desk and thought out loud: "Maybe there is a show here?"

Frank shrugged. "Maybe," he said.

The conversation didn't go much further than that. The idea settled into one of those crevices in the human brain where thoughts are filed and rarely thought of again.

From Cleveland, McCormack had been watching Barry Frank and Roone Arledge's work with a sense of awe. Through the 1960s, Arledge had turned himself into a legend in sports television. He sent camera crews around the world to film track competitions, rattlesnake hunts, and other random sporting events and then turned them into a surprisingly popular show called *ABC's Wide World of Sports*. He spent millions beaming the Olympic Games into living rooms and even televised a few matches from Wimbledon.

Arledge could sit in a control room, stare at twenty monitors showing gymnastics, wrestling, and javelin, and know to cut to gymnastics because there was a fourteen-year-old from Romania about to do her last vault. Then Arledge would tell the announcer through his earpiece that the gymnast's mother was suffering from some life-threatening condition and the gymnast had dedicated her routine to her mother and the friends caring for her in some village no one had ever heard of. Just like that the vault was no longer merely a vault. It was a story about facing down death with an affirmation of life. It was, as the theme of *Wide World of Sports* proclaimed, "the human drama of athletic competition."

Arledge had almost singlehandedly turned ABC into a viable network. In the mid-1960s, ABC was the smallest player in the national television game. It had roughly half the affiliates that CBS and NBC did. CBS ruled news. NBC ruled entertainment. With Arledge, ABC carved out its niche as the leader in televised sports. Sports accounted for just ten hours of programming most weeks, but it produced an outsized percentage of the network's profits.

Like McCormack, Arledge was among the very small minority in sports television who believed there was an audience for something other than American team sports. The trick was to teach the audience about the people who were participating, whether it was at the Olympics or at a barrel jumping competition, so they could feel in their bones the stakes of going ass over teakettle and sliding across the ice. Arledge made auto racing accessible in the same way, putting open-wheel racing on television. It was dangerous and it was exciting, but you also needed to understand the story behind who was winning and who was losing. If you got personal, you could get an audience.

Frank quickly became Arledge's right hand at ABC sports. He sat next to him in the control room at the 1968 Olympics in Mexico City. He helped him turn *Wide World of Sports* into a behemoth, even if they were occasionally covering a barrel-jumping-on-ice competition from a Catskill Mountains resort. As he watched it all unfold, McCormack realized that he needed to do for his clients—and for himself—what ABC could do for ice-skating barrel jumpers. Hiring Arledge wasn't going to happen. So he hired Frank.

Frank got to TWI, IMG's television arm, and opened his Rolodex. He called NFL commissioner Pete Rozelle and MLB commissioner Bowie Kuhn and told them the networks weren't paying the leagues nearly what they deserved. He promised to get them more if they would allow him to represent them. The NFL signed on, and then MLB did, and NASCAR, and the International Skating Union, and before long Frank had a roster of twenty major leagues and federations. Very quickly the rights payments began to climb, because Frank knew firsthand how much money the networks were making off the sports content.

One day in 1972, Frank sat down to lunch with a marketing representative of an auto parts company who told him the company wanted to get more heavily involved with sports to appeal to the sort of adult men who would buy the company's products. He wanted an event with the best-known athletes in the world participating in some kind of competition. He didn't know what shape that competition would take. He was basically agnostic about the sport itself. His mission was to find a vessel with enough big names for the company to attract its target audience.

Immediately Frank thought back to the conversation he'd had with Button three years before: a competition between the best athletes on the planet to determine which one was better than all the rest. When he got back to the office he called Button and offered to make him a 50-50 partner on the show. It was Button's idea, after all. Frank mapped out a proposal for the show, which boiled down to taking the biggest stars in sports and running them through a series of events. They'd call it *The Superstars*. IMG would cover expenses for the athletes and offer a big cash prize to the winner.

McCormack thought it was genius. He already represented some of the biggest stars in sports. Now he could expose them to fans outside their traditional endeavors: a tennis fan could see Rod Laver sprint against Johnny Bench, for example, with cash on the line. It was perfect, especially since IMG would own it, but also because it was going to put to the test McCormack's theory that the star athletes in sports should reside at the top of the pyramid. If they could carry a competition and a show like *The Superstars* that was completely devoid of any legacy or tradition, they could prove they were the equals of the ruling powers of any league or international sports federation.

As the concept evolved, Frank dialed the networks in search of a broadcaster. One by one they passed, still not convinced an audience existed for something so unconventional. Even two of Arledge's junior executives at ABC passed. Finally, Frank got on Arledge's golf schedule at Winged Foot in Mamaroneck, New York. Arledge and ABC had recently lost the rights to the NBA. They needed something to program against it. The obvious move would have been to pick up another winter sport. But Arledge wasn't about obvious. By the end of the round, Frank had convinced him *The Superstars* was worth a shot.

Howard Katz was sitting at his desk in ABC's control room in New York on a Sunday afternoon in February 1973 when the phone rang. A twenty-three-year-old assistant producer, Katz was the low man on the totem pole, and it was his job to pick up the phone. Another assistant producer was on the other end of the line. They needed a body in Florida as soon as possible, because this *Superstars* thing was becoming more complicated than anyone thought it was going to be. Katz was a nice Jewish boy from New Jersey who tried to do what he was told. The next day he got on a plane to Sarasota with no idea what he was getting himself into.

Frank didn't, either. The whole project had started innocently enough. A developer of a new community in Florida called Rotonda that was being built around seven golf courses had paid them $50,000 to film there, figuring the show would be good advertising. Frank got the athletes—Johnny Bench, Johnny Unitas, Joe Frazier, Jean-Claude Killy, the Olympic pole-vaulter Bob Seagren. Everybody did it for different reasons. To some, it was fun. To Bench and Unitas, the first prize of about $40,000 was big money. Jean-Claude Killy wanted to build his name in the United States. Competitors participated in a variety of different sporting events, including a hundred-yard dash, a half-mile run, weight lifting, cycling, bowling, tennis, and swimming. Katz spent the next several days doing whatever was needed: moving cameras; fetching tennis balls; helping out the officials. They ironed out problems on the fly and everyone was managing to have a swell time until Joe Frazier forgot to tell Frank and the producers that he wasn't all that comfortable in water. Frazier nearly drowned during the fifty-yard swim. When it was all over, Seagren had won. No stunner there. He was the reigning gold medalist in the pole vault, a square-jawed Adonis destined for a career as a D-list television actor. Johnny Bench couldn't hold his own in so many Olympic-like events.

When *The Superstars* finally aired, the supposed wise men of sports hated it. These were the grizzled sports columnists and the executives with the old-line leagues and teams. They saw it as a mockery of athletic competition, and they labeled it "trash sports." Sports fans were a different story. The viewers ate it up. When ABC put *The Superstars* on opposite NBA games, it slaughtered the NBA in the ratings, which meant one thing: McCormack and Frank and Katz were going to have to do this again.

By the next year Katz had moved over from ABC to TWI to run *The Superstars* for Frank and build it into a franchise. McCormack connected him with IMG's team sports division in Cleveland to recruit athletes by waving the prospect of prize money. The top athletes were making only a little over $100,000 a year back then. Pete Rose and Reggie Jackson and Lynn Swan signed on. They were among the biggest stars in the country. Wayne Grimditch, the champion water skier, wanted in because he didn't make much money at all. *The Superstars* could provide him with an actual living—and it did. Some guys did it for the free trip to Florida, and later Hawaii, or to attempt to reinforce their notions about the supremacy of their endeavors. Kyle Rote Jr., a soccer player, won three times from 1974 to 1977. That created a rivalry with the traditional stick-and-ball American athletes raised to believe soccer players were wimps. Now a wimp was kicking their butts on national television.

"What became very clear very quickly was that even though this was supposed to be fun, very few of the athletes didn't compete once they got there," Katz said. Most important, *The Superstars* continued to kill in the ratings. After the first two years, Frank and Katz decided it was time to expand. There was already a British version of the show and the thing was starting to take on the flavor of a franchise. *The Superstars* would go on, but so would a spin-off, *The Superteams*. That would pit members of the four teams that had played in the most recent World Series and Super Bowl against each other.

Katz decided the competition would take place in Hawaii in early February, just before spring training and just after the NFL season had ended. After getting ten players from each team to commit, plus former Southeastern Conference commissioner Joe Dey to officiate, Frank rented a 747 and flew it across the country picking up athletes and their wives and girlfriends—or, in Reggie Jackson's case, his mother—before finally touching down in Honolulu. On the plane Frank handed each player $300 to pay for incidentals at the hotel. As he walked down the aisle, he saw the eyes of the athletes grow glassy at the site of a $12,000 roll of bills. It was a window into the mind-set of these men. Most of them had grown up modestly. They were blown away by the stack of cash.

Katz had never set up a competition like this before. He certainly hadn't ever been a professional athlete or coach. But, like so many Jewish kids who grew up in the expanding middle class of postwar America, Katz had been to summer camp, where he had competed in a ritual known as "Color War" as though his freedom had depended on the outcome. In Hawaii, Katz drew on that experience to design a series of running, swimming, and obstacle course relay races, a tandem bicycle competition, a Hawaiian outrigger canoe race through a lagoon near Waikiki's Hilton Hawaiian Village, and, of course, a tug-of-war. Instead of wiry kids, the participants were members of the Super Bowl and World Series teams. "There weren't any rules, so we could just make them up," Katz said.

While there may not have been rules, Katz quickly learned there were substantial physical differences between NFL linemen and the pimply prepubescent Jewish boys from New Jersey who attended Camp Echo Lark. In the days and weeks leading up to the competition, Katz had similarly sized athletes run through the events. The trials didn't go well. They bought bikes for the tandem bike races, but the athletes were so strong they broke the pedals. Katz wanted a boat race, so he got rowboats. Then the trial athletes broke the hinges on the oars. A shot-putter named Brian Oldfield broke five sets of hinges. They put tickets on sale in Hawaii, figuring a huge crowd would turn out to watch some of the country's most famous athletes test their strength and speed against each other or, failing that, make fools of themselves on tandem bikes and obstacle courses. A mere 1,500 tickets were sold.

There was no turning back. A purse of $331,500 was there

for the taking, a guarantee of $3,400 for each athlete, even if they lost every event. Win every event and a check for $15,300 could be had. McCormack had even persuaded a reporter from *Sports Illustrated*, that most staid and respected of sports publications, to cover this little competition. Five team captains—Sal Bando of the Oakland A's, Ray Mansfield of the Steelers, Mick Tingelhoff of the Vikings, and Steve Garvey and Jimmy Wynn of the Dodgers—gathered their troops for a practice the morning after they got off the plane. The next day the competition started.

The tandem bike races went off without a hitch, with the A's and Steelers taking the early lead. But then Bill North of the A's botched his handoff to Reggie Jackson during the running relay even though he was winning the race by ten yards. North blamed Jackson for leaving the handoff area too quickly. The Vikings won their relay on a protest. The athletes were doing exactly what Katz had learned they would almost always do—play hard, whether it was the Super Bowl or a darts competition—as long as money and pride were on the line.

The Dodgers and Steelers took the obstacle course relays. The Vikings took the swim relay, knotting the football competition at 2, while the Dodgers outswam the A's to take a commanding 3–1 lead.

The second day's events took place on Waikiki Beach. The A's stayed alive with a 15–13 win in volleyball. On to the canoes, where the Dodgers got payback and knocked off the A's, but the Vikings once again pulled even, thanks to their canoe captain, Blue Makua Jr., a Hawaiian with experience in the Molokai–Oahu race. That meant everything would come down to the tug-of-war.

Hearing a commotion down the beach, a crowd of curious beachgoers had gathered to take in the action. It wasn't the Kentucky Derby and it wasn't the Rose Bowl. The men wore tank tops and shorts. There were no logos or leagues and there wasn't a historic trophy on the line, but it was the kind of irresistible theater that great athletes can produce: a battle to pull a rope across a four-by-twelve-foot water pit. A flag marked the middle of the rope. Yank the flag onto your side of the water pit, and $44,000 was yours, plus a shot at the $50,000 grand prize. The Steelers brought six men totaling 1,470 pounds with an average age of twenty-eight. The Vikings had 1,398 pounds and an average age of thirty. At the start, the Steelers beat down the Vikes, getting that flag to within thirty inches of victory. But over the next four minutes, inch by inch, the Vikings pulled it back. Franco Harris tugged with everything he had and buried his face in the sand as he tried to get the momentum back for the Steelers.

On the sidelines, Katz watched the tug-of-war play out with a sense of terror. It dawned on him that it might never end—that these athletes were so strong and so determined that the stalemate might last for eternity. He hadn't prepared for that, hadn't written any rules or even considered that the collective wills might be so strong that both sides would refuse to lose. Then he saw that, no matter how hard the Steelers tried to resist, it was hopeless. Near the sixteen-minute mark, the Vikings mustered one final tug and dragged the center of the rope over to their side. The Super Bowl champion Steelers sank into the sand, completely spent.

As the Vikings celebrated, the cameras moved in, showing the massive, sweaty bodies coated with sand. O. J. Simpson, on one of his early broadcasting assignments, leaned down low with his microphone to try to grab a word with Franco Harris. Harris's face rested on the beach, the sand caking his cheek and the side of his head. He couldn't talk. "I'm going to be here for a while, Juice," he said. Dave Osborn of the Vikings said the tug-of-war had taken more energy than two full football games. "It was an hour before I could get my gloves off," Osborn said later. "It was the greatest experience, the greatest victory I've ever had in sport. Better than any football game or anything else. We came here to beat the Steelers, and people who see that tug-of-war on television will remember it when they've forgotten who played in the 1975 Super Bowl."

For McCormack, the tug-of-war crystallized everything he had been working toward since he first tried to convince the best golfers on the PGA Tour that they deserved more than what they were getting for their exhibitions. Like the stars of Hollywood, the athletes mattered more than anything else, he had insisted. In *The Superstars* and *The Superteams*, there was nothing else. There was a rope on a beach and a collection of the world's greatest athletes pulling on it with a jackpot on the line. With the right cast of characters, the competition became as dramatic as the back nine at Augusta National. And the franchise belonged to him.

The Superstars would run for seventeen years. On average, about 65 percent of television series are canceled after a single season. *The Superstars* wasn't just long-lasting, it was prolific, a far more valuable quality if you are in the business of creating, producing, and owning a new genre of sports. *The Superstars* and *The Superteams* spawned a women's version of *The Superstars*, *The World's Strongest Man*, and an NFL arm wrestling competition (won by Tom Condon, who would later become an agent at IMG). In another show, *Survival of the Fittest*, the world's top outdoorsmen climbed and rappelled and raced down a hill and through an aerial obstacle course (think rope bridges over rapids). They raced mountain bikes, held a stick fight on a bridge over freezing water, then embarked on a swim and kayak event in which competitors swam down the rapids for two hundred yards, got in a boat, and paddled back against the current. A ranger warned them of eddies in the rapids, which were dangerous whirlpools that sucked swimmers underwater. A former marine disappeared into one. He stayed under for ninety seconds. To Frank it felt like forever. "I thought for sure he was dead and we were screwed," Frank said. "Finally he popped up."

Frank and Katz tried to build events for traditional sports, too. Through the 1970s, Don Ohlmeyer, then a young producer at ABC and later NBC, became one of Frank's golfing buddies. Like many

amateur golfers, they liked to play for money. If they had four golfers in their group, they split the group and played two-man teams.
If they had two, they played a match. If there were three, they
played skins, a game in which the winner of each hole gets a certain amount of money, and if the hole ends in a tie, the money carries over to the next hole until someone wins the "skin."

By 1982, Ohlmeyer had left NBC to become an independent
producer. He wanted to create a skins game for the best golfers in
the world. He took it to the networks. They passed. The golf audience wanted tradition and history, they said. Then Ohlmeyer called
Frank and McCormack. Frank took about four seconds to jump at
the idea. Even better, he and McCormack had access to the talent:
the golfers in their IMG stable. To Frank, this could be "Big Three
Golf" with big money. Palmer, Nicklaus, Player, and Tom Wat-
son signed up to play the first year. With that sort of star power
committed, Frank knew they had a winner, even if the networks
weren't interested. So Ohlmeyer and IMG bought the time on NBC
and took 100 percent of the risk. They understood how advertisers
thought. In any other golf tournament, each golfer has to share the
stage with as many as 155 others. The Skins Game would have just
a single group that would be on television for four hours. It was
clutter-free television time.

The Skins Game happened on Thanksgiving weekend, when
little besides football was on the schedule. Like so many of the IMG
events, it was simple. People could understand playing a golf hole
for $50,000, just like they could understand a sprint, an obstacle
course, or a tug-of-war. There was no cup; there was no championship. To be champion of the Skins Game didn't mean anything.
It was all about money, and the audiences loved it. They loved the
putt for $100,000. The players loved to one-up each other. The
worst thing that could happen was to get shut out in the Skins
Game.

For years, media executives had been telling McCormack that

the world was too diverse to create a global business. But as he cobbled together clients like Wimbledon and the R&A, selling their rights around the world, then created competitions as varied as the Skins Game and *The Superstars*, McCormack developed something very close to a worldwide network under the umbrella of TWI. People running sports in the US believed the business ended at the water's edge and with the traditional American team sports. Soccer? Who cared about soccer? McCormack, whose mother planned the meals she would eat on European trips six months ahead of time, certainly did. "Mark understood before anyone that the rest of the world was a really big, really interesting place," Frank said.

There were failures along the way. A three-on-three basketball tournament in which each team included a current player, a retired player, and a celebrity produced a lot of uninspiring basketball. But with each success, the McCormack lesson was becoming that much more powerful: sports was a TV show built around its stars. Its main purpose was to entertain an audience and put money in the bank accounts of the athletes trying to make a living at them. Barry Frank's trash sports weren't ever going to replace Wimbledon or the Open Championship or the Olympics or the Super Bowl. But the Skins Game could exist alongside them, and for the marquee events to thrive, they were going to have to look, at least on television, a lot more like *The Superstars* than they had in the past. And they certainly needed the world's greatest athletes front and center or else they were done.

Forty years after Mark McCormack and Palmer started on their IMG adventure, the company was producing and distributing 6,000 hours per year of programming for 240 sports in 200 different countries. It beamed the images of the greatest athletes around the world, broadcasting their feats and failures and transforming them from mortals into legends in the process. McCormack never understood television technology. He had zero interest in learning about it. But as he aged and the technology shifted, McCormack stuck to what he knew and became even more convinced that, to survive, IMG had to own and represent television rights. Let the telecommunications companies battle over transponders and coverage rights. Whoever won that battle was still going to need programming and rights to cricket and soccer matches and golf tournaments and basketball games.

In June of 1980, Alastair Johnston, a Scot who had started as an intern at IMG in 1969 and became one of McCormack's most trusted lieutenants, made the trip that McCormack had made fifteen years before. He set out from Cleveland, flew across the Atlantic to London, and headed over to the All England Club to check up on IMG's business. As Johnston wandered the grounds, he caught sight of the growing number of corporate names in prominent spots throughout the All England Club, like that Rolex sign beside Centre Court. IMG had sold those. When he wasn't watching the matches, he met colleagues and friends in hospitality suites. IMG had created and sold those, too. He followed much of the action on television, a production IMG had sold throughout the world, the riches of which had produced a startling rise in prize money. He watched the defending champion Bjorn Borg defeat John McEnroe in a thrilling five-set final that included an 18–16 fourth-set tiebreaker for the ages. Borg, who captured his fifth consecutive Wimbledon title that fortnight, was a top IMG client who made so much money he had to move to Monaco to avoid Sweden's onerous income taxes.

When Wimbledon finished, Johnston headed to Muirfield for the Open Championship. As he strolled across the historic golf course beside the Firth of Forth near Edinburgh, Johnston had the ultimate déjà vu experience: there were the corporate signs and the hospitality tents, which IMG had mostly sold. There was the broadcast, which they'd sold, too, and every few minutes he'd see another golfer from the IMG stable. He knew the competition would come eventually, but at that moment he and his company sat at the pinnacle of the sports marketing business before most people even knew what sports marketing was. "It just seemed like we were running the whole thing," he said.

Before long the inevitable whispers began: IMG was too powerful, a walking conflict of interest that was controlling and corrupting sports. Its golfers and tennis players were getting the preferred tee times and court assignments at the events where IMG helped manage the operations. The complaints weren't unjustified. At the events it owned, such as the World Match Play Championships, IMG clients took preference. In 1994, Brad Faxon, an IMG client—though hardly a superstar—got invited to the Match Play Championships. Seve Ballesteros and other European greats who were not IMG clients didn't. In 1999 Lee Westwood criticized the IMG-created Official World Golf Rankings system. He'd rattled off eleven wins in thirty-four tournaments, many of them events in Europe that IMG had little to do with, yet Westwood found himself ranked only sixth in the world. He insisted the rankings were rigged against European players, who were less likely to be IMG clients.

After IMG negotiated a multiyear deal for Tiger Woods with General Motors that paid Woods some $7 million a year, the world's top golfer always seemed to appear in the GM-sponsored events despite a schedule that limited Woods's annual calendar to just eighteen to twenty tournaments. At one point Woods even began making noises about dropping off the PGA Tour and playing an even more limited schedule that would include the four major championships and an international slate of tournaments and events that IMG would have been more than happy to set up for him. To a growing number of critics in the sports world, IMG had earned its derisive nicknames—"I Am Greedy," "Incredibly Manipulative Guys," "International Money Grabbers," and "I Manage God."

McCormack rejected the criticism out of hand, arguing that for decades he'd been perfectly clear about his mission: serving his clients. If it was good for them and good for business, he could clear his conscience of concerns about supposed conflicts. Sport was a vehicle, a show, a live-action motion picture to entertain the masses and make the best athletes in the world the wealthiest. His ability allowed him to bring off the World Match Play, in which IMG rented the golf course, took the gate, got the sponsors, produced the television, and sold the hospitality tents. McCormack even commentated on the air and published a book about the event. To him, the event was a matter of pure pride, huge profits, and unending benevolence. "But for us, there would be no match play event," he said. "Is that good or bad for golf in Britain?"

That occasional tin ear was just one of McCormack's flaws. Mark Hume McCormack was not a perfect human being by any stretch of the imagination. He was vastly capable of hypocrisy and contradiction. A shameless braggart, he boasted of his exploits in his books, such as *What They Don't Teach You at Harvard Business School*. He assigned Stewart Binns, the documentary filmmaker who served as his director of special projects for IMG-controlled TWI, to do a documentary about him. During the interviews, he declared that he had no need to brag about his accomplishments. The man who brought commercialism to sport and tore down so many of the traditions of stodgy organizations like the All England Club and the Royal & Ancient Golf Club of St. Andrews started warning of the dangers of commercializing sports. He claimed he was a traditionalist.

McCormack was the ultimate jet-setter. During Wimbledon, his London town house became the place to be and be seen during Wimbledon. Dan Jenkins, the legendary sportswriter who had ghostwritten McCormack's 1967 biography of Palmer, said he looked up from his drink one night and found himself surrounded by Sean Connery, Paul McCartney, and Kiri Te Kanawa, the famous opera diva. Another day, while sitting in McCormack's box, he got introduced to a tall, handsome Swede who happened to be the chairman of the nominations committee for the Nobel Prize in Literature. Yet McCormack rejected all accusations of social climbing. A typical night for him was dinner and a movie at home with his second wife, the tennis player (and IMG client) Betsy Nagelsen. He neglected to say which of his homes—Ohio, New York, Florida, London, or Palm Springs—was his preferred location for such an activity.

McCormack was so meticulous about his daily routine that he kept notes on the number of hours he dedicated to sleep, relaxation, work, flying, and spending time with his family, even recording how many sit-ups he did. After he got divorced from his first wife, Nancy, in 1984, he reasoned the marriage had failed because he had spent only 38 percent of his time with his family. He said this was a calculation, not an estimate. Eventually, one of his sons, Todd, realized that family time really was just another item to be checked off on the legal pad of tasks to accomplish during the day. As time went on, McCormack stopped being able to spend time with his family unless a planned event was involved.

"There always had to be some kind of activity, some sort of structure to it," Todd McCormack said. "He didn't have much confidence in his ability to just spend time with people, he didn't enjoy silence. There always had to be some sort of outcome from an interaction."

In January 2003, McCormack suffered a sudden heart attack during a doctor's appointment and fell into a coma from which he would never wake up. He died four months later. He was seventy-two. In a span of forty-five years, McCormack went from being a shy midwesterner who used to stand around, eyes darting in every direction and often biting his nails, to being a debonair gentleman with a taste for the finest things in life. At his memorial service in New York City, Ray Cave, the former managing editor of *Time* magazine, called McCormack his best friend, a man whose company he delighted in. Then Cave admitted that he didn't actually know

McCormack very well at all, because McCormack didn't really exist beyond the business that so dominated his life. McCormack would pepper his dinner conversation with statements like "Agassi is back" or "Capriati is down." The chatter wouldn't go much deeper than that, with tales about the goings-on of Margaret Thatcher and Pat Riley and Itzhak Perlman told over expensive bottles of wine in the world's finest restaurants.

In 2001, McCormack's penultimate year of work before the cardiac arrest that would lead to his death, IMG recorded $1.6 billion in revenues. The company employed three thousand people in eighty-five offices in thirty-three countries and represented more than one thousand clients. Those clients stretched far beyond sports and included icons such as Thatcher, Pearlman, Placido Domingo, and the Nobel Prize foundation. Nearly fifty years after McCormack's maiden voyage to the All England Club, IMG still sells the worldwide media rights to Wimbledon, in addition to a daily fifty-two-minute highlights show, a twenty-six-minute preview, and the tournament's official fifty-two-minute film. Its archive also offers a series of films on the tournament's legends, from Bjorn Borg to Billie Jean King, and dozens of classic matches, from the 1980 Borg-McEnroe final to the Williams sisters final in 2002. The crossed rackets are synonymous with the oldest major tennis tournament in the world. From 1968 to 1994, IMG helped increase its profits from roughly $55,000 to $43 million per year. The R&A's Open Championship now features thirty-four hours of live coverage in the United States. The R&A has some £50 million in annual revenues, including about $25 million a year alone from ESPN. Players now share £6.3 million in prize money.

Beyond those numbers, there is the lesson he taught the world's greatest athletes and the corporations, team owners, and athletic federations who made money from them, often by taking advantage of those athletes' limited education or the rapturous pleasure they took in the privilege of being able to make a living wage playing games. These athletes, Palmer and Nicklaus and Killy and Bjorn Borg and Picabo Street, were more than simply labor. They represented the essence of sport. They needed to be empowered. By empowering them, he allowed them to transform modern sports.

The transformation carried a price. As we will see later on, the same empowerment movement that put the athlete at the top of the pyramid of sports also helped produce a generation of athletic megalomaniacs. Team play suffers. There are too many moments when it seems money has replaced glory as the end that justifies the means. Athletes whose best years have long passed them by whine about being disrespected because their teams no longer want to fork over $20 million a year for declining production. Seasons and championships have been lost to labor strife.

But what is the alternative? Arnold Palmer and nearly every athlete who came of age before 1970 can tell you what it is: a plantation-style arrangement with monopolistic owners and athletic federation leaders who manage franchises, tournaments, and professional tours like egocentric dictators until someone finally stands up and insists the sports world shouldn't work this way.

By the time McCormack passed away, no one in sports could stop the forces he put into motion, forces that spread through the industry the way free enterprise spreads through a postcommunist society. Those forces changed sports the way Ernest Hemingway said people go broke: very slowly at first, and then all at once.

4

The Pilic Affair

On the afternoon of Saturday, June 2, 1973, the day before the biggest match of Nikola Pilic's life, the lanky lefthander from Yugoslavia decided to lie down on the bed in his Paris hotel room for a nap. Sunday would bring a dastardly test against Romanian Ilie Nastase. "Nasty," as he was known, possessed nearly every weapon in Pilic's arsenal, plus a few more. Pilic, who was thirty-three years old and playing in his first Grand Slam final, needed to rest.

Nikola Pilic may be the most important tennis player almost no one outside tennis has ever heard of, a classic European dirtballer who could make any opponent miserable on clay but was eminently beatable on every other surface. He would occasionally survive into the final eight or even the final four of the Grand Slams of the late 1960s and early 1970s, but then he would run into an opponent who was a little bit faster, hit a little bit harder, served a little more consistently, or knew how to win the biggest matches.

Not that Pilic saw it that way. Over the years he developed a reputation among his peers as a bit of a know-it-all and an occasionally graceless loser. He rarely complimented an opponent who beat him. No one ever played better than he did—according to him. He'd lose a match and say something like *I would have won if I hadn't had to play two days in a row.* He whined about weather and court conditions, about bad line calls and poor lighting, about the balls and his strings and anything else that might have prevented him from coming out on top. Yet Pilic was as tough an out as there was on the tour, an elegant defender with a big serve to go along with his big head. He could work and think his way through singles and doubles matches. To see his name on a bracket with yours was to know you were in for a long, torturous afternoon, a battle of attrition and skill that could be your hardest match of the tournament.

When players like Pilic hang around long enough, eventually they end up in a tournament like he experienced at the French Open in 1973. Unseeded, Pilic was lucky enough to land in a quarter of the draw where the four seeded players were all gone by the end of the fourth round. He hadn't faced any of them. The quarters and semis brought matches against unspectacular Italians Paolo Bertolucci and Adriano Panatta. Pilic won six of seven sets and advanced to the last match having beaten only one seeded player, the eighth-ranked Panatta. Pilic was going to play for his first Grand Slam singles championship at an age when most pros were calling it quits.

As he nodded off in his hotel bed, there was a rap on his door. It was a telegram from the All England Club, hosts of Wimbledon, which would be played later that month. In the telegram the club explained that the International Lawn Tennis Federation, the sport's governing body, had informed its leaders that Pilic was no longer in good standing with Yugoslavia's tennis federation. Under ILTF rules, players who were not in good standing with their national federations were prohibited from participating in the Grand Slam events: the Australian, French, and US Open Championships, and Wimbledon. Never mind that Pilic was scheduled to play in a Grand Slam final in roughly twenty-four hours at Roland Garros. The French had decided to ignore Yugoslavia's decision to put Pilic on its naughty-boys list. In England, however, rules were rules, and they needed to be enforced.

Pilic read and reread the telegram and shook his head in disbelief. It wasn't exactly the sort of thing he wanted on his mind the day before the biggest match of his life. He knew he was on Yugoslavia's naughty list, but he knew he didn't deserve to be there and that nothing would actually come of it.

The trouble had begun earlier that spring. Through twelve years of Davis Cup play, Pilic had become the most successful international competitor in Yugoslavian tennis. He never turned down an opportunity to play under his flag, though he didn't have much choice under Yugoslavia's Tito-controlled government. But that April, after a dozen years of Davis Cup service, Pilic decided he wanted to skip a competition against New Zealand, known as a "tie" in Davis Cup parlance. A tie comprises four singles matches and one doubles match. To win, a country must win three matches. The best players play a singles match on Friday, the doubles match on Saturday, and another singles match on Sunday. Instead, he wanted to play a professional doubles tournament in Canada. The math was simple. Pilic was a premier doubles player. He had a chance to make money in Canada. The Davis Cup barely paid anything. Plus the tie was on home soil. The Kiwis barely knew what tennis was. His team could toss their rackets on the court and win this one.

"They should have won without me with no problem," Pilic said of his Yugoslav teammates. "But then they go and lose 3–2 and they blame me for it, with everyone saying Yugoslavia would have won if Niki Pilic had played."

Yugoslavia's tennis federation was furious. It suspended Pilic for the rest of the year. Pilic stayed out of Yugoslavia and ignored the suspension. He traveled to Paris to start the French Open. The French, who were no friends of the Yugoslavs or anyone else in the Eastern Bloc, had clearly decided to ignore the ban. So, Pilic assumed, no one would indulge the rash judgments of a bunch of Communist Party hacks back home in the Balkans, and as far as he knew no one did—until a hotel bellhop banged on his door with the telegram.

In the weeks following the loss to the Kiwis in Zagreb, Yugoslavia's tennis honchos had gotten into the ears of Allan Heyman, a Dane who was the ILTF president. Heyman had subsequently gotten into the ear of Herman David at the All England Club. To Heyman and David, Pilic's decision to choose money over tradition and patriotism threatened the integrity and foundations of the sport, which the Allan Heymans and Herman Davids of the world believed the Grand Slam tournaments and the Davis Cup embodied. Tennis had "opened" in 1968 and allowed professionals to play on their tours and compete for the hallowed Grand Slam titles. Suddenly there were these flashy American promoters and agents trying to take over the hallowed game, throwing their money around, persuading players to play for cash instead of for glory and country. For Heyman and David, enough was enough. It was one thing for David to make his business deals with McCormack, but when the players got too money-hungry, things were going a step too far. It was time to take a stand against commercialism and these upstart players, who had started the Association of Tennis Professionals and had the nerve to make all these demands about organizing the schedule, increasing prize money, and standardizing work conditions.

Professional tennis had been heading toward this kind of confrontation for several years. For more than half a century, the International Lawn Tennis Federation had ruled the game unchallenged, maintaining a system that prevented professionals from playing in the biggest tournaments. After 1968, when the so-called Open era began and professionals finally were allowed into the Grand Slam tournaments, the pros quickly realized thcy needed to present a unified front if they ever wanted to have a say in how their sport was run. So they formed the Association of Tennis Professionals, a union of sorts that tried to negotiate with the ILTF and tournament organizers over matters like prize money and working conditions. By 1973, though, some pros began to wonder if they even needed the ILTF and its haughty tournaments anymore.

Pilic tried to put the telegram out of his mind. The next day he lost in straight sets to Nastase and headed to Rome for the Italian Open. There, he told Cliff Drysdale, the elegant South African who was the president of the ATP, that the All England club had banned him. Drysdale was apoplectic. This was all about power, Drysdale told Pilic. The ILTF was feeling threatened by the players, who were beginning to skip their events in favor of moneymaking opportunities. The federation was trying to strike back. Now the ball was in the players' court, and Drysdale knew exactly what to do with it.

Sniffing an opportunity to take a stand that might help establish his so-far-ineffective players group, Drysdale wrote up a petition threatening a boycott of Wimbledon and started collecting signatures around the locker room. "It was very simple," he says. "If Niki couldn't play, the rest of us weren't going to play either."

Within days, Drysdale had the signatures of all but a handful of the top fifty players in the world. Eventually, the letter landed in front of the Californian Stan Smith, who was Wimbledon's defending champion. He also faced the most miserable choice of anyone on the tour: give up his crown and stand on principle with his fellow players, or abandon his comrades by competing to keep the championship that everyone who ever picks up a tennis racket dreams of winning. Being Wimbledon champion means becoming tennis royalty. It's the sport's Hope diamond and the last thing anyone in the world would willingly part with, especially Stan Smith.

Throughout the late 1960s and early 1970s, countless college students and athletes grew their hair long, demonstrated against the Vietnam War, or raised their fists in unity with the Black Power movement. Stan Smith may have sympathized with their causes but he was not one of them. He had always been the soft-spoken, well-mannered boy from Pasadena. Yet as Wimbledon's defending champion, Smith was going to be the focal point of any stand the players were going to make, even if he might have appeared the least likely point person in a rebellion. If the defending champion was willing to abdicate, then this little uprising might actually have a chance. If he played, then it would likely fall apart. And then there was this: "I was probably playing the best tennis of my career right about then," Smith says. "I'd won Wimbledon the year before, and I'd won nearly every tournament I'd entered in 1973."

Long before Stan Smith and Niki Pilic, tennis players had a history of facing miserable choices. The first attempts by tennis stars to exert some control over their sport occurred shortly after World War II, when Jack Kramer, the son of a railroad worker who had turned himself into the best player in the world, persuaded a handful of his peers to make a go of earning some real money from the sport, even though they knew that by playing for money they would no longer be allowed to play in the Grand Slams or the Davis Cup. Pancho Gonzalez, Pancho Segura, Bobby Riggs, Tony Trabert, and a handful of others signed up. Kramer and his crew barnstormed the country, playing wherever they could for whatever they could. The players divided the gate among themselves and a promoter, though often the promoter was Kramer himself.

They collected a few hundred dollars here and there for various tournaments and challenge matches. The barnstorming delayed whatever mediocre, wage-making life awaited them—most likely teaching the game at a local club. The mantra of the tour was "Play no matter what." In 1949, Kramer was scheduled to play Gonzalez in an exhibition that was part of a series of matches the two champions were staging throughout the country. Gonzalez had twisted his ankle so badly that he could barely walk. Hours before the match, Gonzalez told Kramer he might not be able to play that night. Kramer knew if there was no match, there would be no money. Bud Collins, the esteemed tennis commentator, wrote that Kramer stared at his young opponent. "Pancho," he said, "we always play." The match went on. They would play more than one hundred matches on that first tour, with Kramer, the seasoned pro, crushing Gonzalez, 96–27.

Life as a professional tennis player hadn't improved much by 1963, the year the legendary Australian Rod Laver, the grandest champion of the twentieth century, turned professional after winning his first Grand Slam. Laver became the first man to pull off the Grand Slam—winning the Australian Open, the French Open, Wimbledon, and the US Open in the same calendar year—since Don Budge managed the feat in 1938. Then he turned professional, essentially banishing himself from the most illustrious tournaments for what he assumed would be the rest of his life. He didn't have much choice. He'd left school as a teenager. He wasn't qualified to do any other kind of skilled labor and couldn't continue playing as an amateur. Tennis was mostly all he knew.

The tennis world as Laver confronted it in the early 1960s was sort of like every other sport, only more so—an awful business for nearly everyone involved. It got a little better in 1968 with the dawn of the Open era. But the pay was terrible for all but the top two or three players, the travel was awful, and the working conditions were often shoddy and sometimes downright dangerous.

The men who ran the sport insisted on traditions that were often stifling and enterprise killing.

It is also not an exaggeration to say that, of all the powerful people in sports who didn't want to change the status quo, no one put up more of a fight than the men who ran tennis. This statement requires a certain context. The stunts that the leaders of Major League Baseball and the National Football League pulled to keep their dominance over the athletes who played on their teams would prove hard to match. However, at least those lords of the realm were ultimately fighting about money—money that wasn't nearly as plentiful as it is today and that they didn't want to share with their labor force.

In tennis, until 1968, the leaders of the sport had a strange approach to maintaining control. They basically starved the sport of money. No money for management and no money for the players. The International Lawn Tennis Federation and the sport's national governing bodies controlled the power over when and where players could play tennis and whether they could make a living playing it, which they couldn't if they wanted to play in the world's biggest tournaments.

The life Laver encountered offered all the glory that greets an indie rock band with a devoted but minuscule following. In 1963, Laver lost the US Pro Championship at Forest Hills to Ken Rosewall. When the final match was over, the promoters explained to the players that there would be no prize money. Attendance was bad, the promoters had gone broke, and there was nothing left over to give.

During the eight-city US pro circuit in 1964, Rosewall led the money list with $8,800. Laver came in second at $6,900, or about half what Arnold Palmer might collect for winning a single golf tournament back then. There were courts overlaid on lumpy wooden gym floors. Laver and company played in warehouses in the winter with no heating, or in auditoriums with roof structures so low the players had to perfect hitting lobs through the rafters. In 1965 several pros traveled to Khartoum, navigating their way through riots and soldiers carrying machine guns to play for a $1,000 purse they had to share. The matches ended when the air became so thick with bugs that it became impossible to play. They went to play in La Paz, the Bolivian capital, where the altitude is some twelve thousand feet. The balls jumped off their rackets as though they were caroming off trampolines. Blood streamed from their noses. First prize was a $600 watch.

The root of the problem was the lingering prejudice against professionals. Whatever other problems golf had, the sport had largely gotten over an anti-pro mentality in the 1950s. Until then, the guys with the phony jobs at a bank or a car dealership who still spent several afternoons a week on the golf course and competing at tournaments where they didn't collect prize money were somehow considered a higher life form than those who dedicated every waking hour to a game they taught or played for cash. Banished from country club locker rooms, the pros often had to change into their spikes in the parking lot before heading out to the country club course. That sounds bad, but in tennis the pros couldn't even get into the country club, and the amateurs had to take whatever non-cash handouts the tournaments felt compelled to provide. Cliff Drysdale, who would become the ATP president, made the semifinals of Wimbledon in 1965. His reward was a voucher for two pairs of shorts at Lillywhites. It was all a bit ridiculous.

After Wimbledon, the amateur summer circuit traveled to exclusive clubs, such as Orange Lawn in New Jersey and others in Southampton, New York, and Newport, Rhode Island, before landing at Forest Hills for the US Open, but no pros could come along. The pros had to head to La Paz to play for a $600 watch.

The strategy of maintaining power by starving the players worked for nearly one hundred years but ultimately collapsed because it relied on three faulty assumptions about elite athletes that the most powerful people in sports would make time and again throughout the 1960s, 1970s, and 1980s—and occasionally still make today:

1. They are stupid and trained from a young age to always listen to a person in a position of authority, whether it is a coach or a tournament director or commissioner of a sport.
2. They don't pay attention to the world around them, even the world of sports.
3. They will always act in their own self-interest when money is involved and won't sacrifice for the greater good of the sport or for those who will come after them.

Elite athletes may be uneducated but they aren't dumb and they aren't uninformed. There wasn't an elite tennis player alive in the 1960s who wasn't paying attention to how Mark McCormack had upended the sport's country club sister, turning Arnold Palmer, Jack Nicklaus, and Gary Player into very wealthy men. Want to know how much a random player got for his last contract or shoe deal? Ask an athlete. No one follows sports and the salaries that other elite athletes make closer than they do. There is a very simple explanation for why Laver, perhaps the greatest tennis player ever, ended up in Cleveland in 1968, practically begging IMG for representation. Laver knew exactly what McCormack had done for Arnold Palmer and golf. Laver was his sport's Arnold Palmer. At the time he had a $13,000-a-year contract with Dunlop that provided no real opportunity for royalties, a $1,000-a-year deal with a Massachusetts shoe company that was barely even making a Rod Laver shoe, and a handshake deal with a South Africa–based apparel company that paid him a 2.5 percent royalty—though he had received only a single payment the previous two years. If only tennis could somehow get organized, Laver believed he could blaze the same trail Palmer had.

So did Donald Dell. Like McCormack in golf, Dell was a top amateur tennis player throughout his teenage years and into college. Dell was born in 1938 and grew up in Bethesda, Maryland. His father was a lawyer in the Department of the Navy. His mother was a lover of tennis who saw to it that her children learned the game at the prestigious Edgemoor Club in their town. Dell got good quickly. By fifteen he was the national champion. He played on the tennis team at Yale. He made the NCAA finals and played for the US Davis Cup team in 1961 and 1963. At one point he was ranked in the top ten in the country, though he doubts he was actually that good, since the rankings were a haphazard mess.

Like McCormack, Dell went to law school and spent the early 1960s playing the occasional tournament. Even though he knew he'd never be a star, Dell wanted something very simple from the game: he wanted to be able to tell people he was a tennis player without having them think of him as some kind of ne'er-do-well—a "sham-ateur," as he and others became known—who might collect a $500 appearance fee under the table when he played. Dell lived in Washington, D.C., and became a close friend and a sort of tennis pro in residence for Robert Kennedy and his family. He would occasionally house-sit and watch the Kennedy children at their home, Hickory Hill, when their parents traveled. And still people would look at him cross-eyed when he told them he was a tennis player. Dell knew the only way that would end was if the cloistered world of international tennis opened its gates to professionals and allowed them to compete for the world's most prized championships.

In 1967, just after striking his deal with McCormack, Wimbledon chairman Herman David decided to make a radical move. He invited the eight top pros—Laver, Fred Stolle, Andres Gimeno, Dennis Ralston, Ken Rosewall, Butch Buchholz, Lew Hoad, and

Pancho Gonzalez—to play in a tournament at the All England Club alongside the amateurs. The pros didn't have to be asked twice to come to the sport's spiritual home. Wimbledon had always set the tone for the game. If it could change, everything could, and the players were going to relish it. A return to the grass of the All England Club was nothing short of reentering the Promised Land.

Wimbledon's connoisseurs welcomed their long-departed professionals back with open arms, packing the stands for their matches, screeching as they hadn't in years as Laver and his cohorts danced across the grass. The momentum toward professionalizing the sport seemed to be growing, but where it all might lead—how the tennis aristocracy felt about that and whether they might cede any of their power to the athletes who played the sport—no one really knew. Regardless, as the calendar flipped from 1967 to 1968, it was as good a time as ever to be blessed with enough tennis talent to turn pro.

More than anything else, Stan Smith, the former tennis champion with the eponymous tennis shoe, has always considered himself a product of ideal timing and very good luck. Born in 1946 and raised in Southern California, Smith came of age during an era of massive expansion in his state. During the first twenty-five years of Smith's life, California's population grew from about eight million to more than twenty million. The boom allowed Stan Smith to grow up in ideal weather among the deepest pool of athletic talent the US had ever produced. Smith was a big kid and an exceptional athlete who would grow to six foot four and nearly two hundred pounds. His father was an athletics coach at Pasadena City College. More importantly, Smith was the third child. He had two older brothers, which allowed him to grow up playing sports against superior competition.

Smith was ten years old when he first picked up a tennis racket. When he was twelve he got his first new racket, a Wilson Jack Kramer model. He took a few lessons and showed obvious natural talent, but he also ran track and played a lot more basketball, football, and baseball than tennis through junior high school and even into his first high school years, when he idolized Elgin Baylor and Jerry West and loved basketball more than anything. By then it was clear tennis had become far and away his best sport, something that almost certainly would not have happened had he grown up anywhere else or at any other time.

When Smith was fifteen, a local group of tennis boosters, the Pasadena Tennis Patrons, hired Pancho Segura to give lessons on the local courts. Segura, one of the top players in the world in the 1940s and 1950s, had quit playing regularly in 1962 to become the head professional at the Beverly Hills Tennis Club. The clinics with Segura began at 8:00 a.m. on Saturdays and ended at noon. The better players, like Stan Smith, got to work with Segura for twenty minutes on their own. Barely five foot seven, Segura had a strange two-handed forehand, a one-and-a-half-handed backhand, and a terrible serve. But he could dart around the court like a deer, hit crisp volleys, and could think his way through a match better than anyone. Into old age he was renowned for his ability to dissect any tennis match at any level.

Before Smith took the court for the final of the 1971 US Open against the Czech Jan Kodes, Segura found him near the locker room and gave him very clear instructions. "He told me to move around on his second serve and try to intimidate him with my forehand, hit kick serves to his forehand, and lob him after he hit his first volley," Smith said. Kodes had a habit of sneaking in too close to the net. On one crucial point late in the match, Smith saw Kodes creep in. He lobbed to win the point and went on to win the match. Segura also played a key role for Jimmy Connors, another of his prodigies, when he went up against Bjorn Borg in the US Open final in 1978. Connors was mainly a baseline player. Segura told him to charge in against Borg, to put pressure on his ground strokes and finish points quickly. Connors upset Borg in straight sets.

If Segura had arrived in Pasadena any later, or if Smith had joined the clinic when he was sixteen or seventeen instead of fifteen, it's hard to imagine him developing into a world class player. But Segura and Smith got in just under the wire—for their era, at least. A decade later, no one who waited until fifteen to dedicate himself to tennis could have sniffed the top of the pro game. But in 1962 tennis was still a niche, largely amateur activity, and Smith progressed quickly.

If he didn't have basketball practice, he would play tennis either at a club in nearby Altadena or at the Los Angeles Tennis Club, which, conveniently for Smith, happened to be the sport's West Coast hub. Jack Kramer, the guy whose name was on Smith's racket, played there. So did former champions Don Budge and Pancho Gonzalez. Laver practiced there occasionally. Perry T. Jones, a leader of the US Davis Cup team, essentially ran the club and made sure Smith got on the right courts with the right players. That included members of the USC tennis team when they were practicing there—a formidable group that included future pros like Dennis Ralston, Alex Olmedo, and Rafael Osuna.

When he first began playing serious junior tennis tournaments at fifteen, Smith noticed that other kids would often grow frustrated and buckle when the pressure became too great. Smith didn't. "I was never afraid," he said. He won two sanctioned tournaments in California that year. But it wasn't just Smith's athleticism and mental approach that allowed him to excel. At the national junior championships in Kalamazoo, Michigan, in 1964, he was down a match point in the round of sixteen. He hit a weak return off a tough first serve. His opponent crushed it with a volley. But the ball hit the top of the tape and somehow didn't roll over. Smith went on to win the match. He survived the quarterfinal despite being down a break in the third set. A semifinal win put him in the final against a tough opponent named Billy Harris, who hadn't lost as a junior as far back as anyone could remember. Harris had destroyed Smith 6–0, 6–1, in a clay court tournament earlier in the year. Fortunately for Smith, Kalamazoo was now a hard court tournament after years of being contested on clay. Smith probably would have lost to Harris on clay but had grown up playing on hard courts. He won and was crowned national junior champion.

Smith desperately wanted to go to USC; he secured a scholarship and spent the next four years there. While the best professionals in the world—men like Laver, Rosewall, and Emerson—barnstormed across the globe for a few hundred bucks a tournament, Smith refined his game against the best young players in the country, such as his future Davis Cup teammate Charlie Pasarell at UCLA. He graduated in 1968, the perfect year for a collegiate champion to do so, since it was the same year that tennis went "open": professionals were finally allowed both to make a living off the game and play in the Davis Cup and the four Grand Slam tournaments. Smith won the 1968 US Open doubles with Bob Lutz, banking half of the $4,200 first prize that would have been unavailable to him the year before. The winnings gave him the seed money to support his first months as a professional.

And the luck didn't end there. Despite leaving college at the height of the Vietnam War, Smith didn't get drafted until 1970, by which time the war was beginning to wind down. He spent much of his military time during the ensuing year visiting hospitals, conducting clinics, and doing other tennis-related activities on behalf of the military.

Since the military hadn't taken Smith, Donald Dell selected him for the 1968 Davis Cup team, an all-time great squad that included Arthur Ashe. They won on Smith's first try, upsetting the vaunted

Australians. Smith won his first professional singles tournament in 1969 and won three more titles in 1970, including the Tokyo Masters, where he beat a thirty-two-year-old Rod Laver. The next year Smith lost his first Grand Slam final at Wimbledon in five sets to John Newcombe, but two months later he reached the US Open final, then contested on the grass of Forest Hills. There he met the Czech Jan Kodes, a clay court specialist, in the final and dispatched him in four sets. At Wimbledon the following year, Smith won a five-set thriller in the final against Nastase.

The only bad luck Smith endured early in his career, if you could even call it bad luck, was the misfortune of having to put up with those bumpy first years of Open era tennis. There was no set schedule, no proven, standardized system for ranking players, and no one looking out for the players' needs, working in concert with them to get the game on television, encourage more investment, and make sure these athletes could train properly and make as much money as possible during a career that in most cases would likely be over by their midthirties.

Players embarked on backbreaking tours that hopscotched the globe from January to December with almost no rest between stops.

Consider Laver, the greatest player of them all, who had a $90,000 guarantee from a promoter for 1969 and ended up collecting a total of $124,000 when it was all over and his prize money was added to his guarantee. (That's about $800,000 in today's dollars, but bear in mind that he covered all his travel and expenses on the road.) Here's what Laver's year looked like in 1969, the season he captured his second Grand Slam by winning all four major titles and became arguably the greatest tennis player in history:

Sydney for the New South Wales Open . . . up to Brisbane
for the Australian Open . . . over to Auckland for the New
Zealand Open . . . off to Philadelphia for an indoor open

at the Spectrum . . . down to Florida for pro tournaments in Orlando and Miami . . . home (in Southern California) for five days . . . up the coast to Oakland, Portland, and Seattle for small pro tournaments . . . home commuting to the pro tourney in Los Angeles . . . a nine-day "vacation" in Hawaii . . . from there to New York for the Madison Square Garden Open . . . a long flight to Johannesburg for the South African Open . . . back home for a few days while commuting to a pro tournament in Anaheim . . . then to Tokyo for a pro tournament . . . home for two days en route to New York for the Madison Square Garden pro tourney . . . on to London for the BBC-TV match . . . over the Channel for a pro tournament in Amsterdam . . . up to Paris for the French Open . . . rebounding over the Channel to Bristol for the West of England Open . . . then settling in for three weeks in London for the open at Queen's Club, followed by the Wimbledon fortnight . . . a jump to Boston for the US Pro Championship . . . home for a few days prior to a pro tournament in St. Louis, Binghamton, New York, Fort Worth, and Baltimore . . . now New York for the Grand Slam climax at Forest Hills . . . back home to welcome the baby and play the Pacific Southwest Open at Los Angeles . . . a hop to Las Vegas for the Howard Hughes Open . . . a few days at home before revisiting Europe for pro tourneys at Cologne and Hamburg . . . home to change shirts, then once more to Europe (via business stops in Boston and New York) to play tournaments in Barcelona, London, Stockholm, Basel, and Madrid. One season, on the road 259 days—nearly 200,000 miles.

Oh, and Laver's wife was pregnant that year, too. If you wanted to design a system that would guarantee burnout, injuries, and short careers, you probably couldn't come up with something more effective than professional tennis in the first years of the Open era. And yet in 1972, when Laver and his fellow Aussie Ken Rosewall squared off in the May final of the made-for-television World Championship Tennis tour, 21.3 million people tuned in to see who would take the $100,000 jackpot. Laver and Rosewall had outdrawn the NBA and NHL playoffs.

This was a moment of triumph for tennis—the match that brought the sport into the modern era. And yet the ILTF, led by Allan Heyman of Denmark, saw it as a threat instead of a boon. If the WCT and its riches became the focus of the sport, what might happen to all that tradition in Melbourne, Paris, London, and Forest Hills? To tennis's ruling class, this was a zero-sum game. The ILTF needed to find a way to make a stand.

And that's when Stan Smith's luck ran out.

When Smith arrived in England in June of 1973, he was on a roll unlike anything an American pro had pulled off before. He'd won seven of the eleven tournaments he entered during the first five months of the year and was arguably the world's best player. He steamed toward Wimbledon as the favorite to defend his championship. Then Drysdale showed him the petition. It was an awful choice, but Smith knew what he had to do.

The players needed to control their own schedules. They recognized the grand slams had their set fortnights, and Davis Cup ties had to be wedged in to allow for the worldwide tournament to be played each year, but the players wanted to have a say on the rest of the calendar that ruled their lives, perhaps even the final word on it. No one was buying tickets to the Italian Open to see the president of the Italian Tennis Federation. They came to see the players. So shouldn't they get some say as to when the tournament might be held, how the purse should be distributed, and what sort of minimum support the tournament might provide for all of its participants when they made their way to Rome? It didn't seem like a lot to ask.

As the players headed north to England for the Wimbledon warm-up tournament at Queen's Club, Donald Dell and Jack Kramer flew to London as well. Dell was representing several of the top players, including Smith and Ashe. Kramer was serving as the director of the ATP. Smith tried to focus on preparing to defend his championship, but he stayed in daily contact with Dell so he could remain up-to-date on any development that might move the boycott off the table. Dell explained his dual strategy: he and the ATP had filed a lawsuit on Pilic's behalf in the British courts while keeping an open line with the ILTF to pursue negotiations for a deal that would save the tournament.

The ILTF board, meanwhile, had no plans to budge. Simply put, they didn't think they would have to. The British judge quickly tossed out the legal challenge. The entire British media ridiculed these upstart players who had the nerve to threaten their beloved tournament. Where the media went, public opinion followed. The powers on the ILTF looked at the ATP and saw an organization that was wobbly at best. Heyman and other ILTF board members, such as Wayne Reid of Australia, believed that when the moment of truth came, the players would buckle and play. As the draw approached, Herman David ran into Bud Collins, the long-time American commentator, who'd been a competitive amateur player in the 1950s. "We're doing the right thing, aren't we?" he asked Collins. "No sir, you are not," Collins told him, but as Collins tried to explain, David waved him off. "He didn't want to hear it," Collins says of David.

Still, in the locker room, support for Pilic was steadfast and nearly unanimous. Drysdale, Ashe, Rosewall, John Newcombe, Roy Emerson, and Laver were all firmly in Pilic's corner. With the days passing and the tournament drawing near, Dell and Kramer holed up at the Westbury Hotel to negotiate with Heyman and a team of ILTF lawyers to see if something could be worked out. It wasn't going well. Heyman kept insisting the players weren't actually going to follow through on their threats. Without that concern over the fate of the tournament, there wasn't much motivation for negotiating a compromise. Smith kept checking in with Dell, who remained skeptical, too. Dell and Smith were fairly certain tournament organizers weren't actually going to be dumb enough to hold the event without them.

With the draw one day away, Dell approached Heyman with a deal. The ILTF would lift the suspensions and accept Pilic's entry into Wimbledon. Then Pilic would withdraw, out of respect for the tournament and the federation. Pilic felt badly that all the players might have to miss the tournament because of him and his backward-thinking federation. With this deal, everyone would save face. The precedent for players being able to decide where and when they would play would be established, but Pilic would leave, so the club didn't have to suffer any embarrassment about caving in. Heyman told Dell it sounded like a good idea. Dell called Pilic at his hotel and made the proposal to him. Pilic agreed to go along with the plan. Then Heyman warned Dell not to get his hopes up. *The ILTF is going to back out of this,* Dell told Smith. "This wasn't about Niki Pilic anymore," Smith said.

The next morning Dell called Heyman to let him know Pilic was on board. Heyman stumbled through his response. He explained to Dell that he still needed to discuss the proposal with the ILTF board. Dell knew then the deal was dead. In fact, just as Dell had predicted, Heyman never presented the proposal to the board and instead let it die an undiscussed death as he waited for the players to cave. At nightfall, Smith went to the Westbury Hotel to be with Dell and Kramer. As he sat there, watching the minutes tick by, he kept thinking somehow this was all going to get worked out. "It just wasn't meant to be," he said.

As the day of the draw broke, there was only one thing left for the players to do: leave. And that's just what they did, in droves. Smith, Ashe, Laver, Rosewall, Emerson, Newcombe, and nearly every other member of the top eight packed up and headed out of town. Just five top players stayed. England's Roger Taylor succumbed to immense public pressure and played. Ilie Nastase of Romania, Jan Kodes of Czechoslovakia, and Alex Metreveli of the Soviet Union claimed the governments of their Eastern Bloc nations had ordered them to boycott the boycott. If they defied the orders, their careers might be over. And a twenty-year-old American upstart named Jimmy Connors, who, later in his career, became well-known for grabbing his crotch and cursing out opponents and officials and would twice sue the ATP, updated his colorful résumé to include the descriptor "scab." Pilic still doesn't buy any of the excuses of the pros who did play, even those from the players who lived behind the Iron Curtain, as he did. "They played because they wanted to win Wimbledon, and they thought this was their chance," he says.

In fact it was. Herman David and the All England Club still had a tournament to run. They called in every decent college and amateur player they could find, guys like Stanford's Sandy Mayer, plus a slew of other no-names—like American Dick R. Bohrnstedt and a Chilean named Pinto-Bravo—who had no business playing on the All England Club's grass during those two weeks. "I think they called in a few guys I had once beaten," said Bud Collins, who'd been a middling amateur. He was only half joking.

Kodes and Metreveli squared off in the final, two clay court specialists who had never come close to winning the tournament before and never would again. Kodes won, 6–1, 9–8, 6–3, lifting the trophy and becoming the answer to the trivia question "Who won history's most absurd Grand Slam title?" Most record books contain no asterisks. As for the fans, they were so eager to show their support for club (and country) over players that they packed the joint as never before.

But the ILTF and All England Club triumph—they did hold a tournament without the big guns after all—was short-lived. Instead of emboldening the ILTF and the leaders of the other Grand Slam tournaments, a no-name-filled draw in the face of a boycott scared the daylights out of them. The players had brought tennis's powers that be to their knees and they would do it again if they needed to. They didn't need Grand Slams or the Davis Cup as much as those events needed them. It was one thing for thousands of English loyalists who had already bought tickets to make a statement by watching the depleted field play tennis. But that wouldn't happen elsewhere, and no television executive was going to pay for the right to broadcast events with a bunch of third-rate amateurs. Any sports official with a brain knew that television was going to be the lifeblood of the sport. And television money followed stars, not dusty clubs. Without the stars and the eyeballs and investments they generated, the Grand Slams were dead. There was only one move to make: negotiate.

In the weeks following Wimbledon, the players and the ILTF worked out a series of rule changes to ensure that such a boycott would never become necessary again. Pilic's suspension was lifted, allowing him to play in the US Open and ending any threat to the year's final Grand Slam. Players won the freedom to play whenever and wherever they wanted without fear of retribution. The players also got three seats on the newly formed Men's International Professional Tennis Council, which consisted of representatives from individual tournaments and the ILTF, guaranteeing them a say in everything from scheduling to work conditions. The ILTF also struck a deal with Lamar Hunt to divide the year. The WCT would dominate the first four months, and what became known as the

"Grand Prix"—the series of more traditional tournaments, with a points system that determined the awarding of a bonus pool—took over for the rest of the year. With a set schedule and a clear understanding of who would be playing when, CBS and NBC would commit to long-term broadcasting deals. Almost overnight, tennis had completely changed. "It flipped," Dell said.

It also boomed. It's always dangerous to connect a single event with a larger, macro phenomenon. But the boom that tennis experienced once the players won their freedom and recognition as the most important people in the sport is unlike anything any other sport experienced during the past fifty years, especially in the US, the country that supplied most of the top players as well as the money that fueled the sport during the next two decades.

Freed to play whenever they wanted and wherever they wanted for whatever money they could rustle up, tennis's best began to put on the kinds of high-stakes, high-profile showcases that became the best advertising the game could dream of. Tennis became boxing. Jimmy Connors took on Rod Laver and John Newcombe in Las Vegas in a series of matches for $100,000 and $250,000 purses that were advertised as "winner-take-all." (They didn't actually turn out to be winner-take-all, which got organizers in hot water with the government, but that's another issue.) These were crowd-pleasers and television bonanzas that spread the buzz on a previously ghettoized sport. In 1970, during a US Open that crowned Australia's Ken Rosewall and Margaret Court as champions, 123,000 people attended the tournament's eleven sessions at the West Side Tennis Club in Forest Hills. In 1978, when Americans Jimmy Connors and Chris Evert won, some 275,000 people attended twenty-one sessions at the publicly built National Tennis Center in Flushing Meadows, while another 15 million watched on television. With those numbers, corporate sponsors and television executives rushed to fill the coffers of the US Tennis Association and others around the world, and the money quickly flowed through the system to the players. From 1968 to 1972—before the Wimbledon boycott—total prize money at the US Open grew from $100,000 to $160,000. By 1983 it was $2 million. An informal study by the Tennis Industry Association found that in 1972 some 21.6 million people in the US played tennis. By 1975 the figure had jumped to 40.9 million.

The new interest revolutionized nearly everything about the game. Seeing a chance to capitalize on the country's tennis-mad suburbs, manufacturers invested in the sport as never before. For nearly a century, tennis rackets were made of laminated wood. Swinging many of them felt like swinging a club. The ball came off the strings with a thud. In the late 1960s, Wilson began to experiment with a steel racket that played more like a spring, most notably the T2000 that Jimmy Connors made popular. But the real innovation arrived in the mid-1970s, just after the Pilic affair and the subsequent tennis boom, when aluminum rackets began to appear. The lighter material allowed Prince, which had started making a ball machine in 1970, to begin producing the oversized rackets with faces that were about 110 square inches, nearly double the size of traditional rackets. Their massive sweet spots freed players at every level to swing harder and play a faster, more athletic game. The 1980s brought rackets made of graphite, another lightweight material that offered even more control than the oversized aluminum rackets. With the balls flying off the rackets at unprecedented velocity, the game required players with world-class foot speed and the endurance of marathoners. Tennis morphed from something effete into a brutal spectacle.

Today the modern tennis champion is almost unrecognizable from the stars of the 1960s and 1970s. They're about six inches taller, ripped with muscles, and armed with a class of speed and power that would allow them to excel in any number of other sports had they chosen to pursue them. But they didn't pursue those sports because tennis offered them the possibility of riches that few other endeavors could.

Any list of the best-known, best-paid athletes in the world would today include Rafael Nadal, Roger Federer, and Novak Djokovic in the top twenty. That concept would have been absurd to think about before the Pilic affair. Then, being able to identify top pros like Ken Rosewall and Rod Laver was akin to being able to speak with authority about French existentialists. Only a tiny segment of the population could have pulled off the feat.

Also worth noting is that the top four highest-paid female athletes in 2013 were tennis players: Maria Sharapova, Li Na, Serena Williams, and Caroline Wozniacki. Each made between $13 million and $27 million in 2013, though they probably owe more to the firebrand Billie Jean King than Niki Pilic.

There is, of course, another legacy of the Wimbledon boycott that went far beyond this country club sport. The boycott marked the first time so many top athletes walked out on their sport at its most crucial moment. Baseball players had gone on strike during the first games of the 1972 season, but they didn't walk out on the World Series. And the Wimbledon boycott truly paid off. Remember, athletes pay attention. They read the sports pages, and they pay especially close attention when the politics of sports drift into the news. They understood long before the owners and league leaders did that what was true for one sport would likely be true for theirs before too long. The tennis players who led the Wimbledon boycott taught their peers in other sports a unique lesson: that standing up for things you believe in, even if it means sacrificing money in the short term, will pay off in the long run—maybe not for you, but for those who follow you. Sure, it's a risk. Life is full of risks, especially for a generation of athletes trying to achieve some level of control over their own lives. But ultimately the benefits outweigh having another trophy to display on the mantel.

*The Pilic affair did have one casualty: a lanky champion from Pas-*adena. After missing Wimbledon, Stan Smith got upset in the semifinals of the US Open that year. He returned to Wimbledon in 1974 as *a* favorite but not *the* favorite. He went up two sets to love in the semifinal against Ken Rosewall. He had a match point in the third set but failed to convert it. Rosewall won that set, then blew through the next two to advance.

"That was my last best shot to win the tournament," Smith says wistfully of 1974. He would never win another Grand Slam title.

His story does have a happy ending, though—sort of.

In 1971 the shoe company adidas approached Smith about putting his name on one of their models of tennis shoe. The German company wanted to break into the US market. Smith was the top American. He wore a canvas shoe made by Uniroyal. Adidas had designed a leather shoe for the Frenchman Robert Haillet. It was a simple, elegant design with perforations on the sides forming the three iconic adidas stripes. The company distributed the product in the US as the Haillet shoe. No one knew who Haillet was, though, so the shoe wasn't catching on like a first shoe of its kind might have.

With Donald Dell advising him, Stan Smith cut a deal with adidas. For the next three years, adidas would put both Smith's and Haillet's names on the shoe. Then Haillet's name would go away and the shoe would become solely a Stan Smith model. Other players had their names on shirts and shorts. Almost no one had his name on shoes. As tennis boomed and boomed after the Pilic affair, owning a pair of adidas Stan Smiths became a statement similar to wearing a polo shirt with an alligator on it: it was a symbol of a certain station in life, a mark of style at once casual and sophisticated, even though the shoe itself quickly lost any technical superiority.

More than forty years later, the adidas Stan Smith remains the top-selling tennis shoe of all time, with more than 40 million pairs sold. Stan Smith has built a small fortune by collecting a royalty on every one. "There are people I meet who say to me, 'I didn't realize you were an actual person, I thought you were just a shoe,'" he says. The tennis gods had found a way to compensate Stan Smith for whatever he lost by skipping Wimbledon in 1973.

5

The Farmer
Named Catfish

Just months before his last season of high school baseball, James Augustus "Catfish" Hunter decided to spend a day the way a lot of children of the rural South passed their time in the early 1960s and still do today: shooting stuff. It did not go well.

Hunter headed out into the countryside with his brother Pete for a hunting expedition near their home in Hertford, North Carolina, a little town tucked into the northeast corner of the state, about fifty miles south of Norfolk, Virginia. As Pete homed in on a target, his rifle fired where it wasn't supposed to. A piece of a buckshot blasted a toe off Catfish's right foot.

At the time, Hunter was a high school pitching prodigy just four months away from the start of his crucial senior season. His father was a tenant farmer. Early in Catfish Hunter's life, which began in 1946, his home didn't have indoor plumbing. The bonus he figured to earn if he could get himself signed by a Major League Baseball team was likely to be more than his family might earn in a decade. A right-hander, Hunter generated much of his power from pushing off that right foot and leg. The timing of this injury couldn't have been much worse. *He* hadn't shot himself in the foot, at least. He gave the honor to his brother.

But as he recovered from the injury and started throwing off a mound to prepare for the upcoming season, Hunter realized there might be some benefit to the mishap even though he was quite literally damaged goods. His pitching motion was now slightly more funky, and the injury hadn't cost him any velocity. Clyde Kluttz, a fellow North Carolinian and a scout for the Kansas City A's, watched Hunter throughout his senior season at Perquimans High School and assured his organization that Hunter's arm was still electric. He argued that an athlete as good as Hunter was—Catfish had also starred in football—would be able to figure out how to pitch with nine toes better than most mortals threw with all ten.

Kluttz was right. A classic hard thrower who could hurl breaking balls for strikes at a variety of speeds, Hunter signed with the A's after he finished high school in 1964. He debuted in the major leagues the following May, when he was just nineteen years old. He pitched a perfect game on May 8, 1968. He won at least twenty-one games each season from 1971 to 1975. He was the heart of a rotation that won three consecutive world championships in Oakland from 1972 to 1974. Along the way, he also figured out how to upend the entire salary structure of sports, teaching not only every baseball player but every team-sport athlete a better lesson in free-market economics than anyone could have gotten at the Harvard Business School.

This was the lesson: a simple rule of labor economics is that the person who gets paid the most sets the market for everyone else below him. If his salary rises, salaries for everyone below him will eventually rise, too. The higher the ceiling, the higher the floor and, most likely, the higher the average, since someone who is half as good as the highest-paid player can suddenly argue that he is worth half as much, assuming he has a forum in which to make such an argument. For the purposes of every baseball player and every team-sport athlete who came after Catfish Hunter, the farm boy from North Carolina was the greatest pitcher and the most brilliant teacher who ever lived.

Hunter won his first game for the Kansas City A's on July 27, 1965, a forgettable 10–8 win over the Boston Red Sox at Fenway Park. Hunter pitched five innings, giving up 7 hits and 5 runs, including a third-inning homer to Tony Conigliaro.

An unspectacular beginning, yes, but there is a sweet symmetry to Hunter breaking into the majors in 1965. It links his career inextricably to the rise of the Major League Baseball Players Association (MLBPA). The same year Hunter broke in, a handful of thoughtful, forward-looking veterans, including Jim Bunning and Robin Roberts, finally decided that their union had a serious problem. Its lead representative, Robert Cannon, was splitting time between the Players Association and his day job on the Wisconsin bench. Judge Cannon, who served as the part-time legal counsel to the MLBPA, had other problems, too—like being a lackey for the owners and angling for the job as the next commissioner. His highest priority was maintaining the supposedly good relations between labor and management in the national pastime. So Roberts and Bunning formed a screening committee to find someone who could work full-time to represent the interests of the players and keep a close eye on the pension and benefit plan the owners had created after the war but was grossly underfunded by 1965. The committee actually offered Cannon the job, but he turned it down when he realized taking it would vastly reduce the pension he could ultimately collect from his work as a judge.

With Cannon out of the running, the committee turned to Marvin Miller, then the senior economist at the United Steelworkers union and a lifelong baseball fan. Miller was an odd choice to lead a group of baseball players, to say the least. The vast majority of professional baseball players in the middle of the 1960s were country boys from small towns, conservative by nature, not very well educated, and so deeply suspicious of the country's labor movement that for years they resented any reference to the Players Association as a union. Unions were organizations for mill workers and bricklayers. Ballplayers were professionals, skilled in the most competitive of games. They didn't need the coddling of some socialist-style, all-for-one-and-one-for-all union to give them dignity. They lived a life that was the envy of men everywhere, traveling the nation and getting paid to play a game, with women in every town happy to keep them company. Then came the off-season, when they went back home and worked as carpenters and housepainters and moving men because they didn't have enough money to carry them through the winter. But spring training was always just around the corner. They'd be back to living the good life soon enough, a life far from the world of the clock-punching steelworkers whose lives this Jewish gentleman, Marvin Miller, had spent the previous sixteen years improving.

Except, on closer inspection, the existence of the average ballplayer and the average steelworker wasn't that different after all. Miller could make a pretty convincing argument that the steelworker was better off, at least when it came to job security and his relationship with management. Miller knew it shouldn't be that way, and he thought Major League Baseball's players ought to realize that, too.

Miller had a pencil-thin mustache. He wore his salt-and-pepper hair slicked back from his forehead. With an economics degree from New York University, he'd worked for the National War Labor Board, the International Association of Machinists, and the United Auto Workers before signing on with the United Steelworkers union. He suffered from Erb's palsy, a condition that rendered his right arm somewhat lame and forced him to keep his elbow bent at a seemingly uncomfortable angle. He was a small man, a shade over five and a half feet tall. He had almost nothing in common with Major League Baseball players.

Miller's colleagues at the steelworkers union told him he would be crazy to go to work for the baseball players. The Players Association was nearly bankrupt. It had little power and members scattered throughout the country, making it difficult to build unity. Miller didn't see it that way. The steelworkers union had roughly 250,000 members. The MLBPA, meanwhile, had only 500 members. Miller knew if he was doing his job correctly he would know each of them personally and be able to speak to each of them individually about their concerns and needs. That was the great allure of the job for Miller and the chance of a lifetime for any labor organizer: to work so closely with a group that had such special talents and so little knowledge of how badly management had been mistreating them.

Every player came to New York three times per season to play twenty-two games against the clubs there. Miller told them to visit the union office in Manhattan. *Let's just talk,* he said. He wanted to be able to tell them face-to-face what was happening and what he was thinking. Sometimes it was personal stuff. Sometimes it was more general, like questions about bargaining. And if nothing was pertinent and players just wanted to chat, he told them to come in anyway, and they did. "I got to know every player, and not just casually," he said.

Miller began meeting with the players during spring training in 1966. He spoke to them in slow, halting, and soft tones that conveyed a kind of empathic seriousness about their situation that they had never heard before. Everyone had always treated them like overgrown kids, a lucky lot who'd never have to grow up. He spoke to them as men, serious men, businessmen. He implored them to think long and hard about their stature in the game they loved, to begin to envision reaching a point where they could deal with their employers as equals.

Miller set out to convince the players that unions weren't only about factory workers—that stars like Bette Davis had thrived through the power of the Screen Actors Guild, and that Clark Gable was an activist. So was Ronald Reagan. Without a union, he would say, management could decide they didn't want to hire anyone with red hair (there's an old baseball scout's myth, by the way, that redheads don't make good ballplayers) or that it wanted to fire all players who parted their hair on the wrong side of their heads. These were all arguments he had made to young workers before. The big difference, of course, was that those workers didn't wear cleats and stirrups to work. They were essentially the same people, though: conservative laborers skeptical of the labor movement of the early 1950s who didn't know anything about the union's history and how it might benefit them. He'd ask the steelworkers how many paid holidays workers received before the union was organized. They would tell him six. The correct answer was none. He'd go through each of their benefits—wash-up provisions, weekend overtime—and make sure they knew that none of it existed before Philip Murray and John L. Lewis had organized the steel industry. It wasn't any different from asking baseball's lords for some consistency when it came to work conditions, like dugouts that didn't smell and visiting locker rooms with running hot water. Players also didn't like to travel after a night game at the end of a series to a city where the next series began the following day. Scheduling these "getaway games" during the day would allow them more rest and result in better performances. It didn't seem like a lot to ask for.

Almost as soon as Miller took office, baseball's owners began to try to undermine him. Since 1960 the owners had helped finance the Players Association with $150,000 in television revenues they received from the All-Star Game. The midsummer classic was a celebration of the players, after all. They didn't get paid extra to play in it. So it was only fitting that some of the money eventually went toward their cause.

But in the summer of 1966, Miller opened a letter from Commissioner William Eckert informing him the owners would no longer grant the money to the Players Association. Eckert and his cronies came up with a lame excuse: that the grant violated federal labor laws. At the time, the Players Association had about $6,000 in its bank account. Worse, the 1966 season was nearly over. Miller and the union's executive committee planned to persuade the membership to vote before the next season to spend a portion of their wages on dues to support the association. But that money wouldn't start coming in for another six months, and the funds would be meager. The average player's salary was $14,000. A lot of the members were just scraping by. They couldn't afford to finance an independent union with a director and, before long, a legal counsel and a permanent office in midtown Manhattan.

Miller had to act quickly or watch the union go bankrupt. He knew there might be some value in the images of his athletes. Perhaps he could capitalize on that the way Mark McCormack had turned Arnold Palmer into a walking Chamber of Commerce. With the help of a former traveling secretary for the Yankees, Miller contacted Coca-Cola and struck a deal that allowed the soda company to put the images of players on the underside of their bottle caps. It was a two-year deal worth $60,000 per year, enough for the union to live on.

Then he went to work on Topps, the bubble gum and baseball card company. Topps had one of the great rackets in the history of sports. It scoured the minor leagues for the most promising ballplayers and signed them to five-year contracts that would begin once the ballplayers made the major leagues. Topps would pay the players $125 a year for the right to use their images on baseball cards. If the players got sent down to the minors, the payments would stop, and the clock would stop running on the five-year deals. So, for roughly $60,000 a year, Topps owned the photographic rights of players on cards that cost pennies to manufacture and generated millions in sales each year.

Miller reached out to Joel Shorin, the president of the company, and invited him to the MLBPA offices for a meeting. Shorin sat down with Miller and the two talked about the origins of Topps's relationship with baseball in 1952. Then Miller told Shorin he was taking advantage of the players. "I want to negotiate another arrangement," Miller said. He suggested the players get a royalty on the sale of every pack of cards. That way they could be partners with Topps. Shorin told Miller his ideas were interesting but he didn't understand the need to change the current arrangement. "I don't see where your muscle is," Shorin said. With that, Miller ended the meeting. The next day he began to plot a campaign to persuade players not to renew their contracts with Topps. Miller told the players the battle could take years, because the contracts were staggered and only about one hundred players would come up for renewal each season. The veterans might not ever reap the rewards of the conquest and would have to do without money they might never have another chance to earn.

The following spring a few players renewed with Topps, but many more of them refused. Joel Shorin had a problem. He called Miller and told him he'd like to schedule a meeting. "Now I see your muscle," Shorin told Miller. Then the two hammered out a deal that gave the players 8 percent of all sales up to $4 million, $250 for each player and 10 percent of sales above $4 million. The MLBPA would never have to worry about money again.

With the union's financial problem solved, Miller could turn his attention to his biggest task: negotiating the game's first collective bargaining agreement. On the long list of employment complaints for the players, two immediately rose to the top.

The first was the reserve clause, that century-old baseball

statute that bound a player for life to the team that signed him to his first contract or, beginning in 1965, selected him in the amateur draft. Players would sign a contract, usually for one year, then renegotiate at the end of the season. If they couldn't reach a deal, the contract gave management the option to renew the contract for one year. Management had always interpreted that to mean one year after another after another. So a contract would expire and management would pick up the one-year option. Then, after the option year expired, the club would pick it up again. Players had never bothered to interpret it differently. The owners told them they couldn't.

The arrangement left the player with no ability to negotiate, while the club had the right to renew the contract and give a player a raise or cut his salary by as much as 25 percent. Ralph Kiner suffered this fate in 1952, after leading the National League in home runs for the seventh consecutive year. His team, the Pittsburgh Pirates, finished in last place. At the conclusion of the season, the legendary general manager Branch Rickey told Kiner the team planned to cut his salary by 25 percent, the maximum allowable at the time. Kiner protested, claiming that he had played hard and led the league in home runs—again. "We could have finished in last place without you," Rickey told him.

If a player didn't like the club's offer, he could refuse to play. If the team refused to give in to his demands—and, really, management had no reason to—the player could either agree to the money being offered or retire, since there was no other professional baseball league in which he could sell his services. It was a ghastly arrangement that halted careers, eliminated competition, and depressed salaries. It was all legal, because in 1922 Supreme Court justice Oliver Wendell Holmes had ruled that the sport's central business was "giving exhibitions of baseball, which are purely state affairs" and therefore not subject to federal antitrust laws. To Miller, the reserve clause turned players into potted plants.

Second on Miller's list was the players' grievance procedure, to the extent that one even existed. The commissioner, the league presidents, and the clubs set the rules. If a club or the league office fined a player for violating a rule, he could appeal the ruling to the league presidents, who were charged with interpreting the rules. But they worked for the owners, who had the power to hire and fire them and set their salaries. They weren't impartial. They had no incentive to rule in favor of a player, and they rarely did.

Somehow Miller had to figure out a way to change both of these rules, and he had an idea that changing one just might help change the other. Change wasn't going to come overnight. Indeed, almost nothing changed when the players signed the first collective bargaining agreement that Miller negotiated for them in 1968. The twenty-four-page deal looked more like a pamphlet than a labor agreement, and it largely codified the existing work rules, the schedule, payments from the postseason, and the pension plan. Owners couldn't cut a player's salary by more than 20 percent, instead of 25 percent, but the reserve clause remained, even though the owners committed to forming a joint committee that would study possible adjustments to it. The commissioner remained the final arbiter of the grievance procedure.

The owners quietly declared victory and went about their business. Little did they know, Miller and the new MLBPA had engaged the owners in a game they didn't even realize they were playing. To the clubs, the negotiations were checkers, a fairly simple game that wrapped up quickly. Miller, on the other hand, understood that labor talks are a chess match that plays out over a series of years and collective bargaining cycles. They require strategic thinking two and three agreements ahead. No union gets everything it wants in its first contract. The first contract is merely a foundation to build upon—a tool to hammer management with in future dealings and negotiations rather than a stone tablet that might stand for all time. If the union couldn't immediately do away with the reserve clause, at least it got the clubs to acknowledge it was an issue and to set up a committee that was supposed to study its relevance and possible problems. Miller knew the committee would do little to address the players' complaints about the system. When the owners refused to budge, that would be a rallying cry for his members, proof that the owners saw them as property with no freedom or inherent dignity.

As for the grievance procedure, Miller had another plan for that. Shortly after the two sides signed the deal, Miller began hammering the new commissioner, Bowie Kuhn, about the absurdity of having someone whose salary was paid by the owners serve as a supposedly neutral arbitrator. Kuhn hated the criticism. He saw himself as a statesman, the man charged with upholding the integrity of the game. One lunch hour Miller ran into Kuhn on a street in midtown Manhattan. They got to talking, and Kuhn complained to Miller that the criticism of him was unjustified. His mission was to represent "the best interests of baseball," whatever that might be. Miller told him that was malarkey and he was going to prove it. Kuhn asked him how he could do that. Miller promised to pile Kuhn's desk so high with grievances that he wouldn't be able to see out from behind it, and as Kuhn ruled on behalf of the owners on each one, he would prove Miller's point for him.

Sure enough, the next collective bargaining agreement, signed in 1972, called for a neutral arbitrator for salary and contract disputes. The reserve clause was still there, but the new deal also included a paragraph from the first agreement that allowed a player to become a free agent if a club ever defaulted on a contract. The paragraph, 7(A), gave the club ten days to rectify the situation from the time of the default. If the club didn't do so, the player would be allowed to get a new contract with another team. This might have been the least contentious issue of any of the first two labor deals.

No one paid much attention to it. Clubs almost never defaulted on contracts. It seemed pretty innocuous—until it wasn't innocuous at all.

At heart, Catfish Hunter was a farmer. That was the job his father had had when he was growing up. Hunter and his siblings all worked on the farm in Hertford, too. It was the job he performed in the off-season, and the job he knew he would return to once he could no longer throw a baseball ninety-five miles per hour.

By the early 1970s, Hunter had helped turn the Oakland A's (the Kansas City A's had moved in 1968) into an unlikely dynasty. In 1972, when Hunter had a scintillating 2.04 earned run average, the A's won their first World Series in Oakland and the first for the franchise since 1930, when the team played in Philadelphia under the legendary owner-manager Connie Mack. A single run decided six of the seven games in that 1972 World Series win over the Reds. Hunter pitched in three games and won twice, including the seventh game, when he pitched two and two-thirds innings of relief on a single day of rest. The following year he held the New York Mets to a single run in game six of the World Series when the A's were down 3–2 and facing elimination. They would win that series in seven games as well. Hunter won twenty-one games in 1971, 1972, and 1973, then twenty-five in 1974.

By the winter of 1974, Hunter was undoubtedly the best pitcher on baseball's best team. That was no small accomplishment, considering his teammates included Vida Blue, Ken Holtzman, and Rollie Fingers, three stellar starters. Hunter led the A's pitching staff with a quiet but loose country demeanor. (He'd occasionally impersonate an FBI agent in random airports, questioning strangers who didn't recognize him.) Reggie Jackson, the fiery outfielder, led the offense, bringing a rare combination of power and speed that would make him one of the great players of his era. Jackson was everything the country-boy Hunter was not. Jackson was a biracial college kid who had starred at Arizona State. He craved the spotlight and had become both the team's representative to the Players Association and one of the union's more radical members. In a profanity-laced speech at a spring training meeting in 1972, he'd urged the union to stand up to the owners and vote for its first strike. Unlike Jackson, Hunter never made waves, and A's owner Charles O. Finley had every reason to give Hunter what he wanted when the two began negotiating his contract for the 1974 season.

Hunter told Finley he wanted a two-year agreement that would pay him $100,000 for his services in both 1974 and 1975, a deal that was less than half the value of the top salary in baseball at the time: slugger Dick Allen's $250,000 yearly take from the Chicago White Sox. Hunter wasn't the sort to measure his worth in dollars and cents or to hold out for every last penny. He and Finley had a handful of friendly exchanges in which they discussed the outlines of the deal, which was an absurd bargain for the A's. A player in Hunter's position today would easily command a five-year contract worth $125 million. Back in 1974, though, Catfish Hunter was just trying to sock away some money for his growing family in North Carolina so in a few years he could retire to a comfortable existence on his farm.

After agreeing to the salary, Hunter told Finley he'd like some part of his salary to be deferred in some way so he could save money on taxes and provide some security for his family. "Fine, how much?" Finley responded. Hunter said he wasn't sure and that he needed to consult with his lawyer back in North Carolina. He promised to get back to the owner soon. And with that, the matter appeared settled.

For Finley, it was a rare moment of smooth magnanimity. In a world of greedy, penurious, and abusive owners who spared no opportunity to take advantage of their players, Finley managed to distinguish himself as perhaps the greediest and most penurious, and also a bit kooky. By 1974 he had also evolved into a thorn in the side of the game's establishment and Commissioner Bowie Kuhn. Finley liked to refer to Kuhn as "the village idiot."

Charlie O., as Finley was known, sported loud plaid fedoras and bright-colored sports jackets and had little use for baseball's traditions. He had purchased the Kansas City Athletics, as they were then known, in 1960. He tried to move in the outfield fence to 296 feet to create more home runs despite a rule that said outfield fences had to be at least 325 feet from home plate. He made a mule the team's mascot and paraded it around the stadium. He changed the team's colors to yellow and green, a radical and much-derided move in a sport where nearly everyone played in some combination of blue, white, and red (or their "road grays"). He phased out the team's nickname, "Athletics," preferring the shorthand "A's" instead. He insisted on giving all his star players flashy nicknames, figuring it was good marketing. Hence, Jim Hunter became "Catfish," not because he ate or fished for catfish more than anyone else but because Finley liked the name. Johnny Odom would be known by his childhood nickname, "Blue Moon." Finley tried to pin the name "True" on his stud pitcher Vida Blue but Blue refused and demanded to be called by his real name. In 1967, Finley suspended pitcher Lew Krausse Jr. for rowdy behavior on a team flight and fired manager Alvin Dark for disagreeing with the suspension. Ken Harrelson, the A's best player at the time, denounced Finley as a menace to baseball. So Finley dumped him, too. Harrelson would sign with the Boston Red Sox and help lead them to the pennant.

Finley moved the A's to Oakland in 1968, abandoning the Midwest for the Northern California territory the Giants had enjoyed a monopoly on for a decade. To his credit, Finley had revamped the franchise's scouting and development, stocking it with budding superstars who would dominate the sport in the early 1970s. With two world championships in the bag and a star pitcher looking for nothing more than a little comfort and security, Finley appeared more than willing to accommodate Hunter's wish to defer a portion of his salary.

Just as Hunter promised, on January 23, 1974, his lawyer, J. Carlton Cherry of the firm of Cherry, Cherry & Flythe in Ahoskie, North Carolina, wrote to Finley to formally request a deferred compensation clause in the contract and to explain that they had not yet figured out the form of the deferral. Cherry told Finley that Hunter was likely to want $50,000 a year deferred.

After receiving the letter, Finley called Cherry from Chicago— the Midwest was the base of his business operations—and told him to go ahead and draft a special covenant that outlined the deferral. Subsequently, Cherry drew up a paragraph that stated the A's would "pay to any person, firm or corporation designated by [Hunter] the sum of Fifty Thousand ($50,000) Dollars per year, for the duration of this contract."

Cherry then gave a copy of the agreement to Hunter in a manila envelope and told him to deliver it to Finley when he arrived at spring training during the third week in February. The envelope contained a letter asking Finley to sign the contract and return it to Cherry, as well as an annuity policy with the Jefferson Standard Life Insurance Company. On February 15, Finley sent Cherry a letter promising his cooperation.

On February 20, Hunter handed the envelope to Jim Bank, the A's traveling secretary. Four days later Finley called Cherry to tell him that he got the contract and the special covenant and had one objection to it: he didn't want Hunter to be able to receive the $50,000 whenever he wanted it. Rather, he wanted to pay him during the season, even if it ended up in some other account. Cherry had no problem with that. He told Finley he should simply type it into the draft agreement. Finley did, signed the special covenant, and sent it back to Cherry.

Meanwhile, being the careful and thorough lawyer that he was, Cherry was also busy discussing the deferred compensation and annuity policy with the Internal Revenue Service. He wanted to get the agency's approval on Hunter's plan not to have to pay taxes on the money, at least not during the year he was earning it. On June 25, Cherry sent the IRS a formal application to approve the plan and sent Hunter two revised copies of the deferred compensation agreement. He told Hunter to show them to Finley and have the owner call him if there were any problems. Hunter took the envelope with the policy in it and Finley's Chicago address on the outside and put it in an outgoing mail basket in the training room.

Twenty days later, Cherry got the IRS's blessing for the agreement. Hunter wouldn't have to pay taxes on the income until the money got paid out to a beneficiary. The catch was the A's were going to have to be both the purchaser of the policy and the beneficiary, and then they would distribute the money to Hunter or whomever he chose to receive it. Cherry figured that wouldn't be a problem, since the special covenant he and Finley had agreed to stated that Hunter had sole discretion over the distribution of the money. In mid-July, Cherry sent Hunter another copy of the application for the insurance annuity and an amended investment agreement that specified the destination for the deferred compensation.

Hunter finally caught up with Finley in a Chicago hotel room on August 1 and handed him the two documents. Finley looked at the application for an insurance annuity and didn't like what he saw. It called for Finley and the A's to put $50,000 a year in a separate account and use it to invest in the policy; half the money would go into a fixed-rate annuity and half would go into a variable-rate annuity. Finley went into stall mode. He said he needed to talk the matter over with his lawyer, but he didn't bother to do that for three to four weeks. "We were missing each other," he later explained.

A week later Cherry still didn't have any signed and executed documents. On August 8, Hunter pitched the A's to a 10–2 win over the Texas Rangers, tossing a complete game to push his record to 16–9 and lower his earned run average to 2.94. That same day Cherry fired off a letter to Finley, asking after the agreement and the signed annuity application. He explained that he was anxious to close the deal. A few days later Finley finally reached out to Cherry. He explained that he was experiencing what he referred to as "domestic marital difficulties" and, since his wife was the secretary of the club, it was an awkward time to ask for her signature on the documents. Cherry reckoned it was pure crap. On August 22 he wrote to Finley demanding that he get a signature on the document. If it was too awkward to ask his estranged wife, then the team treasurer would do just fine. Good idea, Finley told him. The treasurer would take care of it.

Then, on September 4, Finley called Cherry to deliver bad news. His tax lawyer and other partners really didn't want him to sign this deal, and he didn't like anything about it, either. He said he'd assumed the deal would be similar to the one he had with Reggie Jackson. Finley had agreed to pay Jackson $75,000 in total compensation for 1973. But Jackson would receive just $35,000. The rest Jackson would collect over a span of two years after he retired. Such an arrangement might have seemed good for Jackson, who would lower his taxable income. But that was a very nice arrangement for Finley, too, since he was able to use Jackson's money any way he saw fit until Jackson asked for payment. In the deal with Hunter, he couldn't use the money for other expenses. He also wouldn't be able to count the $50,000 purchase of the insurance annuity as a business expense because the A's were both the purchaser and the beneficiary of the policy. And what would happen if other players began asking for similar arrangements? What would he tell them, and how could the A's afford it? Finley didn't refuse to sign the application and the agreement, but he was beginning to sound like he was going to.

The next day Hunter went to the mound for his thirty-fifth start of a season during which he had essentially worked for half pay, since Finley hadn't done what he had promised with the other half of his salary. He shut out the Rangers 3–0, allowing just four hits, to push his record to 22–10. His earned run average shrunk to 2.64. This was becoming an epic season in which he was ending any debate about who the best pitcher in baseball might be.

That same day Cherry sent yet another letter to Finley. He told Finley his relationship with his other players and his tax liabilities were his own problems. He demanded Finley sign the agreement with the Jefferson Standard Life Insurance Company and pay them Hunter's deferred compensation.

Another ten days passed. Hunter won another game and lost one, too. But he gave up just three runs in the loss and the A's had a rare anemic night on offense. His earned run average shrunk further, to 2.58.

Then, on September 15, Finley called Cherry and told him he wasn't signing the papers. Cherry told him to put that in writing. Finley refused to do that, too. Then he told Cherry he couldn't sign the papers even if he wanted to because he'd thrown the documents away. Cherry told Finley he had every intention of enforcing their agreement. Finley told him to go ahead and try.

In the vast catalog of idiotic, bullying techniques baseball owners employed to try to assert their authority over a newly rebellious generation of players, that move probably surpassed every one that came before it. Faced with a client whose employer was refusing to live up to a contract, Cherry did what any intelligent, self-respecting lawyer would do. The day after Finley dared Cherry to enforce the agreement, Cherry wrote a lengthy letter to the A's owner detailing for the record the sordid history of the negotiations and communications between the two parties throughout the year and Finley's rash refusal to sign the agreement.

"For some reason unknown to us and Mr. Hunter, you are refusing to sign the same and we contend therefore you have breached your contract with our client," Cherry wrote. If Finley didn't rectify the breach, Cherry explained, Hunter would be free to sign with any club he desired. It was all right there in paragraph 7(A) of the collective bargaining agreement. Then Cherry picked up the phone and delivered to Marvin Miller something he had been searching for since 1966: a player who could prove to everyone in baseball—and every team-sport athlete on the planet—the value of the open market.

For eight years Miller had preached about human and professional dignity and the riches that a free market for talent would produce. The vast majority of players thought that sounded goofy. It ignored how much competition they had overcome to get to the big leagues in the first place. Miller told them they were special, and many of them were. But countless others felt far less special. They felt replaceable. To them, being a free agent and choosing a team to play for might be nice, but it also sounded a lot like being unemployed and begging for a new job. They saw the game as a buyer's market for the clubs. There were thousands of players in the many levels of the minor leagues. New talent entered the game every year. Even in the minds of some of the better players, the reserve clause brought the benefits of inertia and familiarity, a kind of disincentive for the clubs to replace them with another player whom management might be less familiar with.

Given the ineptitude of plenty of franchises, the reserve clause probably generated a certain amount of laziness. Clubs couldn't pluck players from the other teams to replace the ones they had. Also, developing a quality major leaguer responsible enough to show up and play hard every day took time. In an era before anything approaching sophisticated statistical analysis, the devils many general managers knew were better than the devils they didn't.

Miller knew this thinking was backward, but he needed a

genuine star to somehow become a free agent to prove the players' theories wrong. The players had the right to an impartial arbitrator for salary and contract disputes. Miller desperately wanted someone to challenge the reserve clause in front of the arbitrator, a move he was sure would produce the game's first true free agent because the right to extend a contract "one year" meant *one and only one* year to everyone who was not a baseball owner.

Before Catfish Hunter came along, a player named Ted Simmons seemed to fit the part. The talented young catcher for the St. Louis Cardinals made his big-league debut when he was nineteen, and by twenty-one he had claimed the Cardinals' starting catcher's job. He could hit for average—.304 in 1971—a somewhat rare quality for a catcher. He also had pop in his bat. (Simmons hit 248 home runs during his career, including a high of 26 in 1979—rare production from a catcher.) Simmons was really good, really young, and played with a swagger that often takes catchers years to accumulate. With his shoulder-length hair, he fit easily into the new generation of brash, confident, and outspoken players who had little tolerance for the way things had always been. He also knew he was grossly underpaid, even as a rookie, when he earned $17,500. He'd had enough conversations with Miller and his general counsel, Dick Moss, and other leaders of the Players Association to know what his options were.

So after the 1971 season, when he hit .304 with seven home runs and seventy-seven RBIs, Simmons refused to sign a contract and told anyone who cared that he intended to challenge the reserve clause. It was a gutsy move. Major-league teams generally didn't let players play without a signed contract, but Simmons did, and Miller and Moss began to anticipate the challenge to the reserve clause they had been hoping for.

The Cardinals wised up to the situation, though. John Gaherin, the owners' chief labor negotiator, had been warning clubs to do everything they could to avoid a ruling on the reserve clause. Most didn't take him seriously, but that was a side concern for the Cardinals, who more than anything wanted to keep one of their best young players happy. Midway through the 1972 season, the Cardinals offered Simmons a two-year $75,000 deal. Simmons signed it with Miller's blessing. He had negotiated hard for a fair deal that would pay him what he felt he was worth. When he got one, he didn't owe his union anything more than that.

With Simmons out of the picture, the search resumed for the right player to become the game's first free agent. Then Cherry called, and Miller had everything he could have hoped for. Catfish Hunter wasn't just any player. He was the best pitcher in baseball. For Miller and Moss, Hunter was a revelation. From the moment Cherry reached out to them, getting Hunter his money became an existential matter about the value of a contract. But Moss and Miller had no intention of stopping there, and the last thing they wanted was for Finley to write a check to rectify the situation. Finley was clearly in default and there was no doubt about how that matter should be resolved. It was all spelled out in paragraph 7(A) of the uniform players' contract: when a club defaults on a contract, the player is set free and can sign with any other club. Catfish Hunter, the best pitcher in baseball, was a free agent.

On October 4, a day before Hunter's scheduled start in game one of the American League Championship Series against the Baltimore Orioles, Moss wired Finley to clarify the union's stand on the matter. Finley was in default because he had failed to make payments within ten days of being notified. Thus, Hunter's contract was being terminated after the final out of the season for the Oakland A's. *In other words, Mr. Finley, you're lucky we're letting him start for you in the postseason.*

Of course, having Hunter sit for the playoffs was never really in the cards. Hunter never would have allowed his contract dispute to jeopardize his teammates' championship, even if he was in the right. Sitting Hunter down for the biggest games of the year would have sacrificed the moral high ground. Also, it might very well have forced Finley to honor the contract, and no one on Hunter's side wanted to give Finley the chance to do that.

Finley read the wire from Moss and summoned Hunter to his Oakland office. When Hunter arrived, he saw not just his boss but also Lee MacPhail, the president of the American League. Finley told Hunter he would hand him a check for $50,000 at that very moment, and he'd always been willing to.

"No," Hunter told Finley. "I don't want the money paid to me. I want it paid just like the contract calls for, deferred payments to an insurance company or whoever I designate."

The next day Hunter endured one of his worst outings of the year. He lasted just four and two-thirds innings. He gave up six runs on eight hits as the A's lost game one of the ALCS, 6–3. It was the last game he would lose that October.

Two days later, Moss wrote to Commissioner Bowie Kuhn to detail the issues of the default and request that on the date of the contract's termination Kuhn notify all twenty-four clubs that Hunter had become a free agent, eligible to accept bids for his services. Kuhn denied the request. Two days after that, Hunter bounced back from his game one fiasco and pitched the A's into their third consecutive World Series, giving up just three hits over seven shutout innings.

In the World Series the A's pitching staff worked its magic once again. Their opponents, the Los Angeles Dodgers, managed only 2.2 runs per game. The A's won three of their four games by a single run, including the two Hunter pitched in. With two outs in the ninth inning of game one, Rollie Fingers gave up a home run and a single to right field. The A's manager, Dick Williams, called on Hunter, who finished off the game with a strikeout for his first and only save of the year. Three days later Hunter allowed one run on five hits over seven and a third innings to give the A's a 3–1 lead. Two days after that, Charlie Finley's A's clinched their third consecutive world championship.

As the A's celebrated, Dick Moss did exactly what he told Finley and Kuhn he would do: he filed grievances demanding that Major League Baseball declare Hunter a free agent and that the A's "immediately pay over, as directed by Mr. Hunter and/or his representatives, the sum of $50,000" plus damages.

For three weeks Moss, Hunter, and Miller waited for a response from Finley and Kuhn. Finally, on November 12, Finley got around to responding. He essentially put to paper what he had told Hunter and Cherry in their previous conversations. Then he went one step further. He suggested that Cherry and Hunter had tried to induce him into making investments in the annuity beyond $50,000, what he referred to as a "phantom investment increment." He accused Cherry of strong-arming the A's into an investment mechanism they had no interest in taking part in that had "extremely dubious tax propriety." Somehow he had forgotten the IRS had already approved the arrangement.

And with that, the stage was set for the first hearing of consequence in front of an impartial arbitrator, a test case Miller had been trying to pursue ever since he took over this nearly bankrupt, utterly disorganized, and uninformed trade association of professionals.

On November 26, the parties convened in front of Peter Seitz, the arbitrator the players and owners had agreed to hire. Seitz was a mild-mannered jurist in his sixties, a lot closer to the end of his career than the beginning. He'd hesitated before taking the baseball job, not really sure what use it would be or what impact he might have. He didn't have much of an ego, at least by the metrics of successful lawyers, and he expressed no desire to pursue any sort of agenda on behalf of one side or the other. His instructions were no different from those given to baseball's umpires: call 'em like you see 'em and interpret the rules as clearly and simply as possible.

Over the course of several hours of testimony, Hunter, Cherry, Finley, and everyone who had been involved in the process delivered his version of the preceding ten months in front of a three-person panel. The panel included Seitz, Miller, and John Gaherin, the lead negotiator for baseball's Major League Baseball Player Relations Committee. Moss represented the Players Association. Lawyer Barry Rona represented the owners.

Cherry and Hunter kept their stories as basic as possible. They had agreed to a contract, Hunter fulfilled his part of the deal, and Finley finked out.

When Finley sat down in the witness chair, he delivered a rambling defense of his behavior. Cherry had pulled a bait and switch on him. The deferred payments were supposed to be like Reggie Jackson's. He was going to get screwed on his taxes. Hunter never delivered the papers to him. Rona delivered an additional defense. He argued that the clock shouldn't even start ticking on Finley's default until after the arbitrator issued a ruling that might happen to go against him, so Finley still had time to rectify the situation.

Seitz wasted little time in coming to his decision. On December 13, he issued an evisceration of nearly every argument Finley and Rona used to justify their behavior. It took Seitz only two paragraphs to dismiss Rona's argument about the timing of the default. According to Seitz, it occurred on September 26, ten days after Cherry wrote Finley to put him on notice, and Finley didn't act to rectify the situation. Seitz stated emphatically that paragraph 7(A) of the standard player contract "is pellucidly clear." He wrote that he didn't necessarily think it was the most thoughtful provision. The game might be better served if the remedies weren't so sudden and drastic. But he noted it wasn't his job to rewrite the contracts or the collective bargaining agreement.

Hunter had a contract, Seitz wrote. Finley had an obligation to abide by it, something he appeared inclined to do when he wrote on February 15 that the A's "will be very happy to cooperate in any manner possible to defer any amount of Mr. Hunter's compensation." While Finley later said he thought the deferral arrangement would be like Reggie Jackson's, where he would pay Jackson somewhere "down the line," Seitz said there was no reason why Catfish Hunter should be bound by the contract of another player. He noted that a Reggie Jackson–like arrangement would have contradicted what Finley had agreed to when he insisted the compensation would be paid as earned throughout the season.

Seitz gave Finley the benefit of the doubt on his version of the story about repeatedly not getting the papers that Hunter said he had tried to deliver. "The record supports a conclusion that Mr. Hunter's widely accepted dependability as a pitcher does not extend to his performance as a courier," he wrote. But other than that, Seitz found little wrong with Hunter's behavior. Hunter never promised to come up with a plan that satisfied the A's tax objectives. Seitz then reached the only conclusion that a sane person could reach: Finley preferred the Jackson deal because he got to use the money as he pleased until Jackson retired. He noted that Finley, after receiving the proposal on August 1, could have opened negotiations with Cherry or expressed his concerns that there might be legal problems with it. He could have asked Cherry for other suggestions about deferral processes.

"He did none of these things," Seitz wrote. "Following the August 1 meeting he led Mr. Cherry to believe that the only thing standing in the way of completion of the program was the difficulty of persuading his estranged wife to attest to the regularity of the corporate signature. Then, in their September 15 phone call (a month after the papers had been presented to him) he bluntly stated that he would not sign them; and in response to Mr. Cherry's request, refused to write a letter to that effect and said that the papers had been thrown away."

It's about as close as an arbitrator comes to explicitly calling one of the parties full of crap. With that, Seitz announced he would sustain the grievances. "Mr. Hunter's contract for services to be performed during the 1975 season no longer binds him and he is a free agent."

Some ninety-five years after baseball's owners first created a "reserve clause" to prevent them from cherry-picking one another's players, the fun was about to begin.

*The events that ensued during the next two weeks in North Caro-*lina, near Cherry's office in Ahoskie, were as bizarre as they were predictable.

Baseball's owners had long cited the vitality of baseball's reserve clause. Without it, they said, the game wouldn't survive. Given that, did they balk at doing something so crass as pursuing another team's player, even if the game's version of the high court had declared him a free agent? That would have been the principled thing to do, especially if they believed that creating an open market for a ballplayer would lead to the game's ruin. And these were principled men, weren't they?

Instead, more than a dozen clubs descended on the Tar Heel State. Cherry's work had brought Hunter to this point. Now he was going to see to it that his famous client got the money he deserved. The clubs came ready to write big checks to land the game's best pitcher. Sportswriters filled every little motel and diner Ahoskie had to offer.

No one went with more enthusiasm than the representatives of the New York Yankees, the toy that George Steinbrenner had purchased for the record price of $8.7 million in 1973. Steinbrenner's close friend and partner in the Yankees was Robert Nederlander, one of New York's top Broadway producers. Nederlander had told Steinbrenner that New York loved stars. Now the biggest one of all was available and Steinbrenner wasn't about to pass up an opportunity to grab him.

The only problem was Steinbrenner had recently been convicted of making illegal contributions to Richard Nixon's reelection campaign. He was serving a two-year suspension from baseball, and he wasn't supposed to be taking part in any aspect of the team's business. And yet, as the Catfish Hunter sweepstakes wore on, the Yankees always seemed ready to up the ante; there was little mystery as to where the money was coming from and who was calling the shots.

Word quickly circulated that the Yankees were leading a spiraling auction. In late December, Marty Appel, the Yankees' director of public relations, wandered into general manager Gabe Paul's office at the team's temporary headquarters in a New York parks administration office near Shea Stadium in Queens. (Yankee Stadium was undergoing a two-year renovation at the time.) Appel was puzzled about the million-dollar rumors swirling around the Hunter sweepstakes. That number would quadruple Dick Allen's highest-in-the-game contract at the time. A few other players had multiyear deals. Bobby Richardson had been offered one, but he had been the rare Yankee to get one.

Appel and other executives in baseball assumed Hunter would get a contract that included a salary of $250,000 or maybe $300,000. When he saw Paul, Appel sheepishly asked if Hunter was really about to get a deal worth more than $1 million.

Paul looked up at Appel and proudly pronounced, "You're darn right!"

Beyond the money, the Yankees had a secret weapon. Clyde Kluttz, the scout who had signed Catfish out of high school, was the scouting director for the Yankees and something of a father figure to Hunter. The Indians made a late charge: they sent ace Gaylord Perry to vouch for the organization and lure Hunter to the Rust Belt. But with Kluttz singing the praises of the Yankees and Steinbrenner's surrogates throwing a five-year contract worth $3.5 million at the North Carolina farm boy, there was no doubt where Catfish Hunter was going to end up.

On New Year's Eve, Hunter boarded a jet with tail letters that included "GMS" bound for New York. It was Steinbrenner's plane and its presence dispensed with any pretense that the Yankees' principal owner wasn't involved. Commissioner Bowie Kuhn would later tell Appel that he knew Steinbrenner had taken part in the process. Since the contract was technically worth one-third the value of the franchise, it would be absurd to think he shouldn't take part in the decision. Aboard Steinbrenner's plane, Hunter worked out the details of his deal with Ed Greenwald, one of Steinbrenner's limited partners. The deal included insurance policies for Hunter's children. When they landed, Hunter headed to an event that would soon become as much a part of the game as balls and strikes: the free agent signing news conference.

Appel and a few staff members hastily cleared out the desks in a center room of the parks administration building to make room for the press. Then Appel headed back into the office to crank out a press release on the hand-operated mimeograph machine the Yankees used for the announcement. Most offices had switched over to Xerox copiers by then, but Paul and the Yankees weren't exactly early adopters. The franchise might be ready to commit $3.5 million for a pitcher, but it wasn't about to go waste its money on an expensive copier when it had a perfectly fine mimeograph machine.

The press conference went off without a hitch. Hunter told the assembled press he was thrilled to be a Yankee. New York welcomed him. And then everyone scattered for their New Year's plans.

Catfish headed back to North Carolina but with a promise that he would return in a few weeks for a proper media day.

Sure enough, in mid-January, he was back in New York. He stayed at the Americana Hotel on Fifty-Second Street and woke early for an appearance on *Good Morning America*. In the green room he kibitzed with Jesse Jackson, who seemed very pleased to be hob-nobbing with the country's most famous ballplayer. Hunter shook the young activist's hand and asked him if he was related to his former teammate Reggie Jackson. "You guys sure look a lot alike," Hunter told him. Then it was back to the hotel for lunch with the local writers: pastrami and corned beef sandwiches from the Stage Deli. That night he and Appel had steaks on Steinbrenner's dime at Top of the Sixes, the restaurant above 666 Fifth Avenue.

A month later, Hunter showed up in Fort Lauderdale for spring training in a Brink's truck as part of a segment for Howard Cosell. In the space of three months, Hunter had taught the sports world the value of the open market and changed the way all athletes would think about their careers. Hunter's contract was worth roughly fif-teen times more than the next highest contract at the time. To put that in perspective, imagine a baseball player in 2016 signing a contract worth more than $4 billion.

Hunter immediately became the Yankee leader. Catcher Thur-man Munson would be named captain in 1976, but Hunter had three World Series rings and he pitched like the ace he was sup-posed to be, at least for the first two seasons. He would go 40-29 in 1975–76, leading the Yankees to their first pennant in a dozen years in 1976. Then his arm gave out, and like countless free agents who would follow in his footsteps, Hunter showed the baseball world the risks of breaking the bank for a player when the bulk of the contract covers years on the wrong side of thirty. Still, Hunter showed how much baseball's owners had cost the ballplayers by keeping the market closed for a century. Freedom from a club wasn't akin to unemployment, like plenty of ballplayers thought it might be. It was an opportunity to allow the market to determine a player's value instead of some crony general manager trying to line his owner's pockets.

Within months of Hunter's free agency, Andy Messersmith, another premier pitcher, and Dave McNally, a grizzled veteran, announced they would play out their options and challenge the reserve clause in front of Peter Seitz. That led the owners to their fateful request for Seitz to rule on the meaning of the word "one" even as their top strategist, John Gaherin, begged them to negotiate a compromise with Miller and the Players Association instead of putting their fate in the hands of a neutral arbitrator.

Messersmith and McNally's inevitable victory after the 1975 season led to the 1976 collective bargaining agreement, which put in place the system that largely still exists today: two years of reserve status, followed by a period of salary arbitration eligibility, followed by free agency after six years of service.

Because of Catfish Hunter, free agency became the Holy Grail for every team-sport athlete, *the* cause that all unions would fight for until they got it. It was the line in the sand they would never allow management to cross once it was achieved. The clubs could chip away at it, putting in salary caps—hard ones and soft ones— and limit the size and the length of contracts. But management's support of the idea that a baseball player should go through his entire career without ever attaining control of his own destiny landed the lords of sports on the wrong side of history.

And no, baseball didn't collapse. Rather, it boomed. Yes, salaries skyrocketed, making up quickly for years of under-market compensation, during which players earned less than 20 percent of overall revenues. By 1981 the average salary had climbed to $149,000, from $51,500 in 1976. But so did attendance, and television rights fees, and sales of licensed merchandise, and ticket prices, and every other kind of commerce associated with the game. Forced to compete with one another for talent, owners finally began to treat their teams like going concerns, investing in them the way owners are supposed to invest in valuable assets and the labor that makes them so valuable. "Free agency is responsible for making this a business," said Michael Weiner, the late executive director of the Players Association, who died of a brain tumor in 2013 at age fifty-one. "With free agency, baseball becomes a year-round enterprise. You have to follow all the moves. The newspapers are filled with stories about Reggie Jackson or Dave Winfield or whatever hot free agents are out there. There are lots of people focusing on this. There are debates about player salaries. That furthers the business and it makes the game more popular. Then you also have all the benefits that player movement brings. The simple fact is that in the nearly 40 years since free agency you have more competitive balance than you ever had before. You don't have a situation where a team is stagnant for years because the owner is bad and cheap and doesn't care, or the Yankees are raiding Kansas City every year. You have more excitement, the players are better because they are making more money and they are able to train year-round. The product is better, and then there's more coverage of the game and interest in it."

Today, baseball is an $8 billion business that owns its own cable sports network and Internet company. There are thirty teams, compared with twenty-four in 1976. In 2012 the Dodgers sold for $2.15 billion. The richest contracts are worth roughly $300 million. Indeed, the richest teams have built-in advantages, but from 1901 to 1969, eight teams won 106 of 136 pennants. Since 1979, all but three major-league teams have appeared in the World Series.

Catfish Hunter died in 1999 of a fall in the same small town of Hertford, North Carolina, population 2,100, where he'd been born in 1946. Suffering from the early effects of amyotrophic lateral sclerosis, also known as Lou Gehrig's disease, Hunter had lost the use of his arms. Though balance was becoming a problem, Hunter didn't want to begin using a wheelchair. He fell at his home, banged his head on a set of stairs, and died from the effects of the fall on September 9.

By the time of his death, Hunter's impact stretched far beyond the baseball field. It had begun the minute the clubs started descending on Ahoskie. Team sports had always offered a chance at stardom. Now those sports were going to offer every athletically gifted kid the chance for untold riches, a chance to exert some control over his life through a system where talent is sold on the open market to the highest bidder. An athlete only needed God-given gifts, a freakishly competitive drive, and training—the kind of focused, single-minded training that the sports world was about to create.

6

Academy World

On a late spring afternoon in 1961, a middling tennis coach named Nick Bollettieri wandered down to the courts at Victory Park in North Miami Beach. Until 1959 these tennis courts had been Bollettieri's base of operations. Bollettieri was a law school dropout with an uncle in the local water department who took pity on him. Uncle Walter had gotten Bollettieri a job giving tennis lessons at Victory Park for $3 an hour. Bollettieri knew little about the game. Fortunately, neither did the children he was teaching.

Bollettieri did well, though, well enough to impress a snowbird from Springfield, Ohio, who hired him to run his summer tennis program up north. That job led to a post running the tennis program at the Dorado Beach hotel and resort in Puerto Rico during the winters. On his way up to his summer gig in Ohio, Bollettieri liked to stop in Miami Beach, see his family, and check on the Victory Park tennis courts, just to see who might be hanging around and how the local talent was developing. It was never particularly memorable. And then, suddenly, it was.

On the same courts where Bollettieri used to spend hours trying to figure out what made each kid tick, he noticed an athletic-looking nine-year-old with quick feet and sweet strokes. Instantly he knew he was the most talented nine-year-old he had ever seen. He never looked off balance. The ball jumped off his racket like a line drive off a baseball bat. Bollettieri watched with amazement, then he reacted as only an inveterate coach would: he walked over to the boy and introduced himself. The boy said his name was Brian Gottfried. His parents were nearby. Bollettieri met them, too. He told them who he was, where he coached, about his summer program in Ohio, and then he did the strangest thing: he offered to take Gottfried away for the summer, put him up at his house, and teach him the game. The Gottfrieds checked up on Bollettieri and then did something even stranger: they sent Brian up to Ohio for the summer with the tennis coach they had met at the park.

To Bollettieri, this kid rekindled an idea he'd been pondering about how to turn kids into great tennis players. Money didn't have much to do with it. There wasn't any money in tennis then, even for the top professionals. The Open era was still seven years away. Having Brian Gottfried training with him might help him convince the kids and parents in Springfield, Ohio, that his tennis program was worthwhile, but there was more to this than money. Bollettieri, a former paratrooper, had fallen for the brutal, kill-or-be-killed nature of tennis. Improbable as it sounded, he wanted to be known as the best tennis coach in the world. The only way he could get that recognition was by coaching the best players, and he had watched enough good coaches to know the only way to make good players great was to work with them constantly, day after day, and to pound into them the virtues of the game and the commitment required for mastering it. They also needed other really good and promising players to motivate and push them though. That was what he offered Brian Gottfried and his parents, and that was what hooked them. That and the price: Bollettieri never charged them a dime.

In Ohio, Gottfried was on the court with Bollettieri from dawn until dusk. First Gottfried would have his own lesson with Bollettieri and the other elite players. Then Bollettieri used his star pupil to serve as a human ball machine. He used him to feed balls to other juniors. When they returned the ball, Gottfried volleyed the returns back to the players who were taking instruction on the opposite baseline, ball after ball, hour after hour, summer after summer, until he turned fifteen and could begin traveling to the major junior tournaments. On the junior circuit he quickly became known as the most technically sound volleyer and for having one of the most dangerous forehands around. It wasn't clear why. He had a slight, lanky build, a bushy head of blond curls, deep, academic eyes, and an often knitted brow that made him look like he was always thinking his way through the tennis court rather than reacting effortlessly. Few opponents knew about those long days on the courts of Springfield, Ohio.

Beyond the volume of balls he was hitting, Gottfried also came to know Bollettieri as the first true motivator and disciplinarian of his life. He grew up in a middle-class Jewish home without much yelling, and certainly not at children. Bollettieri yelled constantly. Double-fault a game away and his wrath came down on you like a force of nature. He had a rare ability to be both fiery and critical but to know how to stop just shy of abusive. "You did not want to disappoint him," Gottfried said.

He didn't. Gottfried rose to number three in the world singles rankings and number one in doubles. He was probably the hardest-working pro of his era, the polar opposite of players like John McEnroe and Bjorn Borg, who floated across the tennis court and played as though they were born to do nothing else. Why did

Gottfried become so good? Maybe because he did something almost no one else did at the time, making a radical move that inevitably became central to the development of great athletes during the next quarter century: he uprooted his life to seek out the best coaching and competition he could find.

To understand how an industry dedicated to building the next great tennis players and athletes in every other sport came to be and the role it plays in what would amount to a takeover of sports by the players who starred in them, it's important to understand what existed before it: virtually nothing. There simply wasn't much need or demand for it. The greatest professional athletes have always made out fine financially. In the prime of his career, Joe DiMaggio's salary reached $100,000, about $1 million in today's dollars. (His real fortune came later, from Mr. Coffee.) But for the middling athlete—the journeyman pitcher, the unproven quarterback, the world's thirtieth-ranked tennis player or golfer—sports didn't offer a particularly remunerative life.

No wonder the world of youth sports in the 1960s looks Rockwellian by today's standards. There was Little League and Pop Warner football and after-school sports, which got more serious and publicly funded once kids hit high school. The integration of sports into the high school and college infrastructure was—and to an extent still is—one of the great differentiators for American athletes. Beyond school sports, there were plenty of other affordable opportunities for athletic kids to play. Swimmers could join a local swim club. There were church basketball leagues and Police Athletic League competitions. But the heart of athletic training remained the school, usually a public one. The best of the best played two or three sports in high school and ended up with a scholarship to college, where they could further hone their skills, and the best of them might take a shot at professional sports for a few years—or the Olympics, either during college or as quickly after graduation as possible, since Olympians still had to be amateurs who couldn't receive payments for their athletic endeavors.

For the most part, the system worked. Until the Soviets began to invest in their sports training schools and institutionalize experimentation with performance-enhancing drugs, Americans dominated the Olympic Games, especially in the sports we cared about: swimming (Mark Spitz), track (Bob Mathias, Rafer Johnson, Wilma Rudolph), basketball (Bill Russell). The US produced some of the world's great tennis players (Jack Kramer, Pancho Gonzalez) and its best golfers (Arnold Palmer, Jack Nicklaus). As rudimentary and limited as youth sports during the first three-quarters of the twentieth century might look today, until the Soviets came along, they were far more effective than anything the rest of the world had ever seen.

Consider the upbringing of a kid from Brooklyn named Sanford Braun, who later became a pretty good pitcher named Sandy Koufax. Known as "the Left Arm of God," Koufax is widely considered the greatest pitcher ever to pick up a baseball. He had a blazing fastball, and once he learned how to control it, he was virtually unhittable for six of the greatest seasons a pitcher has ever had before arthritis ended his career at thirty.

Koufax grew up in Brooklyn and Long Island. He played basketball for a local basketball team at the Edith and Carl Marks Jewish Community House of Bensonhurst. He played baseball for a local youth team called the Ice Cream League. He later starred in both basketball and baseball at Lafayette High School, where he was better known for his exploits in basketball. He attended the University of Cincinnati, where he had to try out for both the basketball and baseball teams. He made both. Then, in the spring of 1954, Koufax tried out for three Major League Baseball teams, including the Brooklyn Dodgers, and earned his first professional contract. A year later, just nineteen years old, he was on the Brooklyn Dodgers team that finally beat the Yankees in the World Series. Koufax was too raw and wild to pitch in the Series. And he was so uncertain that he had a future in professional sports that he attended night classes at Columbia University's School of General Studies. Legend has it he even showed up for class one October night in 1955—after the Dodgers had won game seven of the World Series that afternoon.

Imagine how different Koufax's childhood would have been had he come of age today with a fastball that dazzled scouts at a never-ending series of travel team, high school, and showcase-event games. It's doubtful he would have even picked up a basketball once he was in high school. The risk of an injury that might jeopardize his magical arm would have been too great. Given his talents, it's not a stretch to imagine him moving to Florida as a teenager and attending the sports academies that IMG now runs there, where many of the country's top teenage baseball players (and soccer players, and tennis players, and golfers, and basketball players) attend school in the morning and spend the rest of the daylight hours taking infield and batting practice, or in the gym lifting weights, or meeting with sports psychologists. There would have been magazine profiles, scouting reports, scholarship offers, and, more than likely, a tough decision whether to attend college or turn professional right out of high school, since he would have been picked very early in Major League Baseball's amateur draft in June of his senior year.

The reason why Koufax and thousands of American athletes didn't develop like this is very simple: they came of age before Nick Bollettieri dropped out of law school and started teaching tennis full-time.

Bollettieri grew up in Pelham, New York, in the 1930s and 1940s in what was then a largely working-class suburb filled with Italians,

African-Americans, and, in the nicer neighborhoods, a small professional class of comfortable wealth. Bollettieri's father was a pharmacist. Nick played football and basketball and shot marbles as a kid. He barely knew what tennis was; to him tennis was a game played in the neighboring towns of Scarsdale and Larchmont and Rye, where people belonged to country clubs.

Bollettieri attended Spring Hill College in Alabama on an ROTC scholarship. He played a little tennis there, and since he was a decent athlete he wasn't half-bad at it, but it didn't register in the life Bollettieri hoped to attain. His initial focus was fulfilling his commitment to the military. He wanted to join the Naval Air Corps and become a fighter jock. Then he flunked the test, so he opted for Plan B, which was to sign up for the paratroopers, because he liked the idea of an elite unit with a rich history of bravery in battle. He played a little football while he was in the Army, and zero tennis.

Four years later, at the end of his commission, Bollettieri left the service and moved to Miami to attend the University of Miami Law School. It seemed like it might lead to a respectable life. Unable to hack the work, he was done before the end of the first year. It was 1956. Bollettieri had absolutely no idea how he was going to make a living. He'd been making ends meet teaching tennis to kids on a couple of courts at Victory Park in North Miami Beach, the gig his Uncle Walter, a local water commissioner, had hooked him up with, since he knew the folks who ran the public parks. The kids paid him $3 an hour, which is about what his knowledge of the game was worth back then. "Just hit the goddamn ball," he told them. *Hit it like you mean it.*

Slowly, Bollettieri began to develop a following. Uncle Walter noticed and decided that Victory Park needed some new and better tennis courts. As Bollettieri tells it, the following spring, Walter threw a picnic in the park and invited the mayor. He brought a shovel, too. Mid-picnic, Walter got everyone's attention, handed the mayor the shovel, and announced that the park was going to be getting six new tennis courts, enough for Bollettieri to build a burgeoning tennis program in North Miami Beach over the next three years. The program became impressive enough that when a tennis buff from Springfield, Ohio, named Charles Fry wandered by in 1959, he decided his city didn't just need a program like Bollettieri's, it needed Bollettieri himself.

Looking for a new challenge, Bollettieri jumped at the offer and headed north for the summer, trading the oppressive humidity of the east coast of Florida for the sweltering heat of the Midwest. The tennis season was just four or five months in Ohio. Bollettieri figured he could return home to Florida to work in the winter. Springfield, forty miles west of Columbus, seventy miles northeast of Cincinnati, was the middle of nowhere for an Italian kid from New York and Miami. But Springfield was a midwestern tennis hub, the home of the Western Championships and a junior tournament that attracted some of the best young players of the era.

During that first summer, a young Puerto Rican hotshot named Charlie Pasarell arrived in Springfield for the Western junior tournament. He was thirteen and traveling with his parents, Charles Sr. and Dora. They arrived a few days before the tournament and came to practice on the municipal courts where Bollettieri was the tennis pro. Pasarell forgot to bring tennis balls, however, so his mother asked Bollettieri if she could buy a can. He gave them to her for free and the two chatted casually for a while. As the weekend progressed, anytime Dora or Charles Sr. needed a towel or some extra balls, the exuberant pro with the strange last name was there. When Sunday came, Bollettieri mentioned to the Pasarells that he was looking for a job for the winter. He asked them to keep him in mind if any resorts in Puerto Rico might be looking for a pro. He gave them his business card and figured he'd see them again in a year when they returned to Springfield for the tournament.

Three months later, Bollettieri got a phone call from Charles Pasarell Sr., who was a member of the golf club at the Dorado Beach hotel near San Juan. At the time, the Dorado Beach was one of the premier resort hotels in the world. Charles told him that his friend Laurance Rockefeller, the hotel's owner, had asked him if he knew of any tennis pros who might be a good fit at the hotel to replace the outgoing pro. There was a moment of silence on the phone. "Are you really talking about Larry Rockefeller of the Rockefeller family?" Bollettieri asked. He was, and Bollettieri needed to go to New York to meet him.

Bollettieri passed the interview with flying colors, landed the job at the resort, and became something of a personal instructor for the Rockefellers, teaching them the game at their New York estate in Pocantico Hills and during the winters in Puerto Rico. More important, Bollettieri got his first real education in tennis. Wintering in Puerto Rico put him in the same sphere as Welby Van Horn, a top-ten player in the 1940s who moved to Puerto Rico in 1951 to work at the Caribe Hilton Hotel in San Juan. Van Horn became one of the sport's first renowned coaches. He broke the game down to its basic elements and taught with a classical approach evident in players like Pasarell, who began working with Van Horn when he was eight years old. Van Horn's lessons began with teaching the proper footwork that allowed players to attain a sense of balance. Then he taught the proper grip for holding a racket. Mastering the grip led to learning the smooth, low-to-high stroke for hitting the ball. Finally, ideas about strategy to build and win points were discussed. To Van Horn, teaching tennis was just like teaching music to a piano player or a violinist. Too many teachers made the mistake of trying to teach beginning students the improvisational parts of the game. The great players mastered the fundamentals, which allowed them to learn how to improvise. For someone like Bollettieri, a self-taught teacher, being around Van Horn felt like being a young artist getting a chance to spend each winter watching Van Gogh paint.

That first winter, when Charlie Pasarell would head over to the Hilton for his afternoon tennis lessons, he could always tell when Bollettieri was having a slow day at the Dorado. If he was, Bollettieri would park himself next to the court at the Hilton and watch Welby teach. By the time Bollettieri found Brian Gottfried in 1961, he knew enough to teach him the way Welby would have.

That routine—winters in Puerto Rico, summers in Ohio, or later Chicago, or at a sports camp in Beaver Dam, Wisconsin—lasted until 1976. By then, Bollettieri had had enough of Puerto Rico. After nearly twenty years of coaching, the world was finally coming around to him. The men's and women's tennis tours were booming. Jimmy Connors, Arthur Ashe, Chris Evert, and even Brian Gottfried were on their way to careers that would make them millionaires, both on and off the court. Children, and their parents, finally had something to shoot for. There was a real market for someone like Bollettieri, who had the pedigree that came with working at posh resorts.

Needing winter employment, he set his sights on Florida and landed a job at the Colony Beach & Tennis Resort in Longboat Key, on Florida's Gulf Coast. The location was ideal. A dozen tennis courts, year-round tennis weather, and with air travel becoming more affordable, Longboat Key was an easy plane trip from the population centers in the Northeast for the fancy families who wanted their kids to stay sharp through the winter before the junior tennis circuit got going again in the spring and summer. Catfish Hunter was working under a five-year, $3.5 million contract. Stan Smith was about to begin collecting millions in royalties from an elegant tennis shoe. And Nick Bollettieri was living in a comfortable home on the bay side of Longboat Key, across the street from the Gulf of Mexico and just a two-hour drive across Alligator Alley from where his career as a tennis instructor had begun some twenty years earlier at Victory Park in North Miami Beach.

And that's when Bollettieri started obsessing about paratroopers, that elite team he had once been a part of, in which every member pushed everyone else to be the best he possibly could be. Twenty years after his discharge from the service, the paratroopers remained Bollettieri's ideal when it came to taking quality raw material and turning it into something great. The paratroopers weren't a job or an activity. They were a way of life. Couldn't the paratroopers serve as a model for a tennis academy? There was little doubt the pool of American tennis talent was growing deeper. All the best players needed now was a place to play—really play—with and against each other, all day long.

Could tennis be taught that way? Did the world want tennis, or any sport for that matter, to be that way? With the new money coming in, it sure seemed to Bollettieri that it would, but he had no idea whether he was a revolutionary or a kook. Some 1,200 miles north, the Port Washington Tennis Academy on Long Island was churning out hotshots like Vitas Gerulaitis and putting the finishing touches on a teenage John McEnroe. But the kids who trained at Port Washington went to school all day and squeezed in a few hours of training in the afternoons before dinner and homework.

It was a model created decades earlier, before golfers lined up putts worth a half million dollars and baseball players could sign contracts that would allow them never to have to work a day at another job for the rest of their lives. For decades, civil society had pushed the concept of balance in a child's life. A proper education would lay the foundation for what would eventually become a well-rounded adult. He might have a powerful forehand

and a reliable backhand, but he should also be able to read and write and add as well as someone who hadn't been born with his physical gifts.

Bollettieri looked at the model and had a reaction along the lines of *To hell with that*. He had a different idea, an idea perfect for an age in which the prize money available at a single Grand Slam tournament might be triple what a partner in a New York law firm could make in a year. And each year brought four Grand Slam tournaments and dozens of smaller tournaments with tens of thousands of dollars available for the taking. Then there were the equipment manufacturers and clothing companies, suddenly desperate to pay for the privilege of having the top young pros wear their clothes and play with their rackets.

So, Bollettieri thought, why not flip the ratio of school to training and line it up with the earnings potential of each endeavor? Why not take the elite of the elite in junior tennis and make school more efficient? Get the kids tutors, or correspondence courses, or a special school—anything that might allow them to shrink their school day from seven hours to three or four, tops, and spend every other waking hour with tennis shoes on their feet and rackets in their hands, beating balls across the net at each other all afternoon and into the evening, competing to be the best in the eyes of an ambitious, tireless coach, who would rise at dawn to work out himself, give lessons before breakfast, and spend every afternoon watching, training, hoping.

Bollettieri had no doubt that there was a clear correlation between the amount of time a gifted kid spent hitting balls with other gifted kids and how well those kids performed on the junior tennis circuit. What would be the crime of giving them the chance to play as much as they possibly could if that was what they wanted to do? Weren't they training themselves for a professional career—and an increasingly lucrative one at that? Hadn't ballet dancers and musical prodigies lived this way for years? The Soviets had created sports schools in Eastern Europe to train future Olympians. Why didn't that exist in the Western world?

Bollettieri put the word out that he was ready to commit fully to training a new generation of tennis phenoms. The players would attend school in the mornings at a local private academy and beat balls all afternoon. Nine players, all local, showed up, plus a stellar teenager from West Virginia named Anne White, who lived in Bollettieri's home, just as Gottfried had.

At the top levels, the worlds of elite junior sports are rather small. Today, parents of top athletes assiduously scout the competition over the Internet. A serious travel soccer parent knows heading into a regional tournament the records and performances of the teams his child's side will face, as well as the strongest players those teams will bring to the pitch, even if his own child plays in New York and the teams in the tournament are from Georgia and Florida. Same goes for individual sports. Tennis has been this way since long before anyone had dreamed of the Internet. It's a chatty world where people talk and trade gossip about the best coaches and training techniques. And if a couple of impressive young players training under the same coach show up and dominate at the Orange Bowl tournament or in Kalamazoo at the Junior Nationals, or any other gathering of top juniors, the parents of the kids they've demolished will inevitably start asking what those kids might be doing that their kids are not. (I have yet to meet the obsessive sports parent who looks at a kid who has just beaten his own and concludes, *That kid is just plain better than mine.*) That is exactly what happened with Bollettieri and his minions at the Colony in the mid-1970s, especially once the vacationing snowbirds got wind of why those school-age kids seemed to be spending their days on the tennis courts when they were supposed to be in classrooms.

Word quickly spread that Bollettieri just might be up to something revolutionary. After a few months, no one could touch his kids at the local tournaments and high school matches—kids like Rill Baxter, who would go on to reach the top one hundred in doubles, and Mike and Michelle DePalmer, who had first met Bollettieri during a weeklong session. When they started destroying the competition, rival parents began suggesting that the kids be banned because they didn't go to a legitimate high school.

The lesson was perfectly clear for the parents of the children who kept ending up on the losing end of matches against the Bollettieri kids, and to those who saw what Bollettieri was doing firsthand at the Colony on their vacations: if his kids were practicing twice as much as their own, there was no chance their kids were going to be able to keep up. Sure, their kids might be getting a better education and the benefit of being nurtured at home by their parents during their formative years. However, society offers few measuring sticks for those sorts of benefits. There are no rankings for "best upbringing." All these families had to focus on was that when spring rolled around and the junior tennis circuit heated up, the kids from the Colony were spanking their kids and shooting up the national junior tennis rankings.

And that was before anyone had ever heard of Jimmy Arias or seen the magical stroke he called his forehand.

Antonio Arias was an electrical engineer and Cuban émigré born in Spain. In 1978 he was raising a family in Buffalo. His son, Jimmy, had been making noise in junior tennis in western New York since he was eight years old. But Jimmy and Antonio had a problem. Buffalo has two seasons, winter and August, and the city isn't anyone's idea of a tennis hub. When Jimmy first started playing, he landed in a group of decent players who were several years older than he was. He practiced with them nearly every day. Two of them eventually made the pro tour; a few others played at top

Division 1 colleges. But by the time Jimmy was twelve, those players were getting ready to leave Buffalo, and Jimmy wasn't going
to have anyone left to practice with. Antonio Arias started pursuing a relationship with the Spanish tennis federation. In 1977 he
brought Jimmy to the US Open in Forest Hills, showed him off to
the Spanish officials there, and introduced him to Manuel Orantes,
the great Spanish champion. The Spaniards liked what they saw in
Jimmy and invited him to move to Spain and train year-round with
their coaches. One problem: Jimmy had zero interest in moving
alone to a country where he didn't speak the language and would
be three thousand miles and an ocean away from his friends and
family.

So Jimmy went back to Buffalo, and the Spanish proposal
stayed on the back burner until December, when Jimmy traveled
to Florida with the group of tennis players from Buffalo for a week
of practice at the Colony. The Colony Beach & Tennis Resort happened to be partly owned by a Buffalo orthodontist named Murray "Murf" Klauber. Klauber took care of Jimmy's sister's teeth
and had gotten to know his family. On the first day, the father of
one of the boys Jimmy was traveling with approached an assistant
pro named Julio and told him he had a thirteen-year-old stud who
needed another top teenager to hit with. Julio tracked down Mike
DePalmer, who was sixteen at the time and the best of Bollettieri's
minions. He sent them onto the courts. DePalmer and Arias began
beating the ball back and forth across the net. Within minutes
word reached the pro shop that there was a kid Bollettieri ought
to take a look at because he was doing something no one had ever
seen before.

As an engineer, Antonio Arias had a serious beef with the traditional forehand. Every book and every teacher advised bringing
the racket straight back to begin the shot, swinging through the
ball, then stopping the racket head in time to point at the spot on

the court where the player wanted the ball to land. "He figured that to stop the racket and point it somewhere on the court meant you'd be slowing it down while you were still swinging at the ball and long before you actually finished the shot," Jimmy Arias explained. Engineering-wise, Antonio Arias thought that was pretty dumb. Don't slow down the racket, he insisted. Bring it back far and rip it through the ball, finishing the stroke somewhere around your ear. Or, as he'd tell his son, "let it fly."

While everyone else in the world was trying to stroke a tennis ball with elegance, like Rod Laver, Jimmy and Antonio Arias had figured out a way to crush it. While everyone else was trying to perfect the classic techniques that Brian Gottfried had worked on with Bollettieri in Ohio in 1961—closed stance, stand sideways to the ball, Continental grip, racket head above the wrist through the swing, keep the feet on the ground and maintain balance through that controlled follow-through—Antonio and Jimmy Arias figured out how a little twerp from the snow bowl could hit the ball just as hard as a sixteen-year-old Florida hotshot who played all afternoon.

As soon as Bollettieri laid eyes on the method Antonio Arias had come up with, he knew that every aspect of what had been the most basic stroke in tennis was about to change. It started with the feet. Arias never positioned both feet or his body sideways to the ball. Instead, he placed his back foot on a roughly 45-degree angle and he barely rotated his hips, keeping them open to the ball instead. The toes of his front foot were basically facing the net. He rotated his shoulders so they were perpendicular to the net. But by leaving his front foot facing forward, his hips remained open so that the middle of his body was practically facing the ball as it came at him. He held the racket differently, too, placing the top of his palm far lower around the bottom of the grip. In the language of tennis, this is what was called a "heavy Western" grip. The conventional grip, called "Continental," positions the top of the palm about midway around the bottom of the racket handle. Arias also whipped his racket through the stroke all wrong. He dipped the racket head below his wrist then zipped up and through the ball like a slingshot. As for staying level and pointing, that didn't happen, either. His follow-through headed straight toward his left ear. Oh, and he also jumped when he swung, somehow forgetting the basic instruction that every junior in the 1970s heard over and over: do not, under any circumstances, let your feet leave the ground when you swing.

To anyone studying the stroke, it was a tough thing to make sense of. The hips and shoulders were completely out of whack. The racket sagged like a dying flower, then everything whipped together in a violent, jumping whirl. It was a real mess. Until, of course, you caught sight of the ball coming off the strings as if shot from a cannon, a combination of power and spin that sent the ball screaming over the net, rising as though it was going to clear the back fence, then darting down into the back of the court just inside the baseline. And when the ball hit the ground, the violent topspin sent it jumping eye-high in an instant.

"I took one look at that stroke and said, 'That's the new Bollettieri forehand,'" Bollettieri said. "From then on, everyone was going to learn it."

Bollettieri was probably more open to a new approach to the most basic stroke than most coaches. He hadn't come to the game with an allegiance to any kind of orthodoxy. He had barely played as a kid. He knew what he knew because he trusted his eyes, could figure out exactly what would make a kid work his hardest, and kept the message for each of his players very simple. *Hit the shit out of the ball. Just hit the shit out of the goddamn ball.* Being good at tennis meant getting rid of any obstacle that prevented you from attaining that goal, whether it was your feet or your balance or having a fragile mind that made you afraid that your next shot was bound to hit the middle of the net or sail into the back fence. In Arias he saw a kid with a stroke that seemed to solve every one of those issues. Instead of controlling the power of the body in an effort to maintain control of the ball, the Arias forehand was the most efficient transfer of the body's power into the ball, and by adjusting his grip and dipping the racket head and shifting the trajectory of the follow-through, Arias could attain a topspin so furious it pulled down a ball that had been hit with every ounce of power that a sixty-five-inch punk could muster.

Antonio Arias tweaked his son's game in one other unique way. He noticed the distance separating tennis players generally remained constant throughout a point. If one moved up, the other moved back, as if their chests were glued to opposite ends of a metal pole. So he told Jimmy to try to keep inching forward during a point—not with the goal of eventually moving into the net for a volley, but so he could pound his forehand from inside the court, achieve more deadly angles, and push his opponent back in the process. In the era of Borg and Guillermo Vilas, when the ideal maneuver seemed to be to plant yourself six feet behind the baseline and hit moon balls back and forth, the concept was revolutionary. After Andre Agassi burst onto the scene a decade later, pressing forward became the dominant strategy.

By the end of the week, Arias had become a minor celebrity at the Colony. He'd befriended the children of Louis Marx, the toy magnate, who Bollettieri first got to know at the Dorado. Marx told Arias whenever he came to the Colony he could sign the Marx account number for whatever food and sodas he wanted. He'd also received an invitation from Bollettieri to the fledgling academy free of charge. Bollettieri would find a place for him to live.

To Jimmy, the Bollettieri plan sure beat Spain. Four hours of school, seven hours of tennis, free food and soda, plus the beach, and he didn't have to travel three thousand miles alone to a country where he didn't speak the language. He returned to Buffalo and told his father he'd found the perfect alternative to Spain. Antonio Arias listened to the plan and then told his son he was going to Spain. Jimmy said no, he was going to Florida. Antonio told him if he was going anywhere he was going to Spain, and if he refused, he wasn't going to be allowed to play tennis anymore. Jimmy said, "Fine, then I won't play tennis anymore."

And so, January 1978 became the only period since Jimmy Arias first began playing tennis at five years old that he didn't play at all. Father and son had reached a stalemate, and neither one had any intention of backing down. In February, Antonio Arias relented, and Jimmy headed to Florida.

When Jimmy arrived, Bollettieri sent him onto court three for a little workout, just to make sure what he had seen over Christmas hadn't been a fluke. On the other side of the net stood Chip Hooper, a twenty-year-old banger who played at the University of Arkansas. He would later reach the top twenty on the pro tour. Hooper was an intimidating physical presence with a booming serve. He was six feet five inches tall, an African-American from Washington, D.C., and athletic enough to have played college football or basketball had he wanted to. Sensing what Bollettieri was up to, Hooper sent the first ball across the net with a little extra juice on it. Arias creamed it. The ball bounced deep in Hooper's court and took off. Hooper sent it back and Arias creamed another one. Jimmy Arias was no fluke.

He moved in with the DePalmers, whose children had signed on with Bollettieri in the first months of the academy, then quickly fell into the hypercompetitive mix, a setting where drilling took a backseat to matches. "It was all we did and all we talked about," Arias says. Three weeks after his move, Arias tagged along with the rest of the crew to a small tournament at a local college in Manatee. He drew Mike DePalmer in the first round. He'd played DePalmer at the academy a few times but hadn't beaten him yet. They split the first twelve games and the set went to a nine-point tiebreaker. Arias won it 5–4. On the changeover, DePalmer punched him in the stomach. Arias doubled over, then took the next set against a frazzled DePalmer, who fell apart after slugging the kid three years younger than he was. When Arias got back to the academy, he told Bollettieri living with the DePalmers wasn't going to work. Bollettieri moved him into his house. At times as many as eight students were living there, including Carling Bassett, the Canadian beauty and future pro who was the daughter of a media magnate. For Arias, this was definitely better than Buffalo or flying solo in Spain.

In the late summer of 1978, Bollettieri, Arias, and their cohorts headed to Kalamazoo for the Junior Nationals. They went to win but also to recruit. Between matches they told every top junior they could find what they were building on the west coast of Florida. By the time the school year started, another dozen kids, including future pros Paul Annacone and Eric Korita, had signed on for the academy. Bollettieri found them beds to sleep in. His dining room became a mess hall.

Breakfast was cinnamon toast around the Bollettieri kitchen table. Lunch was peanut butter and jelly sandwiches, or something like it. Dinner was whatever cheap mass feast Bollettieri and his pros could rustle up and serve at one of their homes. School wasn't optional, but at Bradenton Preparatory Academy, where the kids attended, if a paper got handed in two months late, no one was going to yell about it.

A story in *Sports Illustrated* brought more kids. A feature on *20/20* showed Bollettieri screaming at a kid who wasn't doing as he was told. More parents called to see if there was room for their kids. By 1981 the kids were spilling out of the homes of the assistant pros and host families. The model was taking hold. Bollettieri realized his academy had outgrown its facilities. He bought a motel and a twenty-one-court complex in Bradenton, a few miles inland from Longboat Key. He hired a former Army Special Forces officer named Bill Baxter—the kids called him "Colonel Bill"—to keep the troops in line. To instill discipline, Colonel Bill would line up the kids and march them around the parking lot and across Manatee Avenue, one of the main drags in Bradenton. Two years later, Bollettieri raised $1 million and bought another forty acres at the site.

In 1983, a little more than five years after his first rally with Mike DePalmer, Arias won the Italian Open. In September of that year he reached the semifinals of the US Open. Just nineteen years old, he finished 1983 as the world's sixth-ranked player. He stood five feet nine inches tall, weighed about 155 pounds, had an average backhand, didn't have much of a serve, and he wasn't much of a net player. But that forehand . . .

Arias wasn't the only Bollettieri project to break out in 1983. That same year, eighteen-year-old Kathleen Horvath was the only woman to beat Martina Navratilova. She reached the quarterfinals of the French Open. Carling Bassett, all of sixteen, made the quarterfinals of the Australian Open and was named the WTA Tour's Most Impressive Newcomer. Bollettieri and his academy had already become known entities—and somewhat controversial ones in junior tennis circles—but the breakout success of these three players, all in the same year, turned Bollettieri and his methods into the hottest story in the sport. Cameras panned to him during his players' matches. His academy was officially the country's top destination for the children of the ever-growing brethren of tennis parents. They all wanted the forehand. But what they really wanted was access to what their eyes and every announcer on television was telling them was the greatest collection of young tennis talent. This was the place—the only place—to learn how to become a pro. The professionalization of training and the athletic development industry as we now know it was off and running.

*Today the Arias forehand has a different name: it's called a fore*hand. Everyone hits a version of it. Continental grips are dead. Open stances rule.

The great irony of all this is that if you ask any of Bollettieri's elite players what they gained from him, no one ever mentions a technical point or a particular piece of strategic advice. There is a reason Bollettieri was able to lead Jim Courier, Andre Agassi, and Monica Seles to the top of the world rankings even though they had almost nothing in common as players. Courier was a relentless defender who pounded balls from deep in the court. Agassi was an immense physical talent with magical hands who was the first in a new generation of players who figured out how to attack from the baseline. Seles played with a bizarre display of strokes. Her two-handed forehand and backhand and swinging volleys found tighter and sharper angles than anyone had tried before. She redefined the boundaries of the tennis court. Bollettieri successfully coached all of them by basically making sure they hit their forehands with abandon and leaving their technique alone. Linda Courier, Jim's mother, once asked him to change the way her son held the racket like a baseball bat. "I said the hell with it, just let him hit the shit out of the ball," he said.

Bollettieri and his academy delivered three utterly nontechnical benefits that every graduate raved about and would become the essential components of athletic development in the new, moneyed age of sports.

First, the alums talk about Bollettieri's unmatched skills as a motivator. As Brian Gottfried said, "You did not want to disappoint him." Monica Seles—who spent two and a half years at the academy, beginning when she was twelve, and later replaced Steffi Graf as the top woman in the world—said the energy level of any session picked up as soon as Bollettieri stepped onto the court, usually shirtless, a lather of sunscreen the only thing protecting his weathered skin from the Florida sun. "He was always the first guy working out in the gym in the morning," Seles says. "You had this sense that as hard as you were working, he was working even harder. So we all knew that if you wanted to be a top professional, this is what you had to do." Bollettieri also had a gift for figuring out very quickly what to say to each kid to make them want to work as hard as they possibly could.

"All day he would tell me how amazing I was," Arias said. "That was great for me, because all my dad ever told me was how much I sucked."

Second, and perhaps more important, Bollettieri alums talk about the intense atmosphere he created at the academy and how their exposure to that pressure every day prepared them for life as a professional. Seles, who grew up in the small city of Novi Sad in the former Yugoslavia, had basically run out of people to practice with in her country. Her city had four courts, none indoors, limiting the time she could practice. She became her country's top junior when she was nine. But while that made her a celebrity, it also made her an oddball. She couldn't go to birthday parties because she was always traveling to another tennis tournament. The kids in her school made fun of her hands, which were covered with calluses. "Then I get to Florida and suddenly I'm with all these kids who were just like me, working day in and day out for the sole purpose of winning a Grand Slam," she says.

Seles was the top female player at the academy. At thirteen she was the top junior player in the world. But she could look over on the neighboring courts and see Andre Agassi, Jim Courier, and David Wheaton, Bollettieri's golden generation of students, and get whatever motivation she needed.

"You're in that sun in Florida," Seles said. "It's 90 degrees every day. You think there's no way you're going to make it to Sunday, when you finally get the day off. But you've got to push through, so it's good to be in that kind of environment and see the others working at it."

The effect was something akin to the slipstream in a cycling race. The first lesson every cyclist learns is that the pack moves faster than any individual cyclist can ride, at least over the long haul. It's a matter of aerodynamics and the physical ability of a larger body—like one hundred cyclists riding within inches of one another—to break down the wind resistance in a way that no single rider can. Likewise, make one kid play in 95-degree heat and humidity for seven hours and you will likely produce a completely burned-out tennis player by the time he turns thirteen. But put fifty of them on a dozen courts and they will battle all day to be the one who works harder than anyone else.

Finally, and most important for both Bollettieri and his players, he offered the best players an opportunity to hit with and play against their peers every day. As Jim Courier once put it, he supplied the balls and the courts and the kids went out and beat the crap out of each other. It didn't mean a player couldn't still get good playing with a coach on a backyard court. But put all that talent together and a tennis complex becomes a battleground where rising stars learn how to try to kill each other. They screamed. They cheated. They came off the courts with broken rackets and the occasional bloody nose. Bollettieri did little to stop it. They were becoming warriors.

The Bollettieri model, like the Arias forehand, is so ingrained across all sports today, we barely notice that it's how we live. Kids with speed and coordination, a good swing, a nice forehand, or an ability to dribble a soccer ball deftly first get spotted sometime around kindergarten, when their parents sign them up for recreational sports. Within a year or two—three or four at most—they are encouraged to join a travel team, which competes at a higher level than a recreational team. If they are pursuing an individual sport such as golf or tennis, a coach will likely tell them to pursue that endeavor to the exclusion of everything else and spend anywhere from two to five hours a day honing their skills. Weekends will be spent at games or regional tournaments, many of them more than an hour away from home. The parents of the most gifted athletes then face a decision in their children's early teenage years: to keep the child at home in a traditional school environment and squeeze in athletics in the afternoons, or to create a homeschooling curriculum that will allow for more time to practice and a more flexible schedule. Alternatively, they could send the child away to an academy that provides expert coaching and a bare minimum of academic balance.

Plenty of families turn their lives upside down in pursuit of athletic greatness. Consider the story of Bowie and Julie Martin, who spent four years shuttling their boys, Zach and Josh, to a series of practices, lessons, and games in a half dozen sports before sitting them down and suggesting that it was time for them to focus on golf, the sport in which they showed the most promise. Zach and Josh were six and eight years old at the time. Two years later the family moved from their longtime home near Raleigh, North Carolina, to a town house in Pinehurst, North Carolina, a golf mecca with proximity to dozens of courses and the best coaching available.

"I just wanted them to be great at something," said Bowie, who was a decent junior table tennis player as a kid. He also played soccer and tennis in high school. But Bowie Martin always wondered how successful he might have been had he pursued one sport to the exclusion of all others, and his children became his way of figuring that out. By 2012 he had something of an answer: Josh Martin had become the country's second-ranked golfer in his age group. Two years later he was the North Carolina Amateur champion.

As he entered his eighties, Bollettieri's impact on elite professional tennis began to wane after working with an unmatched string of players who reached the world's top ranking. They include Jim Courier, Andre Agassi, Marcelo Rios, Boris Becker, Monica Seles, Serena and Venus Williams, Maria Sharapova, and Jelena Jankovic. Bollettieri has long been criticized for training players as though they were in a factory, encouraging them to hit the same big forehand and serve hard, and in the process homogenizing a sport in which the all-time greats are supposed to be artists. Tennis was never art to Bollettieri. It was hand-to-hand combat, where toughness matters as much as serves and volleys and is practiced and honed as specifically as a backhand down the line.

He remained one of the game's biggest names. He still spent eight to ten hours a day coaching at his eponymous tennis school in Bradenton, Florida, on the campus of the IMG Academies. In 1987, IMG bought Bollettieri's tennis academy in a move that was as intelligent as it was inevitable. Bollettieri had access to a treasure trove of young athletic talent. IMG was the leading athlete representation business. Buying Bollettieri's academy would give IMG special access to the next generation of tennis superstars. But IMG also realized the academy model didn't have to be limited to tennis. Today the academy is home to more than five hundred athletes who train in tennis, golf, baseball, soccer, basketball, football, and other sports. The US Soccer Federation houses its junior national teams there. Peter Uihlein, the son of the chief executive of the golf company Acushnet and one of the country's rising golf stars, begged his parents to let him move there when he was thirteen. Seven years later he was the US Amateur champion. It is the first place aspiring athletes and their parents consider training when they hit those formative years and are looking for the edge that will make them that much better than the kids in their region who are juggling school and long rides to lessons and games and everything else that goes along with adolescence.

They are often subjected to ridicule, because an odd double standard remains in the US. The world's most promising young violinists or ballerinas invariably end up in special schools from an early age, many of them far from home, where they spend hours each day in studios and rehearsal rooms learning with and from other like-minded souls. Complaints about this sort of thing are rare. But substitute the words "basketball player" or "tennis star" for "pianist" and "violinist" and suddenly the conversation turns to misguided priorities and robbing children of their childhoods. Such complaints amount to trying to fight back the tide: the Bollettieri approach has overtaken youth sports in the US over the past forty years. The elite are grouped together earlier and earlier. Regardless of the sport, the basic concept is the same. What is most convenient probably isn't good enough. If you want to be exceptional, you need to be with others who are exceptional, or else you will fall behind. It is at once a very simple and very sophisticated pyramid. School sports still exist, of course, but except for football their importance to an elite teenage athlete has drifted so far down the totem pole that the best kids don't even bother playing for their schools anymore.

On the tennis courts in Bradenton, Bollettieri bounced on a blazing afternoon in 2012 from court to court topless in the triple-digit heat. His skin was leathery brown. His paunch hung over his shorts. But his relentless and infectious enthusiasm endured, and the United States Tennis Association now has its own player development program headquartered in Florida. Bollettieri has served as an advisor to the organization.

Brian Gottfried, the first great player Bollettieri trained—the guinea pig for the idea that an elite kid could only thrive if he played with other elite kids all the time—said it was inevitable that Bollettieri's academy would become a massive business with declining results. Gottfried has coached at the academy on and off since his playing career ended. He says Bollettieri and IMG needed to scale the product by bringing in hundreds of kids who weren't as great as the greatest ones so their tuitions could support the scholarships given to the best of the best. While it may be a thriving business that can produce some excellent tennis players, he doesn't see it as an atmosphere that will regularly produce the sort of greatness that can't really be taught. Most parents think it can be, if only their children could play at the right club or be on the right team, or if they could cover the $60,000 annual tuition at the IMG Academy. Gottfried disagrees.

"You can collect a hundred kids and teach them how to paint pretty well, but chances are none of them is going to turn out to be the next Leonardo da Vinci," Gottfried says. "My guess is the next da Vinci is off in the woods somewhere daydreaming about painting."

Perhaps. But probably not. There are few accidental successes in sports anymore. No country and sport is more dedicated to an academy system for developing its best athletes than Germany is with soccer. The Germans centralized the training curriculum for the hundreds of youth soccer clubs across the vast country in 2004. The best kids followed the same regimens and began playing together in their early teens. A decade later, Germany won the World Cup for the first time since 1990.

If Gottfried is right, we probably won't ever know. The parents of that would-be da Vinci will very likely be enrolling their son or daughter in an arts academy before too long, and those parents and that child won't spend much time worrying about whether their decisions are sound. Setting aside all those top-ranked players,

Nick Bollettieri's most significant accomplishment may be making it acceptable for an athlete's training to become all-encompassing, to be pursued professionally to the exclusion of nearly everything else—even if the athletes were preparing for a competition in which professionals weren't supposed to be allowed to participate.

7

Streak: Edwin Moses and the Birth of the Olympic Empire

I n the spring of 1973, at the beginning of his final season of high school track, Edwin Moses arrived at a local meet known as the Greater Dayton Classic filled with teenage optimism. Moses was anything but a star back then. He had three problems: he wasn't very fast, or at least he hadn't been for most of his childhood. He was five eleven, weighed 140 pounds, and didn't have much power—a triple threat of sorts. Yet as the first meet of the spring season approached, Moses was starting to feel like he could run faster—eventually. He knew whatever dreams he had of a college track career—perhaps even a scholarship from a small school that valued his brain as well as his feet—rested on his performances early in this spring season, before the colleges made their final decisions on admission.

During his junior year he won the triple jump at an Ohio state competition. He'd trained through the fall and winter and won the quarter-miler's spot on his high school's ladder relay team. The race required the first two runners to run 220 yards, the next to run 440 yards, and the last to run 880. Individually, he was focused on the 120-yard high hurdles.

At the Greater Dayton Classic, the 120 hurdles came first, and the day started as well as he could have hoped. Moses burned it and took first place. As he lined up to run the quarter-mile leg in the ladder relay, he felt, if not fast, then faster. He grabbed the baton and took off, feeling like he could do this. As he turned onto the backstretch he felt a sharp, stabbing pain deep in his hamstring where the muscle met the bone. As soon as he felt it, he knew his high school running career was over. He also knew that no college was going to be interested in him now. His dream of having even a mildly successful career as a runner after high school had all but evaporated. By the time he graduated three months later, he was little more than a marginal athlete. The best kids in Dayton were running quarter miles in just over 47 seconds on slow dirt tracks. His best time was a 51.3. In the 120-yard high hurdles, the best kids turned in times between 13.8 seconds and 14.3. Moses's best scholastic time was 15.1.

The apparent end of Moses's running career was of little concern to his parents. For them, the body part that took priority didn't have a pair of running spikes attached to it. Moses's father, who had been a Tuskegee Airman, ran his family like a unit of the military. He had a master's degree in elementary education and was a school principal. Moses's mother had a bachelor's degree in education and worked as a reading specialist and curriculum advisor in the local school system. She had planned to get a PhD but got sidetracked raising three children. Chores, respect, and work were all that mattered in the household. Bs were not looked at very highly. Cs were unacceptable. As soon as the grades slipped, athletics got taken away. No football, no basketball, no track. Nothing. The brain needed to be as finely tuned as the body.

That discipline would pay dividends for Edwin Moses both on the track and off when his body blossomed like no one could have predicted. Over a period of thirty months he became very fast, at which point he realized he wasn't going to be satisfied simply being a great Olympian; he needed to change the definition of what it meant to be an Olympian as well—and along the way teach the Olympic movement how a modern sports empire was supposed to operate.

When people talk about the growth of the Olympic movement, bureaucrats and television executives are usually lavished with the most extravagant praise. Baron Pierre de Coubertin, the French idealist who dreamed up the concept of the modern Games, deserves plenty of credit. ABC's Roone Arledge created the model for the Olympic television extravaganza. Juan Antonio Samaranch, the Spanish president of the International Olympic Committee from 1980 to 2001, pulled the Olympics from the verge of collapse and the grips of Cold War political turmoil.

Lost in the story are the long-exploited athletes, including one especially good hurdler, who got sick of watching other people get rich from their labors while their ascetic lifestyles were turned into a symbol of purity. Scraping together the necessary pennies by holding down two jobs and maintaining an exhausting training schedule whose payoff comes once every four years may make for a good television profile during an Olympic telecast, but it's a miserable way to live. And in an era when nearly every aspect of sport had become professionalized, the concept of amateurism at the highest levels of competition was downright anachronistic, although the athletes had to teach everyone exactly why that was so.

For Edwin Moses, the Olympics were never about purity or

amateurism. The Olympics were about the best competing against the best. The sooner everyone accepted that, the better off the Olympic movement was going to be, even if the figureheads leading the Olympics had to be dragged kicking and screaming into modernity by someone who could run the 400-meter hurdles like no one had ever run them before. Moses won a gold medal in Montreal in 1976, lost a race in 1977, and then didn't lose again in his next 122 races over the next ten years. By the time his absurd streak was over, he'd improbably led Olympic athletes down the same path to liberation, both financial and otherwise, that Arnold Palmer and Stan Smith and Catfish Hunter had followed.

As a child, Moses was always fascinated with science. He collected fossils, plants, and anything else that might broaden his knowledge of the natural world. He went to summer school from the end of sixth grade on, taking special classes in biology, chemistry, and math. He took a computer science class at Wright-Patterson Air Force Base, where the military had one of the few mainframes available for public use. Those classes allowed him to carry a high school schedule filled with what are now referred to as advanced placement classes. When the summer classes ended, his mother would pick him up and take him to volunteer with the local Head Start program she helped run, or he'd work with his father, who ran the summer school.

It wasn't a particularly carefree childhood but the work paid off. While no one bothered to consider Moses for an athletic scholarship, Morehouse College in Atlanta, one of the leading historically black institutions, offered a full academic scholarship for him to study chemistry in a five-year undergraduate and graduate program with Georgia Tech. Morehouse, the college of Martin Luther King Jr. and dozens of other African-American leaders in government, entertainment, and business, didn't have much of a track program in 1974. The team had an annual budget of about $4,000. That had to cover all coaching salaries, equipment, and travel. The team practiced at a nearby high school. After his less-than-stellar high school athletic career, Moses was fine with that. Track would be his hobby, along with another interest of his: photography. Studying chemistry would be his job.

That was the plan, anyway. Then fate—and speed—intervened. While rehabilitating his pulled hamstring during his senior year, Moses began trying to hurdle leading with his left leg. A person who is right-handed often wants to lead with his right leg, but Moses's tight right hamstring made it impossible for him to clear a hurdle leading with his right leg. It sounds counterintuitive but, when hurdling, the body sometimes naturally wants the dominant leg to rise off the ground first and use its momentum to clear the obstacle. That's how Moses had hurdled ever since he first entered a 480-yard shuttle relay event as a sophomore in high school.* With a tender hamstring, however, the act of exploding his right foot forward while he was airborne would have put too much strain on the injured muscle.

Moses had always been a righty. His right leg was significantly stronger than his left. Once he got over the awkwardness of leading with his left leg, he realized how much more powerful his hurdling became and how much easier it was to clear a three-foot hurdle because he was pushing off his stronger leg. In retrospect, he was lucky to get injured young, before his hurdling technique had

---

* The shuttle hurdle relay is an incredibly cool race that is rarely run anymore. Four runners each do the 120-yard high-hurdle sprint. First one runner darts down the straightaway, then his teammate takes the baton and sprints back the other way. Two more runners repeat that. It looks like a minute of pure chaos.

become ingrained, because it was easier to switch legs. By the time he got to Morehouse, he was a better hurdler than he had been six months earlier.

At Morehouse, life didn't exactly follow Moses's plans. First he had a series of disagreements with the head of the chemistry department. The teacher didn't like the methodology he was using to get his answers and punished him with poor grades—at least, poor by Moses's standards. Work that he believed deserved As came back with Bs and Cs on it. That infuriated his father, who prohibited him from competing on the track team. Moses became a physics major and, despite his father's prohibitions, continued to train with the Morehouse track team every day. It wasn't a fancy outfit, but the team was turning out to be better than he had expected. One teammate was even an Alabama state scholastic champion who had run a quarter mile in 46.1 seconds in high school. That's moving.

Moses got faster, and bigger, too. After graduating high school at five foot eleven, he went through a late growth spurt and was well on his way to reaching six feet two inches as a sophomore in college. The height and the daily training with the other Morehouse runners—cross-country in the fall, indoor in the winter, outdoor in the spring—were paying dividends. Moses worked with a friend named Steve Price, who had specialized in hurdles for several years. Price labored to clean up Moses's technique.

Like Moses, Price was a science buff and an enginner, and he approached the hurdles scientifically, taking the motion apart to understand how to clear the obstacle with the least amount of interruption to the runner's horizontal momentum down the track. Price looked at Moses and immediately saw his knee was too high, bringing him too far off the ground. Price showed Moses how to lean into the jump and stay low; how to come out of the starting blocks to arrive at the first hurdle in the perfect position to make the jump; and how to keep his lead arm from swinging out of position. It worked. His 110-meter high-hurdle time dropped from 15.1 to 14.2.

Broken down to its core, clearing a hurdle requires nothing more than an exaggerated step. But a high hurdle is forty-two inches off the ground, and only seven-footers like Shaquille O'Neal have a step like that. So a hurdler has to generate horizontal momentum and have as little lift as possible. The idea is to limit the vertical rise and clear the hurdle by less than three inches, but it's scary running full speed and seeing an obstacle that high. Hurdling is about managing the fear of hitting the hurdle and transferring the horizontal force through the air. Every hurdler knows the price of failure. "You hit that hurdle and you hear the noise and know it's going to hurt before you hit the ground," Moses said.

Moses didn't just improve as a hurdler. His quarter-mile time dropped from 51.3 at the beginning of his freshman year to 49.2 at the end of it. In the fall of his sophomore year he dropped into the 48s. Then he ran a 47.5 to win the conference championships the following spring. He had started the year at the back of the pack and chased down the competition. This was the essence of what had drawn his scientific mind to the sport in the first place. Everything was measurable. To Moses, track was becoming an extension of science.

When his sophomore year ended, Moses traveled to Coatesville, Pennsylvania, where he had an engineering internship with Lukens Steel Company. He lived in Philadelphia that summer. Each evening after work he trekked to the University of Pennsylvania to train at Franklin Field, home of the Penn Relays and the East Coast hub for track. There, Moses ran, but he also studied the top hurdlers, observing the positions of each of their body parts as they bounded over the hurdles, and stealing technical hints from them.

By the start of his junior year, he felt certain he could run 13.6 in the 110-meter high hurdles, and that a quarter mile under

46 seconds was within his grasp with the right rabbit setting the pace. And yet he still hadn't experienced the epiphany of combining the two events. In late March, after seven more months of daily training, Moses and his Morehouse teammates traveled to the 1976 Florida Relays, the first major meet of the outdoor season. Moses registered to run the 110-meter high hurdles and the "400 flat," as the runners called the quarter mile, and, on something of a whim, he entered the 400 intermediate hurdles, a race he'd barely run. In each race he turned in times good enough to qualify for the Olympic trials coming up in June. He ran a 13.6 in the high hurdles and a 46.1 in the 400 flat. But his 50.1 in the 400 hurdles, a mere 1.5 seconds off the US record, made everyone at the meet take a second look at their race programs and try to figure out the name of the guy with the big Afro and the big glasses who walked over the hurdles like they were small orange traffic cones. Moses's previous best time in the 400 hurdles had been a 53.1.

After the meet, Moses did a little research on the competition he would face to make the Olympic team. Mike Shine of Penn State had decent times, but he took fifteen steps between the hurdles. Most runners took fourteen. Moses was on his way to mastering a thirteen-step technique. Shine was beatable. Jim Bolding out of Oklahoma State had set a US record in the event, but he'd underperformed at the US trials in 1972 and failed to make the team. It wasn't clear that he had the mettle for the pressure cooker of the trials. Quentin Wheeler at San Diego State figured to be the most formidable competition. He would win the NCAA championship and set the American record that year, but Moses was within shouting distance of Wheeler in a race he'd barely run.

Before making a decision on which race to focus on, Moses decided to see if his 400 intermediate hurdles time was a fluke. In his next race Moses dropped his time to 49.8. Then he ran a 49.2.

In early May he ran a 48.8. With just two and a half months to go before the Olympics, he was three-tenths of a second off the US record. The 400 hurdles was his ticket to the Games.

What was going on? How was the kid who couldn't even get a college scholarship banging on the door of the Olympic Games? In short, Moses's body had caught up to his mind and his dedication. Now it was coming together at the perfect moment. All those hours sitting at the track and watching the hurdlers at Franklin Field had meshed with a body that was a lean six foot two, 165 pounds, and had trained twelve months a year at distances ranging from 60-meter sprints to 10-mile cross-country runs. Moses could stretch like a rubber band, too. What might have looked like an overnight sensation was really the result of ten years of training and learning and running.

Moses went to the Olympic trials in Oregon in June and won the final in 48.30 to break the US record. He beat Wheeler and Shine with little difficulty. Wheeler finished nearly four-tenths of a second behind. Shine ran more than a second back.

Next came the Olympic Games in Montreal. Moses arrived as the favorite, then broke the world record, finishing in 47.64, more than a second, or about ten meters, ahead of Shine. Yevgeni Gavrilenko of the Soviet Union won the bronze. Wheeler finished fourth.

Moses isn't sure how many 400-meter hurdle races he'd completed when the gold medal was draped around his neck. Including all the heats, probably more than six, but probably not more than ten or twelve. Yet on the track in Montreal, Moses was arguably better than the competition at his event than any of the other athletes were at theirs. And that's when the fun started for Moses. Since he had a gold medal to flaunt, promoters all over Europe wanted the man with the Afro and the goggle-sized glasses. Moses still had a year of college to complete, but there was money to be made. He'd have to get it under the table, of course, because NCAA rules and the laws of amateurism prohibited him from taking a single dollar for showing up at a track.

The rules never did make much sense to Moses, especially in 1976, when athletes in nearly every other sport suddenly seemed to be able to cash in on greatness, and the power in sports seemed to be shifting to the athletes and away from the bureaucrats. Moses believed he deserved his piece, too, as did every Olympian. The promoters were all making money off the events, and they were the same guys who were running the International Association of Athletics Federations, world track's governing body. They were supposed to enforce the rules against professionalism. If they were willing to break the rules and pay the runners under the table, why shouldn't he accept it as long as he followed the unspoken guidelines? *Don't sign anything. Don't put anything in writing. Don't talk about the money, and don't put it in your own bank account.* Sure it was an idiotic system, but it was the system the all-powerful International Olympic Committee had forced everyone to live with ever since Baron Pierre de Coubertin had dreamed up the modern Olympics at the end of the nineteenth century.

It's worth noting that participants in the ancient Greek Olympics weren't amateurs. They received financial support while they trained and reaped the rewards that went with glory when they returned home from the Games. The concept of amateurism developed in the nineteenth century to prevent "the working classes from competing against the aristocracy," according to David Wallechinsky, one of the foremost Olympic historians. Wealthy people could remain amateurs because they didn't need to take time off from work to play. The working class had to get paid to live, even if it was for playing sports. Barring professionals from competitions such as the Olympics saved the idle rich from mixing with (and probably losing to) the unwashed. De Coubertin had a solution to get the good athletes involved, however: wealthy people would come forward to support working-class athletes just as they did starving artists. It's hard to fault De Coubertin's idealism, to which the Olympic movement owes its existence. Unfortunately, eighty years later, idealism wasn't covering the living expenses of aspiring Olympians.

The laws of amateurism actually started causing controversies and scandals almost as soon as they were enacted. Jim Thorpe lost his 1912 Olympic medals in the decathlon and the pentathlon after it was discovered he had earned $2 per game to play semiprofessional baseball in 1909 and 1910. In the 1920s, the British complained that the US was creating a generation of professionals by awarding college athletic scholarships, and in the 1930s the participation of gym teachers and trainers came under scrutiny, since their livelihoods were closely tied to athletics. Dick Pound, the Canadian swimmer and longtime member of the IOC, said he didn't take summer lifeguarding jobs because he was scared it might cost him his amateur status.

In 1952, the American industrialist Avery Brundage was elected president of the IOC. During what would become a half-century career as a sports administrator, Brundage showed a special knack for landing on the very wrong side of history. In the early 1930s he spoke admiringly of Hitler, complimenting the Führer's work at uniting and raising the spirit of the German people. As the leader of the United States Olympic Committee in 1936, he saw to it that certain Jews did not compete in Berlin so as not to embarrass Hitler if they won. He was an outspoken member of the isolationist group America First, which opposed intervention in World War II.

During his two-decade reign atop the IOC, Brundage ordered American sprinters Tommie Smith and John Carlos banished from the 1968 Olympics after they raised gloved fists and bowed their heads on the medal podium during the national anthem as a protest against human rights violations. The gesture was misinterpreted as a Black Power salute. When the USOC refused to ban them, Brundage threatened to dismiss the entire US track team.

Brundage saved his greatest ire for the enemies of amateurism—that is, anyone who would suggest that an Olympic athlete had the right to earn a living playing sports. He divided the sports world simply: there were people who played sports for sports' sake and people who participated for financial reasons. "Olympic glory is for amateurs," he declared. The International Ski Federation (FIS) became Brundage's biggest enemy, since it was clear that all the top skiers in the world had deals with equipment makers. Austrian Karl Schranz, perhaps the best alpine skier of the 1960s, founded his own company, Kneissl. Their so-called super skis helped him win the overall world titles in 1969 and 1970. Brundage viewed this as an attack on the foundation of the Olympics and everything the rings stood for. Three days before the Sapporo Olympics in 1972, Brundage convinced the IOC to ban Schranz for violating its code on amateurism. If Brundage had had his way, he would have eliminated alpine skiing from the Games, and he actually floated the idea of canceling the Winter Games entirely because of the growing commercialism.

When Brundage finally stepped down as IOC president in 1972, a former journalist and Irish baron named Michael Morris and known as the third Baron Killanin replaced him. Killanin, who wasn't nearly as exercised about the cause of amateurism as Brundage, created a working group to study the potential effects of money and professionalism in the Olympics. The task force performed like a task force: it studied the issue and discussed it but did little to change anything. The Soviets were the biggest obstacle to change, and with good reason: all their athletes were soldiers and guards in the army who did little soldiering or guarding and a lot of training, which was the real job they were getting paid to perform. The arrangement gave the Eastern Bloc countries a terrific competitive advantage, one they really didn't want to give up. The

Soviets had won the races for most gold and overall medals in the Summer Games in 1956, 1960, 1972, and 1976, and in the Winter Games from 1956 to 1964 and in 1972 and 1976.

"They could literally look you in the eye and with a straight face tell you their athletes were not professional," Dick Pound, who eventually became an IOC vice president, said of the Soviets. "It was a special talent." The leader of the Soviet bloc was the Russian Konstantin Andrianov, who first got onto the IOC in 1951. Andrianov spoke for the Soviet government. Since the Soviet government controlled the Eastern Bloc, all the representatives from the Eastern Bloc voted as Andrianov and his young sidekick on the IOC, Vitaly Smirnov, wanted them to. Change didn't seem likely anytime soon. The rules Moses ran under in 1976 were largely the same as they had been in 1972. When the European track circuit's under-the-table payments started to flow his way, he didn't turn them down.

When Moses arrived in Europe, Lasse Virén, the Finnish champion in the 5,000- and 10,000-meter races, was the biggest attraction on the track-and-field circuit and perhaps the highest-paid Olympic athlete of the mid-1970s. Virén, who captured the gold medal in his events in the 1972 and 1976 Olympics, could command $2,500 a race. If he ran the 5K and the 10K in a single meet, he could collect $5,000. After the 1976 Olympics, promoters started offering Moses $1,500 plus expenses to show up and run the hurdles, all cash, all under the table, in total violation of the rules of collegiate and Olympic track. That was real money, far too much to turn down for the child of a school principal and a reading specialist who was still supporting himself in college. He could run fifteen times during the summer and fall seasons and take home as much as his father made in a year. Moses says he never thought twice about accepting the money. He was considering medical school.

The track money would pay for it. He was the best in the world at his event. As far as he was concerned, he deserved every penny. Everyone knew the routine. After the meet, the runners would make their way down to the office of the promoter, who, sitting with his banker, would divvy up the cash and pass out a series of envelopes. Sometimes, if a promoter didn't like how a runner had raced, he'd cut the pay and there wasn't anything the runner could do about it.

Back at Morehouse the following spring, the college track team got a chance to cash in, too. The team got an all-expense-paid trip to the Mt. Sac Relays near Los Angeles. The meet wanted Morehouse there for one reason: to have Moses running the hurdles and the 4x400 relay.

At Mt. Sac, Moses met Larry McVeigh, a director of the meet who was also an executive with the defense contractor General Dynamics. McVeigh took a liking to Moses and his friend Steve Price, who had honed Moses's hurdling technique. General Dynamics wanted to hire more minority engineers. With McVeigh's help, Moses landed a job with the company as an associate test engineer after he graduated in 1978. With an Olympic gold medalist on its staff, a company building missiles might seem a little warmer and fuzzier.

The job was real. The Olympic rulebook prohibited a company from paying an employee for anything other than actual work that was performed. Moses could not receive a full-time salary for part-time work or take a salary merely for serving as a spokesman for the company. Also, as a defense contractor that was charging the government for its work, General Dynamics had to account for Moses's time. A no-show job wasn't an option.

Moses didn't mind. His office was ten minutes from the world-class track in Walnut where the Mt. Sac Relays were held. He could head to the track in the morning, do his usual three-hour workout, and get to his office for his 4:00 p.m. to 11:00 p.m. shift that would include work on cruise missile and rocket systems to help the US win the arms race against the Soviet Union. The Cold War was on and General Dynamics had enough work to keep three shifts of engineers busy twenty-four hours a day, every day.

When spring and summer rolled around, Moses would take time off and head to track meets in Europe. The double life felt normal. Plus there was no long-term future in track and field. The money was decent, though not the kind of money he could retire on. The biggest challenge was making sure to get enough rest, especially since so many of the European athletes had cushy postings with their national sports federations, working as coaches and gym teachers.

In August of 1977, Moses lost a race to Harald Schmid of West Germany. Moses was nursing a leg injury at the time. After winning, Schmid declared himself the favorite at the World Championships in Düsseldorf later that year. There, Schmid stayed with Moses for all of ten feet. Then Moses bolted past him and won by ten meters with a time of 47.58, just an eighth of a second off his world record 47.45. "Took care of that," Moses said as he walked off the track. He wouldn't lose again for a decade.

In 1980, he lowered the world record to 47.13. Two years would pass before one of his competitors broke 48 seconds. Moses credits his training methods for his supremacy. A cross-country runner since high school, Moses kept up his long-distance work and combined it with middle-distance training he'd done with his college buddies. He could still run the 800 meters in 1:43.5, about a second off the world record. He trained like a sprinter, too, as though he might one day return to the 110-meter hurdles. He tracked his diet and his regimen like a scientist, thinking every day about how he might lower his time. He flirted with doing multiple events and even ran the occasional leg on the US quarter-mile relay team. But he ultimately decided to stick with his bread and butter, the 400-meter hurdles, when he realized the subtle alterations in training for the other races might jeopardize his streak. Running the 400-meter hurdles requires a long gait and the ability to rise quickly. The quarter-mile requires a much shorter gait and favors runners who can stay close to the ground.

Ever the physicist, Moses figured out how to run the hurdles in the most efficient manner possible. Most hurdlers led with their right legs, which forced them to leap over the middle or the outside half of the hurdle. That placed their running paths on the outside halves of their running lanes. Moses had led with his left leg ever since his injury in high school. That allowed him to leap over the left, or inside, edge of the hurdle. It also placed his running path on the inside edge of his lane. What is the difference between running along the inside or the outside of a running lane on an oval track in a 400-meter race? About four or five meters, depending on how meticulous he could be. Beating Moses when you were running the same distance was hard enough. Spot him four or five meters and the race became a competition for second place.

Moses's dominance became the stuff of legend and gave him a position of authority less dominant runners could never achieve. He didn't shrink from it. Since 1977, Moses had been speaking out against the hypocrisy in international athletics and the unfairness of a system that forced most of the athletes to serve as free labor. He'd gone to the college of Martin Luther King Jr. He knew exploitation when he saw it. Most runners did, but most runners kept their mouths shut. "If you were too outspoken or controversial as an athlete, bad things might happen to you," says Pound, the longtime IOC member. Avery Brundage had shown that.

Moses didn't worry all that much about repercussions. He didn't have to. He had a gold medal and a college degree and a job as an engineer. If speaking out cost him his Olympic eligibility, life would go on. He didn't get much support from other Olympic athletes, even those from his own country. Many of them were afraid to confront an entrenched system and risk their own eligibility. Moses didn't care.

Then, in the summer of 1980, President Jimmy Carter ordered a boycott of the Moscow Olympics to protest the Soviet invasion of Afghanistan. Practically overnight, thousands of athletes from more than sixty countries that honored the boycott, who had toiled for under-the-table cash or nothing at all for years, became pawns in the Cold War. Four years or, in some cases, a lifetime of training went up in smoke. For Moses and the other American track-and-field athletes, the only good thing about the summer was that the British middle-distance runners Sebastian Coe and Steve Ovett staged two duels for the ages in the 800 and the 1,500 in Moscow. They became two of the biggest stars in international sports. Their appearance fees skyrocketed, and that brought Moses's fee up, too, to nearly $20,000 for a meet. Suddenly the money was simply too good to continue working at General Dynamics. Moses took an indefinite leave of absence that summer and never returned.

There was one other side benefit to the 1980 boycott. US Olympic athletes, especially the track-and-field athletes who were expecting to clean up in Moscow, were furious at both their government and the US Olympic Committee for keeping them from their shot at glory. If they were going to stick around for another four years for Los Angeles, they certainly wanted to get paid for their efforts, and the only way to do that was to change the rules on amateurism.

That stance still wasn't very popular. Few were holding the banner of purity anymore, but much of the world believed the amateurism rule leveled the playing field with the mighty Americans. The US had 250 million people, enormous wealth, and a seemingly bottomless pool of talent. The Eastern Bloc and some Western European countries had training schools that employed and supported their athletes with coaching jobs, but the US had college athletic scholarships. The higher minds running most of the sports federations didn't want the system to change. Other than the ski federation, most of them had largely free labor at their disposal. The last thing they wanted to do was start paying the participants any more than they put into those envelopes at the end of a competition.

Fortunately for Moses, the newly elected president of the IOC, Juan Antonio Samaranch, had a problem that went far beyond athletes who didn't have enough money to pay their rent or cover the costs of their training, although his problem was directly related to theirs. After nearly ninety years, the modern Olympic movement was dying.

In an era when cities wage $100 million campaigns and their representatives hopscotch the globe to beg for support for their bids to host the Summer Games from the various princes, sheiks, masters of the universe, and former athletes who make up the IOC, it's difficult to imagine a time when almost no one wanted to host the Olympics. Denver gave up the 1976 Winter Olympics when the city hit financial turmoil, forcing the IOC to send the Games to Innsbruck. Tiny Lake Placid (population 2,500) was the lone bidder for the 1980 Winter Games. Moscow and Los Angeles bid for the 1980 Summer Games. Moscow won. Then the US and sixty-four other countries boycotted. Only Los Angeles bid for the 1984 Summer Games. Just two cities bid to host the 1988 Summer Games: Nagoya, Japan, and Seoul, South Korea—not exactly Paris and London.

Samaranch had plenty of faults. He'd been a pal of Spanish

dictator Francisco Franco. He served as Franco's sports minister and president of the province of Catalonia, where Franco's leading enemies resided. He liked to be addressed as "Your Excellency." In the 1990s he oversaw an organization that became mired in the Salt Lake City bribery scandal, in which IOC members received cash, gifts, and college scholarships in support of Salt Lake's bid to host the 2002 Winter Games. But on the issue of allowing athletes to receive money for their performances, Samaranch got it right, even if he acted purely out of self-interest.

The IOC that Samaranch took over had little money in the bank. The Montreal Olympics had lost more than $1 billion—a debt that lingered for decades—and Samaranch understood there was only one way out of the hole: turning the Games into the greatest television show on earth and persuading broadcasters, especially those in the US, to pay through the nose to televise them. Great shows need great stars. The Olympics had plenty of those. But great shows don't boot their biggest stars off the stage after one season. Samaranch knew the Games needed American stars to appear over and over. That way, people would get to know them, watch them evolve, and grow attached to them. The rules of amateur athletics essentially did everything possible to prevent the best of the best from coming together every four years to compete like hell for a hunk of metal.

Meanwhile, there was Moses, winning race after race, taking money under the table so he could sustain his excellence and make it back to the Olympics in 1984. He was educated. He could speak intelligently about everything from civil rights to missile defense systems, and he could run like the wind. If the IOC was going to listen to anyone's ideas about change, they would listen to Moses. So Samaranch asked him to serve as part of a commission of athletes to help craft a proposal for a system that would allow athletes to make enough money from their pursuits to feed themselves, put a roof over their heads, and cover the costs of health care and a coach or two. There was one catch: the proposal couldn't horrify the IOC's old guard.

Moses wanted to trash the whole concept of pseudo-amateurism, but he knew that would never fly. He had to come up with something that would allow athletes to live and train and compete like professionals while still nodding toward the Olympic ideals of sports for sports' sake. The plan Moses and his allies came up with worked like this: athletes who wanted to continue competing in the Olympics could win prize money and collect fees from commercial endorsements, but the money wouldn't go directly into their bank accounts. It would go into trust funds overseen by their national Olympic committees. While they were still competing, Olympians couldn't buy fancy cars or speedboats or vacation homes. They had to spend their winnings on essentials for living or training. Athletes had to keep track of the expenditures from the trust fund and get them approved. When they retired, the leftover money would be there for them. The system could also be jiggered to allow national Olympic committees to provide direct support to their athletes, which so many of them already did anyway.

This was exactly what Samaranch was looking for. There was something for everyone. With Samaranch throwing his weight behind the plan, the IOC approved the athletic trust fund in 1981. After nearly a century of Olympic vows of poverty, "Olympian" became a viable job description, allowing stars like Carl Lewis to compete every four years. By the end of the 1980s the IOC had gotten so hooked on the concept of having the biggest stars in sports in its Games that it got rid of the trust fund farce, too. Of course, the staid IOC didn't want to be so crass as to state that it was really allowing professionals in its Games, so it essentially punted the decision on eligibility to the individual federations. If an international federation allowed an athlete to compete at the world championships, then he or she could be eligible for the Olympics as well.

Pro soccer players arrived in 1984. Tennis pros arrived in 1988. In 1992, Samaranch and the IOC welcomed the so-called Dream Team to the Olympics, a basketball team that included NBA stars Michael Jordan, Magic Johnson, and Larry Bird. With a growing roster of millionaire athletes competing, nearly overnight the meaning of the Olympic rings transformed from amateur sport in its highest form to the world's premier professional athletics competition.

By allowing Olympic athletes to earn money and support themselves, the Games embody a competition between the best of the best. In the process they have also changed our understanding of human development and the peak of athletic performance.

For three years and fifty weeks, swimming is ignored by the vast majority of sports fans. It may be the most ignored of all the major Olympic sports, which is partly what makes it a good sport to examine in order to understand the evolution of the modern Olympics. Unlike track, there was no under-the-table professional circuit that existed in the amateur era of Olympic competition. There is barely an over-the-table professional circuit that exists in 2016 that will allow an athlete to live on prize money. Anyone who makes money in swimming makes it from sponsors, not prize money. Swimming was once dominated by American college and high school kids, and at certain times by juiced-up East Germans. It was thought to be a young person's game. There were theories about the lung capacity of a twentyish male and of a late-teenage female. Pablo Morales didn't qualify for the 1988 Olympics, and he was considered well over-the-hill for his sport when he dropped out of law school and won a gold medal in the 100-meter butterfly at the 1992 Olympics in Barcelona at the age of twenty-seven. He became the oldest Olympic swimming champion ever and was considered the ultimate outlier. In reality, Morales was part of a vanguard.

If one were to compare the ages of the world-record holders in swimming events before Moses burst onto the scene at the 1976 Olympics and the ages of the winners of those same events at the 2015 World Swimming Championships, an obvious pattern would emerge. Many of the 2015 world champions are far older than the swimmers considered the best in the world in swimming in the pre-professional era. Even wunderkind Katie Ledecky, who was eighteen and a half years old when she won the 200-, 400-, 800-, and 1,500-meter freestyle races at the 2015 Swimming World Championships in Kazan, Russia, was between one and three years older than her counterpart in each of those events in the mid-1970s. At thirty-one, Ryan Lochte, who won the 200 individual medley, was thirteen years older than the world-record holder in 1976.

The women's records of that era are particularly absurd, considering just two of the women were of legal drinking age in the US then—back when the legal drinking age was eighteen. Also, even younger women broke several of the records within the next three years. In 1978, American Tracy Caulkins, then just fifteen years, eight months old, set world records in the 200- and 400-meter individual medleys. A year later Mary Meagher broke the world record in the 200-meter butterfly. She was fourteen years, nine months old. Would these women have been the best swimmers ever in their events had swimming careers not ended with college graduation when they were setting those records? Doubtful.

What happened? Swimming became professionalized, and better performances by older competitors began to carry the day— especially in the US, which ended up being the greatest beneficiary of the rise of the professional Olympian. The pattern of older, better champions holds for the American Olympic team as a whole and the US medal winners as well. From 1972 through 2014, the trend line for men and women, whether they competed in winter or summer, won gold medals or silver or bronze, was undoubtedly upward, even if there might have been a slight dip from quadren-nial to quadrennial. The average age of a female gold medalist from the US in the Summer Games has risen from 19.5 years old in 1976 to 25.5 in 2012. For men who won gold medals, the average age jumped from 22.6 to 26.4. For all medals, the average age for men and women jumped from 24 to nearly 27 for the Summer Games and from 22.4 to nearly 26 in the Winter Games. Americans have won the races for most gold and overall medals at every Summer Games since 1996, when the advantages of population, money, and the fall of the Soviet empire combined to make the US nearly un-beatable.

The explanation for what happened is really what didn't hap-pen. With money coming in, even if it was just enough to buy food and pay the rent, the athletes didn't quit. Mark Spitz was only twenty-two when he won seven medals in 1972, but staying in the sport after Munich didn't even enter his mind. He had to figure out how to cash in on his fame. Instead of trying to duplicate his feat in Montreal, he got a supporting role on one episode of the television show *Emergency!* Could Bruce Jenner have won another decathlon? Frank Shorter tried to win a second gold medal in the Olympic marathon in 1976. He won the silver instead. Pretty good, but did the fact that he had to spend part of the intervening four years pursuing a law degree instead of training full-time become the difference between first and second place?

In other words, Americans often "win the Olympics," so to speak. And since they do, Americans tune in in record numbers even as the television audience for nearly every other form of pro-gramming fractures. Those results have produced a massive escala-tion in US media rights fees. Here's a look at what has happened to the price of the US media rights for the Games since Edwin Moses and Juan Antonio Samaranch helped convince the IOC to let the athletes earn money and continue to compete in the Games:

THE OLYMPICS ON TV

SUMMER GAMES				WINTER GAMES			
Year	Location	Network	US Rights Fee	Year	Location	Network	US Rights Fee
1960	Rome	CBS	$390,000	1960	Squaw Valley, CA	CBS	
1964	Tokyo	NBC	$1.5 million	1964	Innsbruck, Austria	ABC	$600,000
1968	Mexico City	ABC	$4.5 million	1968	Grenoble, France	ABC	$2.5 million
1972	Munich	ABC	$7.5 million	1972	Sapporo, Japan	NBC	$6.4 million
1976	Montreal	ABC	$25 million	1976	Innsbruck, Austria	ABC	$10 million
1980	Moscow	NBC	$87 million	1980	Lake Placid, NY	ABC	$15.5 million
1984	Los Angeles	ABC	$225 million	1984	Sarajevo, Yugoslavia	ABC	$91.5 million
1988	Seoul	NBC	$300 million	1988	Calgary	ABC	$309 million
1992	Barcelona	NBC	$401 million	1992	Albertville, France	CBS	$243 million
				1994	Lillehammer, Norway	CBS	$300 million
1996	Atlanta	NBC	$456 million	1998	Nagano, Japan	CBS	$375 million
2000	Sydney	NBC	$715 million	2002	Salt Lake City	NBC	$555 million

SUMMER GAMES				WINTER GAMES			
Year	Location	Network	US Rights Fee	Year	Location	Network	US Rights Fee
2004	Athens	NBC	$793 million	2006	Turin, Italy	NBC	$613 million
2008	Beijing	NBC	$894 million	2010	Vancouver	NBC	$820 million
2012	London	NBC	$1.18 billion	2014	Sochi, Russia	NBC	$775 million
2016	Rio de Janeiro	NBC	$1.226 billion	2018	Pyeongchang, South Korea	NBC	$950 million
2020	Tokyo	NBC	$1.43 billion				

Why does this matter for the Olympic movement as a whole? The money from US broadcasters is the mother's milk of the IOC. Television rights fees accounted for 47 percent of all Olympic revenues of some $6 billion from 2009 to 2012. Fees from the US accounted for $2.15 billion out of a worldwide total of $3.9 billion, or 55 percent. It should account for at least that much through the Tokyo Games in 2020. In 2012, NBC paid $4.4 billion for the rights to the Olympics from 2014 to 2020. In 2014, NBC committed to spending another $8 billion for the media rights through 2032. Without professional athletes from the US winning a lot of medals, there is no way NBC pays that kind of money, and the IOC is a much smaller and poorer organization.

On the morning of August 16, 2008, Michael Phelps emerged from the turn in the 100-meter butterfly at the Beijing Olympics half an arm's length behind Milorad Cavic of Serbia. Over the next forty meters, Phelps inched closer, then fell back, then began to surge again until, just before the wall, he made one last desperate stroke to try to reach the wall first. On the line was his chance at breaking Mark Spitz's thirty-six-year-old record of winning seven gold medals in a single Olympic Games. As Phelps burst toward the wall, stretching his fingers as far as they could go, Cavic glided through the water and finished a fingertip short. The moment is the iconic image of twenty-first-century Olympics—that underwater shot of Phelps beating Cavic at the wall by one one-hundreth of a second. The victory gave Phelps his seventh gold medal, tying him with Spitz, a record he would go on to break the next night when he swam the butterfly leg in the 4x100-meter medley relay.

Phelps's triumph encapsulated everything the world loves about the Olympics and why they become an obsession in the US every two years, even though most people don't follow swimming or, say, beach volleyball when the same athletes aren't competing for Olympic medals. The best swimmer in the world did something no one thought anyone ever would, and he did it at the most important moment. NBC rode the Phelps story to unprecedented success. The Beijing Olympics were the most watched television program in history, seen by 217 million unique viewers over the course of seventeen days. More than 30 million people tuned in when Phelps swam for the gold, a phenomenon that repeated itself in 2012 during the London Olympics, even though his races were shown on tape delay and nearly everyone knew the results before turning on their televisions.

The lords of the IOC in Lausanne, Switzerland, ought to be very happy that Michael Phelps had every possible resource available to him on his road to becoming the most decorated Olympian in history with twenty-two medals. Most elite swimmers take one day off each week. The respite is part of a routine ingrained in the sport, the way baseball pitchers take the mound every fifth day and NFL teams take off Tuesdays during the season. After the 2004 Games in Athens, when Phelps set his mind on breaking Spitz's record, he decided to skip the rest day and train seven days a week instead. He figured it might make him one-seventh better than everyone else, or at least make him think he was.

"We practiced seven days a week, 365 days a year, including Thanksgiving and Christmas, for four years," said Bob Bowman, Phelps's coach. That's what it took to break one of the most hallowed records in sports by a fingernail.

But Phelps had something more than dedication. He had money, including more than $1 million each year in sponsorships with Visa and Speedo. And he had almost no distractions, because that money allowed Phelps to skip college and train exclusively without the distraction of passing sophomore English. Instead, Phelps became the most fitting Olympic hero of his era. If Michael Phelps had been born a generation earlier, when Olympians were prohibited from getting paid, and the best Americans usually gave up their pursuits by the age of twenty-three or twenty-four, he almost certainly wouldn't have appeared in four consecutive Olympic Games, or won twenty-two medals, or set out on a quest to win eight medals in a single Games after winning six in 2004, or come out of retirement to shoot for the 2016 Games. But he did, and he delivered exactly what most people want to see when we tune in to the Olympics: the best of the best, even in sports whose rules are often a mystery for a vast portion of the viewing public. The Olympics feel different than they did fifty years ago—because they are. Since 1994 they have been happening every two years, a move made so that they would be more attractive to corporate sponsors who demand a more consistent advertising vehicle.

Indeed, athletic progress has its costs. Nothing is free. But amateurism as the IOC defined it had its costs, too. Just ask the several hundred US athletes forced to boycott the 1980 Games who couldn't afford to train another four years for their shot at a medal.

In 1981, after leading the charge to change the rules for Olympic athletes, Edwin Moses returned to the business of being the most dominant track-and-field athlete of his era. Part of that meant becoming integral to the promotion of the 1984 Olympics in Los Angeles. Shortly after the IOC enacted the trust fund program, Moses's phone began to ring. Kodak wanted him. So did adidas. Peter Ueberroth, who led the Los Angeles Olympic Organizing Committee, was steering his sponsors toward the athletes who were nearly guaranteed to become the stars of the show. Like Mark McCormack, Ueberroth realized that most people, including the people who ran major corporations, were drawn to the Olympics because of the athletes who participated in them. By the time the Games began, Moses was on some nine thousand Kodak billboards across the country.

Entering the Games, Moses hadn't lost a race since August 26, 1977, and he didn't have any intention of losing one anytime soon. The same summer he lost his Olympic title because of the US boycott, he lowered his world record to 47.13. That left no doubt the results in Moscow would have been different had he been allowed to participate. He won at the World Championships in Helsinki in 1983. That same year, he beat his world record again, in Koblenz, West Germany, where he ran a 47.02.

In the late-afternoon sun of August 5, 1984, Moses stepped into the starting blocks of lane six at the Los Angeles Memorial Coliseum. As he and seven other runners leaned into the track, the stadium fell silent. Harald Schmid, the German champion, was in lane five. Next to him was Danny Harris, an American upstart who had only started running in the event a few months before the Olympic Trials, just like someone else had eight years before. At the click of a trackside camera, the runners exploded out of the blocks, but just as quickly they had to pull up. Moses, who had waited eight years to return to this stage, appeared to have false started. The runners reloaded. Finally the shot from the starter's pistol. This time the start was clean, and the eight men bolted for the first hurdle. Nearly every eye in the Olympic stadium fell on one hurdler. After fifty meters, Moses had already passed Michael Zimmermann of Belgium in lane eight, despite the staggered start that gave each successive runner about a five-meter head start. As Moses bounded over the fifth hurdle, he took control, sprinting down the red track in a different gear than the rest of the field. Nearly two hundred meters remained, but the race was over. Chest up, head high, knees firing over the hurdles every thirteen steps, Moses won the way he always did, with three meters between him and the closest competitor.

After the Olympic triumph, Moses continued to race with barely even a close call. Before a race in Poland, he got food poisoning. He got in the blocks and won by just 1.5 meters, but the streak endured. During the 1986 season, he landed hard coming off a hurdle. The impact jarred his body, as though he'd been twisted around while driving a car and got rear-ended. Although he didn't realize it at the time, he'd ruptured a disk. The pain was brutal. Still he went on, and so did the streak.

Then, in June of 1987, Danny Harris nipped him by 0.13 seconds in Madrid. Moses had led the race through the first two hurdles, but Harris caught him midway through. When Moses hit the tenth hurdle, Harris moved a few steps ahead. Moses closed in the final yards, but ran out of track. He took a lap of honor that night before a standing ovation from twelve thousand Spaniards. A half hour later, they were still chanting his name. "I ran a good race, and the guy that beat me is ten years younger and ran the race of his life," an ever-defiant Moses said when it was over.

Later that summer, he beat Harris at the world championships by 0.02 seconds. The world was catching up with him. The Seoul Olympics were just a year away. By the time the Olympic flame began to blaze in South Korea, Moses and Carl Lewis were the stars of the US team. NBC had acquired the US broadcast rights for an unprecedented $300 million. The deal included a split in advertising revenue between NBC and the IOC, an arrangement that could increase the ultimate payment to nearly $500 million. Since advertisers wanted the final races of the biggest events to be shown live at night in the US, NBC persuaded organizers of the Games to schedule marquee events in the early afternoon in South Korea, which is thirteen hours ahead of eastern daylight time.

In his semifinal heat on September 24, Moses cruised to a first-place finish in 47.89 in Seoul's early evening. To accommodate NBC's desired television schedule, the final was set for the following afternoon at 1:00 p.m., a turnaround of just nineteen hours, much shorter than the usual twenty-four to thirty hours Moses was used to. (Runners now often have a full day between the semifinals and the final.) Moses knew his recovery was going to be tight, especially at age thirty-two. The semifinal had taken more out of him that he had expected. The Olympic Stadium in Seoul wasn't equipped with the ice baths and treatment rooms that all major venues have now. So, instead of getting his usual post-race treatment at the stadium, Moses went to a local hospital to treat his cramping legs. By the time he got back to the Olympic Village, it was nearly 1:00 a.m. Seven hours later his alarm went off. He rolled out of bed and struggled to his feet. He felt like someone had strapped a ball and chain to his ankles.

"My legs were dead," he says. "It was one of the only times in my career I had a day like that. It just happened to be on the day of my last Olympic final. I needed eight more hours to recover."

Moses arrived at the stadium and carried his metric tape measure to the starting line so he could place his blocks in lane three in exactly the position he'd come to prefer during his remarkable thirteen-year hurdling career. He walked down the entire backstretch to get a feel for the breeze he would confront during the race. He didn't have to look far to see his biggest challengers. The West German Harald Schmid was in lane one and American Kevin Young was in lane two. In lanes five and six stood Amadou Dia Ba of Senegal and Andre Phillips of the US, who had actually been the top-ranked 400-meter hurdler in the world in 1985 and 1986, although he had never beaten Moses.

At the sound of the gun, Moses darted out of the blocks and appeared to beat everyone to the first hurdle. By the second hurdle, however, Phillips had pulled at least even and he appeared a half step in front as they headed down the back straight. Then on the far turn Phillips improbably edged into the lead.

In every race there is a moment of truth as the runners enter the final straightaway. There's something about the finish line coming into sight that separates the weak from the strong, or in this case the quickly weakening from those weakening less quickly. Coming off the eighth hurdle, Phillips found enough gas to stretch his lead to two steps and then three. Suddenly Moses was moving backward. That's how it looks on the tape with the finish line forty meters away. Ba darted from the pack to catch Moses just ahead of the wire and finish just off Phillips's left shoulder. Phillips had been lining up against Moses since 1979. Finally he had beaten him and taken his gold medal, leaving Moses with a bronze medal and the taste of bitter disappointment in his mouth.

Moses became a victim of the world he had helped create. Had he not pushed for professionalism in the Olympics, he probably never would have made it to the 1988 Games. It's doubtful he would have stuck around for 1984. He had, though, and he'd become one of the Games' biggest drawing cards and a major part of the growing appeal that drove a twelvefold increase in the fee for the US broadcast rights for the Games in just twelve years. But everything comes with a cost. For Moses it was eight hours of recovery so his race could be shown at night in living rooms across the US.

"I beat the odds by being here," Moses told a trackside reporter as he headed for the locker room. He had. After a dozen years of international track, he just couldn't beat the competition anymore.

8

The Quarterback Club

In January of 1985, Frank Vuono, the NFL's newly hired director of licensed merchandise, made his maiden voyage to the NFL Pro Bowl in Honolulu. For Vuono, a football junkie from Lyndhurst, New Jersey, the trip figured to be something of a dream come true. Like any number of kids who grew up in the 1960s and '70s, glued to their television sets on Sunday afternoons and Monday nights, Frank Vuono could get weak in the knees from one look at the NFL shield. Born and raised just a few long passes from the swamp that became Giants Stadium, Vuono played tight end for Princeton during the 1970s—heady stuff for a kid whose father spent thirty-one years working on the Westinghouse factory floor.

After graduating from Princeton, Vuono began his career in business as an assistant account executive with Young & Rubicam, then gambled on a more entrepreneurial role at Integrated Barter International. The company gobbled up excess inventory of nearly any kind—office supplies, sneakers, trucks, computers—at huge discounts and then found a customer to buy or trade for it at a slight markup. The experience gave him a graduate-level understanding of the retail market and consumers' endless search for good products at a decent price. Vuono never got rid of the football bug, though, and every time he wandered through a sporting goods store, he wondered why it was so hard to find a decent jersey, one where the numbers wouldn't disintegrate the second week you owned it, or a sweatshirt that wasn't 50 percent polyester and paper-thin. Vuono was still buddies with the equipment manager at Princeton, so each year he could get another ultra-heavy Reverse Weave Princeton Football sweatshirt. The NFL didn't produce anything like that.

One day in 1984, Vuono ended up at a lunch with a few guys he knew from the NFL. Feeling punchy, he started telling them how crappy their licensing business was, a venture that seemed focused on selling foot pajamas at Sears. This wasn't complicated, he explained. They needed to sell the jerseys the players wore on the field. The NFL guys looked at him incredulously. "You really think there'd be a market for that?" they asked.

"I'm thinking, 'Jesus Christ, how stupid could you be?'" Vuono said. "Do I think that people would buy game quality uniforms, the same ones worn by NFL players? Yes, I think they would." Then he told them they should sell the Reverse Weave sweatshirts the players wore on the sidelines. Their response: "What's Reverse Weave?" Vuono couldn't believe what he was hearing. Arguably the most popular league in the world's wealthiest country had no idea what its product actually was. Before the end of the year, the NFL guys came back to Vuono with a challenge: if you're so smart, why don't you run our merchandise business for us? Vuono didn't have to be asked twice. The NFL's licensing business did $300 million in sales at retail, providing maybe $20 million a year for the league. He figured he could triple the business without breaking a sweat simply by using the players to market the clothes they wore and redirecting the business toward adults. He scheduled his start date for Pro Bowl week in Hawaii.

Vuono had a plan to do something truly radical in the annals of the NFL. He wanted to build a sales and marketing campaign around the league's heroes, the stars playing in its version of an all-star game. From a business standpoint, the plan was about as simple as handing the running back the ball and sending him up the middle. You hand the players their uniforms, shoot pictures of them, then go sell replica jerseys and practice shirts in every sporting goods store in the country, since players wore their own team's jerseys in the game. By the time back-to-school shopping season rolled around, all the kids and their dads would be able to buy replicas of the game and practice jerseys that quarterback Joe Montana and linebacker Lawrence Taylor had worn during Pro Bowl week and in the game itself.

Vuono hired a photographer and headed to the Aloha Bowl for the first day of practice. His first hint that life in the NFL might not be as it appeared on television arrived when he walked into the locker room at Aloha Stadium. Water leaked from the pipes above his head. The dank air reeked of mold. On the side of the room he found a collection of metal chests with uniforms inside them. The worn-out clothing looked like it was twenty years old. Half the jerseys were ripped and darned back together. For a moment he wondered where the actual Pro Bowl uniforms were. Then he realized these were the actual uniforms. As he handed the practice jerseys to the best football players in the world, men like Walter Payton and Mike Singletary, he could see the disappointment in their eyes. "They were looking at me like, 'You're giving this to me again?'" So much for building a catalog. Vuono was flabbergasted. The NFL, this grand sixty-year-old league, with its austere shield at the pinnacle of American sport, was a chimera.

The mythology around the National Football League's rise to world domination goes something like this: once upon a time the NFL was a sputtering mess. Then, in 1961, a new commissioner, this marketing whiz named Pete Rozelle, negotiated a deal with CBS for $4.65 million for the national television rights to NFL games. He persuaded all the teams to share the revenues equally, and everyone lived happily ever after.

There's one big problem with this story: it's not true.

In 1966, the NFL was forced to merge with the rival American Football League, which had a network television contract that paid about double what the NFL was receiving. The AFL developed a nasty habit of taking some of the best college players, such as Heisman Trophy winner Billy Cannon and the Alabama star Joe Namath. The mega-product of the merger was the Super Bowl, the showdown between the respective champions of the two leagues. About one-third of the ninety-three thousand seats at the Los Angeles Memorial Coliseum went unsold for the first Super Bowl in 1967 between the Green Bay Packers and the Kansas City Chiefs. In 1977, sixteen years after the revenue-sharing vote, NFL teams averaged 56,218 fans per game, down 5 percent from the 1973 season. Owners outside the big markets struggled to break even. Players were suing the league over free agency. Two NFL owners were suing the league over a bylaw that prohibited them from owning a team in another sport. The NFL was a mess—and not much of a moneymaker, either. It was slightly profitable as a whole, and it was the most intensely followed sport during its season; but Major League Baseball's revenues were significantly higher, because the NFL played so few games and the modern sports television business was still in its infancy. Strangely, that didn't seem to bother the owners very much. The only one who seemed to focus on money was Carroll Rosenbloom, who owned the Rams. At one owners meeting in the 1970s, Rosenbloom suggested they raise the price of a Super Bowl ticket from about $20 to nearly $100. It was the premier one-game championship in American sports, after all. "Everyone thought he was crazy," said Jay Moyer, Rozelle's right-hand man and general counsel. No one really saw an NFL team as a way to get wealthy, not even Rozelle. He was more focused on running the game properly, getting good write-ups in the papers, and keeping gamblers and bookies who might try to fix games out of the locker rooms.

By the late 1970s, the NFL had another problem besides sluggish finances: the game itself was just plain boring. On the opening Sunday of the 1977 season, five teams failed to score a single point. There were shutouts eleven out of the fourteen weeks that season, often more than one. It wasn't just the expansion Tampa Bay Buccaneers or the awful New York Jets. The Bills, Browns, Chargers, Bears, Giants, Packers, Lions, Falcons, Seahawks, 49ers, Eagles, and Cardinals all failed to score in at least one game that season. Teams averaged just 17.2 points per game. The Falcons allowed 9.2 points per game in 1977 and went 7-7. The Bucs scored 7.8 points per game that season. The 2007 New England Patriots scored more than that every quarter. To one football lifer in Texas, this was no way to sell a sport.

Gil Brandt, the Dallas Cowboys' vice president of player personnel, was sitting in his office at the team headquarters on Tuesday morning, September 20, 1977, when his boss, general manager Tex Schramm, stopped by. Schramm had spent nearly his entire adult life working in the NFL. He'd been with the Cowboys since the team's inception in 1960. He came of age in an era when NFL football was a distant second in popularity to the college game. He knew there was only one way the league could continue to grow and remain successful—by giving fans what they wanted—and he was certain they didn't want shutouts, like the four the NFL delivered on Sunday, September 18, 1977, or the 27–0 Steeler beat-down of the 49ers on Monday night.

Schramm poked his head into Brandt's office and asked if he had noticed anything peculiar about the season-opening games. Brandt knew exactly what Schramm was talking about. The weekend had been a complete disaster, Brandt told him. The Bengals scored three points. The Rams scored six. Schramm said enough was enough. If the NFL didn't find a way to get more scoring incorporated into the game, people would stop buying tickets and showing up. Fans wanted to see touchdowns, Schramm said. Brandt said he was with him all the way, although he had no idea exactly how Schramm might manage to effect change in the stodgy NFL, with its sepia-toned nostalgia for ground-and-pound, three-yards-and-a-cloud-of-dust-style football.

Schramm wasn't just any football lifer, though. Sensing that the games needed a little life pumped into them, he essentially invented the famed Dallas Cowboys Cheerleaders. He also ran the league's competition committee, which was charged with changing and adjusting the game's rules. To Schramm, that mandate meant an existential fight to favor offense over defense. Fans had come to love the NFL for the same reason they loved any other sport. At its best, it featured breathtaking athleticism and suspense until the final whistle, both of which were sorely lacking on Sunday, September 18.

While his Cowboys marched to a Super Bowl championship that season, Schramm began to wage a campaign to change football by making it easier for players to thrill fans. NFL rosters were stocked with some of the fastest men on the planet—men like Bob Hayes, the Cowboys receiver who won the gold medal in the 100 meters at the 1964 Olympics in Tokyo. But in the NFL of 1977, a defensive back could keep his hands all over a wide receiver and keep bumping him all the way down the field. That made it awfully hard for even the fastest receiver to break into open space, much less catch a pass thrown at fifty miles per hour. How hard? In 1977, the average quarterback completed just 51 percent of his passes. Today a quarterback can't keep his job if his completion percentage isn't above 60 percent.

Schramm started working the phones, harassing everyone on the competition committee: Oakland Raiders owner Al Davis, the Chicago Bears executive Jim Finks, Dolphins coach Don Shula, and even that most traditional of NFL owners, Wellington Mara of the Giants. Schramm was acting partly out of self-interest. The Cowboys had a pretty good quarterback in future Hall of Famer Roger Staubach. Any rules that favored offense were certainly going to help the Cowboys.

In March of 1978, Schramm and the NFL announced the most radical reforms in league history. Defensive players could no longer touch a receiver beyond five yards from the line of scrimmage, where the play begins. Offensive linemen would be allowed to extend their arms when trying to block a rushing defender. Defensive linemen could no longer slap offensive linemen in the head. Imagine trying to block Deacon Jones (six foot five, 270 pounds, nasty as a pit bull) if you weren't allowed to extend your arms and he is permitted to slap you in the head.

It worked. Slowly, scoring began to return. But the rule changes had an even more significant effect than generating more scoring and excitement. The league of Lombardi, where the coaches were lionized as sideline generals who oversaw a form of legalized warfare, handed the keys of the ship to its players—actually, to one player on each team: the quarterback. The NFL desperately needed offense. Empowering the quarterbacks was the easiest way to create that, even if it meant putting in motion a system that would ensure they would become stars on an unprecedented scale. Making the players the stars of the show had long been anathema in the NFL, where the teams and the people who ran them endured, while the players came and went. They were little more than anonymous guys in helmets and huge pads that most people wouldn't recognize in the supermarket.

Now the quarterback was going to shift from a sort of middle manager to the prime mover of the franchise, the embodiment of the club and the public face of what the game and each of its teams was about—or, in a few cases, aspired to be about. Out in San Francisco, Bill Walsh was wondering what had taken so damn long.

Bill Walsh never set out to revolutionize the game of football. He grew up playing football in Southern California and Oregon, then attended the College of San Mateo and San José State. After a stint in the Army, he landed a job as an assistant football coach at San José State. Impatient to be in charge of a team after just a year, he took over as head football coach at Washington High School in Fremont, California, where he stayed for three years. He wanted to become a head coach at a top university, though, so he hooked on with Marv Levy at Cal, then landed an assistant coaching job at Stanford. A series of opportunities in pro football led Walsh to the Cincinnati Bengals in 1968, where he coached the offense on the staff of the legendary Paul Brown and began to change the game of football.

In Cincinnati, Walsh had a quarterback named Virgil Carter, who had been terrific at Brigham Young University. Only six feet tall, Carter could barely see over the defensive linemen and linebackers, and he didn't have a strong enough arm to throw the ball deep. Worse, Cincinnati's offensive line stunk. The team could barely run the ball. Walsh decided that, given the team's limitations, the only way the Bengals could hold the ball long enough to convert the requisite twenty-five first downs that were usually needed to win a football game would be for Carter to think on his feet, throw a series of short, high-percentage passes, and hope his receivers and backs could pick up yards after they caught the ball. The game plan made Carter the central figure and decision maker in the offense. What became known as the "West Coast Offense" was born—in Cincinnati. The Bengals went 28-14 from 1973 to 1975, far better than if they had been running a traditional attack.

Walsh got passed over for the Bengals' head-coaching job in 1976. He became the San Diego Chargers' offensive coordinator for a season, then fulfilled his original coaching goal when he returned to Stanford as head coach. In Palo Alto, Walsh found plenty of talent. Quarterback Guy Benjamin, wide receiver James Lofton, and offensive lineman Gordon King had all-American athleticism, but they were still raw, even as seniors, especially Benjamin. Benjamin was a scrambling quarterback who relied on his athletic ability and his arm but didn't know how to think. Walsh drilled Benjamin in the art of footwork, showing him how his feet could buy him more time behind his blockers. He taught him the mechanics of throwing the ball on a line and of thinking through his passing options, seeing the primary, secondary, and alternate receivers in quick succession. Benjamin led the country in passing. Stanford went 9-3 and beat LSU in the Sun Bowl.

The next year Walsh had the unenviable task of replacing three All-Americans and four NFL draft picks on the offense alone. Yet quarterback Steve Dils led Stanford to 435.5 yards in total offense per game and set school records with 2,943 yards passing and 22 touchdown passes. The team battled to a 7-4 record that included close losses to Oklahoma, USC, and UCLA. It was good enough for a berth in the Bluebonnet Bowl in Houston, at the time a second-tier postseason game, against heavily favored Georgia. Georgia pounded Stanford early, stacking eight men on the line and pressuring Dils whenever he dropped into the pocket. Early in the third quarter Georgia led Stanford 22–0. Walsh told his quarterback to stop looking down the field, let the pressure come, and drop quick passes over it. Stanford scored 25 unanswered points and won 25–22. Nine days later the San Francisco 49ers gave Walsh his first professional head-coaching job.

Walsh attacked his new gig the way a graduate student goes after his PhD in neuroscience. To Walsh, coaching football wasn't about riling up the locker room with inspirational speeches. It was about paying attention to minute details and rethinking every traditional approach to building a winner. For years Walsh had watched coaches run bruising practices through every month of the season. "Bring 'em in and beat 'em up," it was called. To let up was to invite players to slack off. The flip side of this approach was increasing the risk of injury through a brutal season. Walsh wanted to figure out how to keep players healthy, fresh, and productive. So he eliminated back-to-back practices in which players wore pads and banged into each other. He kept the sessions short—no longer than ninety minutes. Special teams practices often took place without pads and hitting.

On the field, precision was paramount. Brian Billick, who led the Baltimore Ravens to the Super Bowl in 2001 but got his start as Walsh's press liaison, said in one early practice in 1979 quarterback Joe Montana threw a swing pass and hit the receiver in the numbers. Everyone on the field thought it was a pretty good throw. Walsh stopped everything and launched into a mini-tirade. He ranted about wanting the ball to hit the receiver's hands as he moved his feet forward. The ball needed to be thrown one foot in front of the body so that the throw could produce the necessary yards after the catch.

Walsh and his quarterbacks coach, Sam Wyche, evaluated fourteen quarterbacks that spring. They caught up with Montana in Southern California. He didn't have the strongest arm, but he could move, "almost like a ballet dancer," Walsh wrote. He initially wanted Phil Simms but figured Simms wasn't going to be available by the time the 49ers picked. He grabbed Montana in the third round, as an insurance policy for Steve DeBerg, who'd been injured. (In the tenth round he picked Dwight Clark, the tight end who would catch the pass that sent the 49ers to the Super Bowl in 1982.)

Walsh picked Montana because he knew the NFL was changing. Playing quarterback didn't simply require being able to throw the ball far down the field anymore. Walsh immediately went to work on teaching Montana a new way to play the position in the new NFL he saw evolving, given the previous year's rule changes. The game was going to be about pace and efficiency. The pass would set up the run instead of the other way around. Short, intermediate passes were going to move the football down the field most effectively. Having a quarterback with a 60 percent completion rate would be essential. Teams needed to keep the chains moving and be more multifaceted. Success wouldn't be about being the most physical team. It would be about everyone being healthy at the conclusion of the season. To Walsh, the rule changes after the 1977 season were just the tip of the iceberg. He believed the rules were going to continue to change because the league and the television networks wanted more offense. Walsh assured Billick the old NFL was dead. The new NFL was going to be about money and offensive talent, which was going to come together and produce a different kind of game that was about scoring and offense. "That's what people want to see," he said.

Success didn't come immediately. The 49ers were an awful 2-14 Walsh's first year, but by 1982, Walsh and Montana had won the Super Bowl and everyone wanted what they had. A year later NFL teams selected six quarterbacks in the first round, an indication that there were a lot of quality quarterbacks in this draft and of the importance teams now placed on the position. By 1984, Schramm's changes had increased scoring on average by eight points per game.

Total yards had risen from 286 per game to 330. The quarterback era was under way.

The question now was whether the owners could figure out how to avoid having these stars become so big they would rob them blind. Their relationship with the players had become increasingly confrontational. In 1982 the NFL Players Association had gone on strike to try to gain the kind of free agency that baseball players had. The effort failed and the players returned to work after fifty-seven days in part because the union didn't have a large enough strike fund to hold the players together. Now a former too-slow tight end from Princeton had a few ideas for how to keep the players' union poor and powerless and in the process send the pendulum that had been swinging in the direction of athlete power and players' rights for roughly a quarter of a century back in the opposite direction.

By the 1986 Pro Bowl, Vuono had learned his lesson. This time he ordered all the game uniforms and practice gear on his own, far ahead of time, and had it shipped to the Hilton Hawaii Village hotel in Waikiki. Each day he loaded up a van with hats, T-shirts, sweatshirts, and practice jerseys and stocked the locker room before the players arrived. Then he took their pictures in the gear. Finally he had his catalog, which he carried around to the country's big retailers and sporting goods conventions so they could begin selling high-end gear to adults.

Vuono then started to turn his attention to the rest of the league's marketing and merchandise deals. He was curious how much the teams' jersey and equipment suppliers were paying to associate with the league. But when he looked at the budgets of the individual teams, he quickly realized that shoulder pads, practice uniforms, and equipment accounted for one of their biggest line items—several hundred thousand dollars each year. He was flabbergasted yet again. How did these people not get it? The relationship was supposed to be the other way around. Suppliers should be paying the NFL and its teams for the privilege of outfitting their players. In exchange, the suppliers would get their emblems on the gear and get the right to advertise themselves as official suppliers of the country's most popular league. The suppliers didn't like the idea at all. *Giving* pro teams the equipment was going to kill their very profitable professional division, they said. Somehow they missed the big picture: NFL players were going to wear their logos all day Sunday in front of millions of people. "It was the best advertising they could ever get," Vuono said.

Vuono met resistance from his own bosses, too. No player had ever gotten paid a dime for his identity or a jersey sale with his number on it. The league and the teams claimed it was part of their rights of publicity. The league had never tried to build a real business from jersey sales, so whether the players should get any money from such sales had never been a major bone of contention. Now Vuono was going to do that, which might open up a can of worms. But Vuono sensed the union had a more immediate problem. Another strike was on the horizon. It needed money. Giving the union a piece of the jersey business would produce much-needed cash. He proposed giving the Players Association a cut of the royalties on jersey sales: $1 for every jersey that was sold. Desperate for cash, the union leaped at the deal. Vuono knew plenty of his owners wouldn't like helping the union, but league officials were willing to gamble that they could handle whatever work stoppage the union planned. They were right. The players walked out two games into the 1987 season. Free agency remained the main sticking point. The players wanted to get rid of the so-called Rozelle rule, which allowed the commissioner to compensate a team if a player signed somewhere else when his contract expired. The threat of onerous compensation essentially eliminated the possibility of an open market for free agents. The strike lasted twenty-four days and collapsed after stars like Joe Montana, Doug Flutie, and Lawrence Taylor crossed the picket line and played with replacement players.

Having failed to make any headway using the tools of collective bargaining and the picket lines, the union turned to the courts, filing an antitrust lawsuit against the NFL to try to break the cartel. The NFL beat it back on procedural grounds before the merits of the litigation had been heard. On November 1, 1989, the court of appeals ruled that the union could not sue on antitrust grounds because of something called the "labor exemption." That exemption prohibited lawsuits between unions and management while a union was still intact. The union had proven inept at conducting a strike. Now it had failed in the courts, too.

Just days after that decision, Gene Upshaw, the executive director of the NFL Players Association, sat on a couch in the midtown Manhattan law firm of Weil, Gotshal & Manges. For Upshaw, the destination was about as far from his upbringing picking cotton in rural Texas as he could get. Upshaw had risen from little-known Texas College of Arts and Industries, a public university without much of a reputation for athletics, to become an all-pro lineman and one of the leaders of the championship Oakland Raiders teams of the 1970s. He famously wrapped his arms with tape and gauze from his shoulder pads to his fingertips, making him appear like a giant, terrifying mummy. As he became a veteran, Upshaw emerged as one of the leaders of the Players Association, and after he retired from football he'd become its executive director. So far Upshaw was proving to be as bad at leading a union as he was great at leading a football team. He'd led two disastrous strikes.

With the union and his own reputation in tatters, Upshaw traveled to New York in search of a strategy to combat the seemingly unconquerable NFL owners. Jim Quinn and Jeffrey Kessler, the two lawyers assigned to meet with Upshaw, didn't offer a lot of expertise in sports. They were experts in antitrust law. Kessler was developing a particularly obscure expertise in antitrust as it related to the electronics business. However, they had handled a few matters on behalf of the NBA Players Association. Kessler had even been involved in the lawsuit against the NFL in 1977 when two owners sued the league because they also wanted to own soccer teams, which league rules prohibited.

Upshaw listened closely and silently as Kessler and Quinn explained his problem. His opponent operated as a cartel. With the collapse of the World Football League in the 1970s and the United States Football League in the early 1980s, the league faced no competition. A top-tier football player had no other marketplace in which to sell his talents. Then there was the "Rozelle rule," which required substantial free-agent compensation for any teams that lost a player on the open market. Even the annual draft, which prohibited a college player from selling himself to the highest bidder, could be viewed as an antitrust violation. The top law firms in the country couldn't set up a draft to divide the best legal talent emerging each year from the top law schools. Why should NFL teams be allowed to do that? The league was clearly functioning as a monopoly, Quinn and Kessler explained. It didn't have an antitrust exemption from the US Supreme Court, like baseball did. No reasonable judge could ignore this. Given the difficulty of building player unity in the NFL, the courts represented the only way to get the Players Association closer to the triumph they sought in their ultimate fight for a fair collective bargaining agreement that included free agency.

Upshaw knew all this. He sat stoically on the couch. He wasn't a lawyer. He preferred to face his enemy directly, across a line of scrimmage or a collective bargaining table, rather than through years of legal briefs and courtroom hearings. He was desperate, though. He asked Kessler and Quinn what the hell he was supposed to do.

Well, Kessler said, you might want to consider shutting down the union.

At first Upshaw didn't believe what he had heard. How could he possibly serve the players' interests by dissolving the only organization ever created to protect them? Kessler explained that the union didn't actually have to be a union. It could dissolve and re-incorporate as a business created to raise money and represent the legal interests of football players who happened to play in the NFL. It couldn't collectively bargain contracts, file grievances, or do any of the other basic functions of a labor organization, but it could pursue an antitrust case that it could finance by getting players to sign over their marketing rights to the association. The association would then license those rights to trading card companies, clothing manufacturers, and any other entity that wanted to sell products using the players' likenesses. It was a cockeyed plan with no guarantee of success and no existing funding source. It relied solely on applying pressure to the one weak spot that the NFL and every sports league and team owner shared: their collective fear of being labeled a monopoly.

The office fell silent. Upshaw spent perhaps a minute, but not longer, absorbing what Kessler and Quinn had just told him. Then he spoke.

"Well," he said. "Looks like we got to get out of the union business."

As the 1980s drew to a close and Upshaw, Quinn, and Kessler plotted the players' next moves, over at the NFL offices on Park Avenue, Vuono was noticing a clear pattern in the league's licensing business, in particular the jersey sales, which served as the bread and butter for the business. Most of the jerseys fans wanted to buy were worn by a very small number of players. The vast majority of those players played one position: quarterback. In theory, that didn't surprise Vuono, but the level of dominance was a little startling. People bought the jerseys of Joe Montana, Phil Simms, Boomer Esiason, Jim McMahon, Dan Marino, and John Elway—and that was about it. A running back or a wide receiver might get hot for a season or two. There were a couple of big-time defensive guys. Lawrence Taylor. Mike Singletary. But the numbers made it clear that if you controlled the quarterbacks, you controlled something like 80 percent of the licensing business. Quarterbacks had always been popular, but this level of domination was startling. It didn't take a Princeton diploma to figure out exactly what was happening. All those rules Tex Schramm pushed through a little more than a decade before had transformed the NFL into a quarterbacks' league in every way. To an executive helping to shape the league's financial strategy, it meant one thing: whoever controlled the quarterbacks would control the football licensing business.

For Vuono and the NFL, that concept quickly became urgent. Following Kessler and Quinn's advice, Upshaw and the NFL Players Association had indeed decertified as a union for collective bargaining purposes in 1989 and registered as a trade organization that would represent NFL players in litigation and group marketing rights. Remember that $1 per jersey deal that Vuono cut with the NFLPA? The primary purpose of the new decertified NFLPA would be to collect that money, as well as revenues from a few other group licensing deals made on behalf of NFL players. It would then use that money to finance antitrust litigation. If there was any money left over, it would be divided among the players and distributed to them. Given the expense of the legal case, which was going to take several years, there wasn't going to be much money left over. As Vuono looked at the monthly reports on the top-selling jerseys, he hatched a plan to make sure there wouldn't be much money at all.

Every great athlete is, in part, a greedy egomaniac. It's what makes some of them want to take on the responsibility of playing quarterback in the first place, and it allows them to perform heroically under intense pressure and scrutiny. Vuono's strategy was to tap into the greedy egomaniac in the best quarterbacks and channel those qualities in a direction that could serve the purposes of the league. Instead of treating all the players as equals, Vuono proposed creating a separate entity called "the Quarterback Club." To do that, he had to convince all those top jersey sellers that they would be better off if they stopped assigning their group licensing rights to the Players Association. Instead they would enter into a partnership with the league to market the league's most popular players, the ones responsible for selling nearly every NFL jersey.

Vuono's plan was star driven for a simple reason: that was the direction the entire sports business had shifted to. By 1990 the NBA was threatening the NFL for supremacy, largely because the NBA had created massive promotional campaigns around stars like Michael Jordan, Magic Johnson, and Larry Bird. In contrast, through the 1980s, the NFL continued to promote its fabled shield and its franchises. It treated its mostly anonymous players like a marketing afterthought.

The problem was NFL players wore helmets and they didn't really register with the public. Joe Montana barely made top-ten lists of the country's most popular sports stars. Athletes from other sports were much better known. To an extent, that's how the NFL owners wanted it. The league wanted to promote the teams. If it promoted the athletes, they might get big heads and demand the salaries of Hollywood stars or even baseball players. To Vuono, that thinking was backward. If the league could get big companies to sign sponsorship deals with the league's biggest stars, those companies would use those players to promote their products in commercials, which would serve as free advertising for the league. It also might leave the NFLPA without any money to fight its antitrust litigation.

When Vuono presented the plan to the owners, he received only lukewarm support. Several thought he was heading down a slippery slope of player promotion that was eventually going to cost them a lot of money. But he had one important figure in his corner: the new commissioner, Paul Tagliabue.

Tagliabue succeeded Rozelle as commissioner in 1989. A former Defense Department lawyer, Tagliabue was a partner at the law firm Covington & Burling and had spent the previous decade overseeing the NFL's legal strategy as its outside counsel. Tagliabue had taken over at a time of great turmoil. The ongoing labor problems were beginning to take a financial toll on the league. The litigation was expensive and the television networks were using the uncertainty as leverage in negotiations for their broadcast packages. The payments to the league actually dropped in the broadcast deals Rozelle had cut with the networks in 1986, to an average of about $340 million per year over the next three years, compared with $420 million in the previous deals. To make the owners whole, Rozelle had sold a new Sunday night package to ESPN for $135 million.

Tagliabue brought to the job the idea that lingering legal problems, such as labor strife, could often be solved with business opportunities. In the 1980s he sued countless small-time bar owners on behalf of the NFL because they had purchased early-generation satellite dishes and were using them to pick up the signals of every NFL game, not just the games in their home markets. The bars would televise the games to attract the most rabid NFL fans. The endless litigation was an inefficient strategy. The better solution to that problem was "Sunday Ticket," which DirecTV now pays the NFL $1.5 billion a year to distribute and gives anyone willing to part with $250 access to all NFL games.

To Tagliabue, a "quarterback club" represented another business opportunity that could solve a problem. The labor litigation looked like an albatross that would hang around the league's neck for years. He also sensed the league's case might be a loser. The league did operate as a cartel that thwarted competition between clubs and didn't have an antitrust exemption. The sooner the players could be convinced to agree to a new collective bargaining agreement, the better off the league would be. Creating a business that might make some money for the owners while cutting the legs out from under the antitrust litigation looked like the ultimate win-win.

Tagliabue sent Vuono on the road with a proposal that guaranteed the top quarterbacks anywhere from $20,000 to $100,000 in additional annual income. That was real money at a time when the average NFL salary was still only about $300,000. Starting quarterbacks averaged about $1 million per season—a nice living indeed, but not enough to eschew what might amount to a 5 to 10 percent raise.

His main targets were agents Marvin Demoff and Leigh Steinberg. He knew he had Steinberg's support. His quarterback corps included Warren Moon, Steve Young, Tony Eason, Ken O'Brien, Wade Wilson, Eric Hipple, and Neil Lomax. Steinberg, who claims to be the basis for the Jerry Maguire character in the 1996 movie, had little taste for the labor wars. An antiestablishment law student at Berkeley in the 1970s, he had evolved into a true friend of NFL management by the late 1980s. The idea of a "quarterback club" was music to Steinberg's ears. Because he represented all those quarterbacks, he knew a disproportionate amount of the endorsements went to them and they were the star attractions of any group licensing deals. Mixing their rights with the other 1,500 or so players in the Players Association inevitably diluted their value. Steinberg saw Vuono as an ally.

Demoff was the key, though. He represented Dan Marino and

John Elway, who were the biggest stars aside from Montana. Marino had been an officer in the Players Association. Yet here was a chance to gain equity in an invitation-only company whose only partners were the elite of the elite of the National Football League. He bit.

"Once we had Marino and Elway, everyone else fell into place," Vuono said. At the end of 1990, the NFL announced that John Elway, Warren Moon, Bernie Kosar, Jim Kelly, Troy Aikman, Randall Cunningham, Phil Simms, Jim Everett, Boomer Esiason, Bubby Brister, and Dan Marino had assigned most of their group licensing rights to the new entity now officially known as the Quarterback Club. (Vuono didn't actually want Brister, but he had the same agent as Randall Cunningham, so Brister got in on the Eagles star's coattails.) Soon, Jim Harbaugh and Steve Young would join, too. Montana never signed on, but not because of a sense of solidarity with the rest of the rank and file. Montana thought he deserved a bigger cut than the rest of the members of the club, since he was the league's biggest star.

There were quarterly meetings, golf outings, sportswear lines, and, of course, millions in sales of the league's most popular jerseys, which was the best advertising the Quarterback Club and its members could receive.

"They set it up so that you could do whatever you wanted on your own but if there were three or more players involved from the club all the money would go to the Quarterback Club and then it would be divided among the group," Demoff said. "The Players Association had nothing that was competitive."

No one mentioned the other part of the equation: that creating a separate licensing division for the league's biggest stars was going to bleed the union dry. Steinberg certainly wasn't bothered by it. "Football was built with the quarterback as the leading man," Steinberg said unapologetically. He believed a franchise quarterback was the vital part that the teams could build around for ten to twelve years.

Predictably, the Players Association, or what was left of it, was livid. The quarterback was supposed to be the leader of the team. For thirty years the best athletes had come together to demand to be paid their fair share. That unity had produced unimagined riches for both the players and the owners because it had forced sports to start acting like real businesses that deal with labor as a partner. The Quarterback Club showed that the modern athlete's greatest strength—his understanding of how special and valuable his talents are—could be turned into his greatest weakness. Under the right circumstances, he would cross a picket line and he would cut a deal that would jeopardize the future of his teammates and fellow athletes. He would act like a jerk. And that was before most of them had any idea who Mike Ornstein was.

Mike Ornstein grew up in a largely Italian section of the Bronx near Fordham Road and Jerome Avenue. Nearly every day some kid called him a "kike" or a "Jew boy." Ornstein rarely turned the other cheek, even when he was outnumbered. He took his share of lumps. The beatings taught him that saying what he had to say wasn't all that scary. He could deal with the consequences. Ornstein speaks in the "dese" and "dose" vernacular of a New York street tough. It gives the distinct impression that Ornstein has done some very bad things in his life, some of them criminal. In fact, he has. In 2006, he went to prison on charges related to selling scalped Super Bowl tickets and fraudulent NFL jerseys.

Ornstein got his start in the NFL with the Oakland Raiders in 1975 just as the franchise was becoming one of the NFL's best. He began as John Madden's administrative assistant and morphed into a jack-of-all-trades, helping out with scouting and film work. He then became the team's director of marketing when it moved to Los Angeles in 1982.

Ornstein idolized Al Davis, the combative owner who was willing to do whatever it took to win, and Ron Wolf, the team's main player personnel executive. Wolf researched every player's personality and took risks on the ones other teams shied away from. The Raiders took on unstable types who weren't known to be good citizens—players like John Matuszak, a former first-round draft choice released by the Washington Redskins after the 1975 season. In that era, the Raiders had Gene Upshaw functioning as the locker room sheriff. He kept everyone in line. But Wolf also spent significant time on the road scouting and getting to know players before he brought them in. From Wolf, Ornstein learned the value of travel, of seeing players in person and getting to know them.

In 1989, Ornstein moved to the NFL offices to serve as a marketing cop for the league. His main responsibility was to make sure that teams weren't signing deals with local companies to give away space on NFL sidelines that national sponsors had already paid for. Then the league came up with another job for him. A year after the NFL started the Quarterback Club, the Players Association was still pushing ahead with its litigation. Settlement talks were going nowhere. A dozen quarterbacks had been persuaded to turn over their marketing rights to the league. League executives wondered whether there was a price at which the rest of the players would flip. Surely that would bankrupt the Players Association. It was going to require confrontational work—nasty, union-busting stuff at camps and in locker rooms, the sort of roadwork a fiery, confrontational guy like Ornstein would be perfect for.

Ornstein hit the road armed with a virtually open checkbook. Initially, Vuono went along with him, but Vuono was more of a wine-and-dine, play-eighteen-holes-and-make-a-deal type. This was trench warfare that required getting up in front of the team with the head coach as Players Association loyalists screamed to toss him from the locker room. Ornstein's approach wasn't complicated. He would explain to the players they were making maybe $1,000 for their marketing rights through the Players Association. Then he'd offer $10,000, promising to write a check on the spot. That got the players' attention. It was instant gratification.

Ornstein's first stop was the Denver Broncos. Mike Shanahan was the coach, and John Elway, who had already signed on with the Quarterback Club, was the team's leader. As a result, Denver did not prove particularly hostile. But then he went to the Arizona Cardinals. "That was bad because they knew we were coming and they were prepared for us," he said. "They had this big defensive lineman who was the player representative. Their general manager was so nervous he was smoking one cigarette and had another one in his hand ready to light. The guys were screaming at me. It was brutal."

By the time he left, however, roughly the same number of Cardinals and Broncos had signed on, about twenty-five guys from each team. Soon word got around to the other camps that Ornstein was on his way with an open checkbook. He said the San Diego players came out to meet him in the parking lot. Hall of Fame caliber players like Marcus Allen and James Lofton knew Ornstein's arrival would mean an extra $50,000, while linemen and kickers figured out how to be happy with $10,000.

Not everyone took the cash. Ornstein offered Barry Sanders $200,000 a year for two years for his group licensing rights. He passed. Ornstein had never seen a guy walk away from $400,000. Reggie White, who was becoming a leader in the Players Association and was a lead plaintiff in one of the lawsuits, held out, too. Other Players Association figures proved far more malleable. By the time Ornstein's spending spree was over, he had signed 1,100 players, spending $36 million over two years. The spigot funding the Players Association's antitrust lawsuit hadn't run dry yet, but at the rate Ornstein was signing players, it was going to before too long.

*On a winter morning in 1993, Judge David Doty of the US Dis-*trict Court in Minnesota called the top NFL and Players Association executives and lawyers into his chambers for a conference. A stack of papers sat on Doty's desk. Doty had spent most of the fall listening to arguments in the antitrust suit, a class-action case in which the Eagles' star defensive lineman Reggie White claimed the NFL had illegally limited his freedom throughout his career.

The previous summer, the nearly bankrupt Players Association had scored a huge victory when a Minnesota jury ruled unanimously that the NFL had violated antitrust laws with its "Plan B" free agency system. That system had replaced the so-called Rozelle rule under which the commissioner determined compensation for any team that lost a player to free agency. Under Plan B, teams could protect the best thirty-seven players on their roster. The other sixteen, the ultimate runts in the litter of fifty-three-man rosters, could become free agents. The Players Association had argued the system was too restrictive and violated the rights of the league's top players. Frank Rothman, the league's chief outside counsel, had told owners the case was a slam dunk for the league. After the decision, which went the other way and put the league on the hook for the Players Association's legal fees, the owners started referring to Rothman as "Slam-dunk Frankie." It was not a compliment. The NFL received one reprieve: the decision covered only the eight players who were part of the lawsuit. Almost immediately, White filed his class-action suit on behalf of all players to force universal free agency.

Now, as that litigation wore on, the two sides remained far apart on a settlement. As the lawyers and executives filed into Doty's chambers, they could see the judge wasn't happy. Doty pointed to the stack of papers on his desk. *There's a decision sitting right there,* Doty told them, *and no one is going to like it. Do yourselves a favor before you subject yourselves to God knows how many more years of litigation. Settle your differences so I don't have to settle them for you.* No one in the room needed to hear anything else—not the owners, who weren't having much luck in court, and not the Players Association, which was quickly running out of cash and couldn't afford more years in court.

Before long the two sides unveiled the first collective bargaining agreement in six years. The players got free agency, but they paid a heavy price for it after so many of them had signed away the union's war chest and leverage. Payrolls were capped at $34.6 million, or a little more than 50 percent of NFL revenues. That ceiling was hard, too. Unlike the NBA, where teams could exceed the salary cap without repercussions by re-signing their own players, the NFL limit had no exceptions. Also, true free agency could be achieved only after four years, which became the definition of an NFL veteran. But teams could still tie up one veteran, presumably their best one, by giving him their "franchise" or "transitional" player tag. That entitled the player to the average salary of the top players at his position, but it also allowed the owners to prevent top players from setting the market through open bidding the way Catfish Hunter had. Contracts weren't guaranteed. Top players could be cut at any time. Individual teams didn't have to turn over audited financial statements to the Players Association. Salaries would rise as league revenues increased, but the owners would figure out ways to make their revenue growth look far less substantial than it was. The agreement would be extended four times with little pushback from the players. As the concussion crisis would later reveal, pension and post-career health benefits would remain de minimus for most of the next decades. Indeed, the NFL system would become a model for other sports, but not in the way any athlete would have hoped.

The NFL had figured out the weakness of the modern athlete and how to use that greed and ego to its advantage. The NFL's biggest stars had read all the hyperbolic headlines about their talents and believed every word. Money and fame and the power they can produce were suddenly available and proved absurdly tempting, even irresistible, just as they still do. NFL players had understood they were the golden geese, and then they allowed themselves to get cooked. They wouldn't be the last great athletes to make those mistakes. Fortunately for their sakes, and for the sakes of so many others in a variety of sports who made similar missteps, the industry was so big and so mature that it had ceased to be a zero-sum game. Labor wars were about to become battles between millionaires and billionaires, and, barring some disastrous personal misjudgment or mistake, ultimately everyone was going to make out all right.

9

The Joy of Shooting and the Nike-ization of Sports

In 1962, a former college runner by the name of Phil Knight began selling running shoes he imported from Japan out of the trunk of his car at track meets. Knight was a disciple of Bill Bowerman, the legendary track coach at the University of Oregon, who believed that American-made shoes were too heavy and clunky to help produce optimal performances. Together, they began to spread the gospel of a company named Blue Ribbon Sports, which had footwear that could make athletes run faster and stay healthier than ever before. Then one morning after breakfast, Bowerman took a close look at the waffle iron his wife used in their kitchen. There it was—the design of the sole of a lightweight running shoe that could provide the cushion, spring, and responsiveness that all serious runners searched for in the only piece of equipment that mattered in their sport. He poured rubber into the waffle iron, and an amazing thing happened—his idea turned out to be right. By the 1970s, Blue Ribbon Sports had become Nike, a company based in the progressive wilds of Oregon, and the company's shoes were on the feet of America's greatest middle-distance runner, Steve Prefontaine. By the end of the decade, John McEnroe, suddenly the greatest tennis player on the planet, was wearing them. To wear a Nike shoe meant something more than being very good at a sport and wanting the best equipment. It was about being an individual, even a rebel—or better yet, a superhero. But team sports don't allow for individuals and rebels. Or do they?

The basketball game was a blowout from the start. After just five minutes, the collection of well-groomed, well-read, and well-led players from the elite northeastern university were up 16–4. Their opponents from the state college in the heartland never had a chance.

The game was basically an exhibition, a third-place contest from back in the days before the NCAA realized that forcing the two semifinal losers to hang around and play again after their dreams of a championship had been dashed bordered on cruel and unusual punishment. That the game meant almost nothing only made the experience worse for the guys on the short end of the scoreboard. At halftime, the deficit stood at 14. With nine minutes to play it had stretched to 84–58, and the star of the game had 32 points.

This was supposed to be the moment when the coach of the team in the lead began to replace his veteran starters, especially his seniors, to let them bathe in the adulation as they made one last walk from the court to the bench at the end of a fine career. But on this day, this coach and his star player had something else in mind: a triumphant exit that would celebrate the act of the ball falling through the basketball hoop as it had never been celebrated before.

Despite the 32-point lead, the star did not take a seat on the bench. He returned to the court and very quickly dropped in another 8 points. The lead stretched further, and still he kept shooting. There were buckets from the left side and the right, a jumper from the top of the key, a wild hook shot from the right corner, a short pop from the middle of the lane, and then one more from the right corner before finally, mercifully, the coach called for his hero's walk to the bench.

When the final buzzer sounded, the score of this mostly meaningless game was 118–82. The hero had dropped in 58 points, including 26 in the final nine minutes and 16 in the final five minutes. The scoring spree allowed him to rewrite the NCAA tournament record books. He finished with 177 points, a stunning accomplishment for an era when college basketball had no three-point shot and no shot clock.

Even more stunning, perhaps, is the identity of the man who put on that exhibition. It wasn't some playground showboat known for hot-dogging his way across the hardwood. It was Bill Bradley of Princeton University, whose image as the ultimate gentleman and student-athlete somehow survived the beating he and his Princeton Tigers inflicted on the Wichita State Shockers in March of 1965. A Rhodes scholarship at Oxford, two NBA championships with the Knicks, and a distinguished career as a three-term US senator from New Jersey probably had something to do with that.

Still, what does it say about the nature of basketball if even someone of Bradley's pedigree, the son of a banker whose identity has always been intertwined with the highest standards of sportsmanship, can so easily turn a consolation game into a stage for personal accomplishments and showmanship?

Bradley grew up in Crystal City, Missouri. He was an A student and excelled in both baseball and basketball, which he played

about nine months a year, taking off three months for spring baseball season. He spent hours each day shooting and dribbling alone,
imagining game situations in his head. A coach named Ed Macau-
ley told him whenever he wasn't practicing, someone else was.
Once he heard those words, Bradley could never get them out of
his head.

About sixty schools recruited Bradley. He chose Duke during
his senior year and graduated from high school with every intention of matriculating in Durham at the end of the summer.
Bradley's parents wanted him to travel a little before he started
college, though, and they sent him to a summer program at Oxford University in England. Bradley, who was the only boy in
the program, fell in love with the university. He grew determined
to figure out how to get back. That's when he learned about the
Rhodes scholarships, given to college seniors who exemplify academic excellence and leadership. Being a great athlete doesn't
hurt, either. Rhodes scholars spend two years at Oxford. They
study whatever they want. For a book nerd like Bradley, that
sounded like heaven.

Bradley did a little research and learned that Princeton produced more Rhodes scholars than any other college. When he got
home, he persuaded his father to help him secure last-minute admission into Princeton's freshman class, a spot he'd been offered
months earlier when basketball coach Butch van Breda Kolff recruited him. Bradley didn't contact van Breda Kolff, however. The
coach didn't know the young star had decided to attend Princeton
instead of Duke until he ran into him on campus during the first
week of classes.

Bradley became an All-American at Princeton, a campus hero,
the subject of newspaper and magazine profiles and writer John
McPhee's first book. He won his Rhodes scholarship, and when the
Knicks drafted him in the spring of 1965, he told them he was done

with basketball. He was headed to Oxford to begin his path toward a career as a diplomat.

During Bradley's first months at Oxford, an Italian club team asked him to play with them. He figured *Why not?* and helped the team win the European championship. Along the way they beat a Russian squad made up mostly of the players who had won the silver medal at the 1964 Olympics, where Bradley and the Americans had won the gold. After that, Bradley decided he really was done with basketball. He read books. He wrote. He barely exercised. He put on thirty pounds. A man who had set his calendar and daily clock according to a series of games and practices since the time he'd been a small boy was suddenly free.

Some nine months later, Oxford opened a new gym that had an actual basketball hoop, a rarity in England, where the game has never caught on. Unable to resist, Bradley began making his way down to the gym a few times a week, not to play in any kind of organized game, but to run around alone and shoot. In his mind, an announcer would narrate his movements: *Bradley dribbles into the corner, shoots from twenty feet—it's good . . . Bradley drives the lane, fakes to his left, and lays it in with his right hand . . .*

It felt good to shoot again—really good. He was twenty-three years old, a gifted athlete with a chance to make a living in a way most people would kill for. He began to accept the idea that basketball accounted for more of his identity than any other thing he did. He decided that to not play would be to deny an essential part of his being. Diplomacy and politics could wait. Professional basketball could not.

Bradley put in a call to the Knicks, who still owned his rights. The two sides discussed a contract that would pay Bradley one of the highest salaries in the league at the time. Bradley wanted nearly $200,000 a year. It was far more than the Knicks wanted to spend. When the negotiations stalled, the Knicks proposed a solution: a salary of $180,000, but the team wanted 25 percent of all commercial endorsement income that Bradley received. A Princeton graduate, a Rhodes scholar, a white star in the country's largest market at a time long before Madison Avenue began partnering with black athletes, Bradley seemed like a lock to earn nearly as much in ancillary income as he did on the court. Bradley saw the situation much differently. He had no interest in hawking toothpaste or soft drinks or beer or a bank or anything else. Commercials would detract from the game and his enjoyment of it. He had already decided he wouldn't do any commercial unless it used the whole team. For Bradley, conceding 25 percent of his endorsement income was easy, since 25 percent of nothing was nothing.

Few who remember the glory years of Bradley's career, those championship springs of 1970 and 1973, realize just how ramshackle the NBA was back then, or recall the early failures, those first months as a Knick when he looked too slow and plodding, too unathletic, too prone to missing easy shots. For the first time in his life, Bradley failed at something. There was only one solution: work harder. Bradley believed he could be a great NBA player, although the life of even the greatest of NBA players in the 1960s wasn't all that great. At home, the Knicks' locker room attendants took care of laundering the uniforms. On the road, the players did. Each player got two road uniforms and bore responsibility for keeping them clean. In those less-than-glamorous days, Bradley usually went through three pairs of canvas high-tops in a season. LeBron James and plenty of other NBA stars today wear a new pair every night.

In his book *Life on the Run*, Bradley described the apotheosis of his sport as a communal ballet. "I believe that basketball, when a certain level of unselfish team play is realized, can serve as a kind of metaphor for ultimate cooperation. It is a sport where success, as symbolized by the championship, requires that the dictates of community prevail over selfish impulses. An exceptional player is simply one point on a five-pointed star. Statistics—such as points, rebounds, or assists per game—can never explain the remarkable range of human interaction that takes place on a successful pro team."

So how does the man who penned those words, the ultimate gentleman/scholar/athlete/senator/writer, reconcile all the values he represented with the player who ran up the score on an outgunned Wichita State team in a meaningless game to set personal records? That answer provides a context for how the NBA evolved to today's spectacle that is at once both incredibly thrilling and incredibly irritating. When Bradley thinks back to the Wichita State game, he sees a twenty-two-year-old trying to go out on top. "It was about midway through the first half and I was playing my game, passing and trying to get the other players involved. Then van Breda Kolff calls a timeout and with everybody standing in the huddle he looks at me and he says, 'It's your last game, your last opportunity to score in your career. Shoot the damn ball!' So that's what I did, and that's what that game became. I guess you'd say it was the joy of shooting."

For some, basketball is about the joy of passing and rebounding. But at its core basketball really is all about the joy of shooting. That's what it was for Bill Bradley, and later for Larry Bird and Michael Jordan, and now that's what it is for LeBron James. That's also what it was a for a slew of eighteen-year-olds who rejected the traditions of a sport in which the best teams have always been able to balance the cooperation required to break down an opponent with the magical talents of an individual player. The game, the National Basketball Association itself, was built around that balance—until suddenly it wasn't.

Jumping to the NBA from high school as an eighteen-year-old,

a trend that lasted from the mid-1990s until 2006, came to symbolize the environment that drove it. A collection of teenage phenoms
believed their stories and their sneaker commercials were at least
as important as how they actually played. That's the story the numbers on the paychecks told them. Then, after all those temptations
and emotions that were writ so large in the NBA of Michael, Magic,
and Larry, it also became the story that corrupted so many others
in so many other sports.

The modern NBA—the league that has existed since about 1980
or so—may be unique among the major US sports in that its creation myths are actually extremely accurate.

In the late 1970s there was a pro basketball league that had
image and financial problems. Recreational drug use was rampant.
Teams hemorrhaged money. The league's main television partner
broadcast the championship series on tape delay. Corporations
thought the league was too black for white America to embrace it.
Then a sharp New York lawyer named David Stern became commissioner. Stern believed in the extraordinary athletic talents of
the league's players, these oversized men who could fly through
the air like ballet dancers and hit jump shots from thirty feet away
with an opponent's hands in their face. He thought they were un-
derappreciated and the world should embrace them regardless of
their skin color. Then came two terrific players, Magic Johnson
and Larry Bird, who could carry that message to the people who
needed to hear it most: America's television networks, packaged
goods conglomerates, banks, and car dealers. Stern wanted to
recruit them to invest in the league. He persuaded them to buy
sponsorships, commercials, pricey courtside seats, and luxury
suites. A few years later the greatest player and greatest messenger
of all arrived. Michael Jordan flew like no one else flew, smiled

like no one else smiled, and possessed an unmatched fire to win basketball games.

Jordan entered the league in 1984. By the time he and the Chicago Bulls got good enough to win championships, in 1991, NBA basketball had become the hottest sports property in the world. Soccer was more popular internationally and probably always will be. NFL football had its lock on the American autumn. But the NBA had become the ultimate growth stock, a captivating, aesthetically remarkable mix of sports, art, and theater perfectly presented by the NBC Sports chairman, Dick Ebersol, in a neat, immensely profitable corporate package. Within a span of fifteen years, the drug-riddled NBA that couldn't get its championship on live television became the world's model sports organization. Jordan stood at the pinnacle, a $50-million-a-year juggernaut who hawked everything from Gatorade to underwear. Once Michael Jordan took over, everyone wanted to be Michael Jordan, or rather the idea of Michael Jordan, the modern superhero who ruled the world in basketball shoes. It was just how Sonny Vaccaro thought it should be.

John Paul "Sonny" Vaccaro is a fast-talking Italian-American gym rat from western Pennsylvania. He may also be the most overlooked character in the creation of Michael Jordan, or at least the Michael Jordan who the public came to know. In 1965, Vaccaro started a high school all-star game called the Dapper Dan Roundball Classic, which began in Pittsburgh. The Dapper Dan became a launching point for a series of high-performance basketball camps Vaccaro ran. The camps and the Dapper Dan gave Vaccaro a view of basketball's growth from the ground up. Interest in the game and the athleticism of the players were undoubtedly growing, but Vaccaro could see the essential piece of basketball equipment, the shoe, was stuck somewhere in the late 1950s. Basketball shoes of the late 1970s were canvas or suede and offered little support to the feet of the biggest human beings on the planet.

Sensing an opportunity, Vaccaro called an Italian friend who was a shoemaker. Vaccaro proposed making leather sneakers with a Velcro strap around the ankle to provide additional support. Once he had a prototype, Vaccaro bought a plane ticket to Portland, Oregon, where he met with executives of an upstart company named Nike. He hoped to persuade them to manufacture his shoes. The trip turned out to be a good one for Vaccaro, though not for his shoes. Nike didn't care much for Vaccaro's prototype. The company had its own ideas about footwear technology and didn't need any guidance on that front. But Nike liked Vaccaro. The company needed help getting its shoes onto the feet of kids who were hooked on Converse and Pumas, like the ones Walt Frazier wore for the Knicks. Nike knew Vaccaro ran the Dapper Dan. If Nike could somehow persuade the best high school players in the country to wear its basketball shoes, they just might catch on.

Vaccaro told Nike this was an easy problem to solve. College basketball coaches were the key. A company couldn't tell a kid what shoes to wear, but a college basketball coach could. Vaccaro spent a lot of time talking to these men about recruits. Vaccaro told the assembled Nike executives they could simply pay the coaches and give the shoes away for free. It was simple, cheap marketing, because college kids would wear Nike sneakers on television.

Vaccaro started with Jerry Tarkanian at Nevada–Las Vegas. Then he got Norm Ellenberger at New Mexico, then Jim Valvano at North Carolina State, and then he got everybody. By 1981, Nike had roughly eighty college teams wearing its shoes. The only problem arose when the best players left college and started wearing a different shoe in the NBA. That damaged Nike's credibility and led to an obvious conclusion: it was time to start thinking about trying to sign some high draft picks to major endorsement deals.

Executives scanned the 1984 draft class. The company had set a budget of $500,000 for signing the new crop of future NBA stars. Now they had to figure out where to place their bets. Pro drafts are a crapshoot. No one really knows with any certainty who will become the next Michael Jordan or the next Sam Bowie, the Kentucky center the Portland Trailblazers drafted before the Chicago Bulls took Jordan. Bowie suffered from a series of leg injuries and barely had a pro career.

The Nike brain trust gathered at an off-site meeting to go through the alternatives. Rob Strasser, the company's second in command, was there, as was Howard Slusher, a longtime confidant of Nike founder Phil Knight. So was Vaccaro. A huge Georgetown fan and a friend of then head coach John Thompson, Vaccaro had been in the stands when Jordan hit the winning shot in the final seconds against the Hoyas in the 1982 NCAA championship game. He'd known Jordan as a high school star. He liked his smile. Conventional wisdom said to take the $500,000 and sign a few players. Vaccaro had another idea: give it all to Jordan. That's how the revolution started.

Vaccaro is occasionally prone to overstatement, especially where his own impact on the sports world is concerned, but there is a pretty solid consensus that Vaccaro persuaded the Nike power structure to put all its eggs in Jordan's basket. Far more important than who did or didn't want to make the bet on Jordan is what happened once the bet was placed. When a company like Nike, even the 1984 version of Nike, commits all of its basketball resources to a single player, the investment goes well beyond a player wearing a Swoosh on his sneakers. It involves billboards and television commercials and personal appearances and a near-obsessive commitment to make the company and the player synonymous. Almost overnight, and certainly once he started flying through the air dunking basketballs in the fall of 1984, Jordan morphed into the symbol of the company, encapsulated by that spread-eagle icon that remains ubiquitous long after he last shot a basketball. Jordan averaged 28.2 points and 6.5 rebounds his rookie year. Two years after that heroic debut, Jim Riswold, a creative director at the Portland ad firm Wieden + Kennedy, began crafting a series of Spike Lee–directed ads depicting Lee's alter ego, Mars Blackmon, from the movie *She's Gotta Have It*, and his obsession about his favorite basketball player. "It's gotta be the shoes" that made Jordan so good, Lee/Blackmon insisted. The cinematic commercial campaign was an instant hit.

Jordan was quickly becoming a new kind of star. He perfectly fit Nike founder Phil Knight's vision of the athlete as superhero, someone who can inspire the masses like no one else—and persuade them to buy a lot of sneakers and sportswear. In the fall of 1987, when Nike and Jordan signed his second contract, the deal called for an $18 million guarantee over seven years and a 5 percent royalty on all Jordan shoe sales. Knight didn't bat an eye. Neither did the seventeen other companies that would sign Jordan up during the next ten years, with fees beginning at $500,000 a year and rising, depending on Jordan's level of commitment.

Jordan was an easy sell. By the early 1990s he was very simply far better at basketball than anyone else in the world. He and the Bulls won the first of three consecutive championships in 1991 while Jordan pulled in roughly $30 million per year in salary and endorsements. Three decades after Arnold Palmer won his battle with Wilson, Jordon was following in that tradition by collecting what the market would bear for his extraordinary talents. What separated Jordan from nearly everyone who came after him is that somehow a generation of basketball players misinterpreted what it meant to "Be Like Mike." Even Jordan himself noted at the height of his superstardom in the 1990s that something very strange had happened: "Phil [Knight] and Nike have turned me into a dream."

Jordan averaged more than 30 points per game from 1986 until 1993. As astonishing as Jordan's individual statistics were, his Bulls didn't win a championship in any season in which he led the NBA in scoring. Jordan truly emerged as a world beater once he began playing in the triangle offense, a system of passing and ball sharing that involves constant motion to create a series of offensive options on every play. That story line doesn't sell shoes, or Gatorade, or underwear, though. Superheroes do, and creating the myth that a basketball player can be a superhero, and a very wealthy one at that, shifted not only the way kids began to think about basketball but how the game itself would evolve over the next fifteen years.

How do you tell an extraordinarily talented teenager that he should risk tens of millions of dollars toiling for a season or two at a college where he has to study subjects he has never been interested in and probably never will be instead of signing a life-altering professional contract with both a basketball team and a shoe company? You can't. Well, you can, but it's a safe bet he won't listen to you. Jordan shifted the way teenage basketball players thought about how they might be able to develop their talents and build their careers. Then he changed the way athletes in other sports began to think of themselves and how they could develop both commercially and athletically. The kind of money that Jordan was making off the court suddenly made college seem like an unnecessary risk. It wasn't that NBA starting salaries were so terrific, but with Jordan producing hundreds of millions of dollars in profits for Nike, every shoe company became desperate to find "the next

Michael Jordan." That made them willing to place Jordan-sized bets on eighteen-year-olds they believed could become NBA stars without going to college.

"Our money was more than the NBA was paying," said Vaccaro, who jumped from Nike to rival adidas and later Reebok with orders to find the next M.J. "Of course they were going to skip college."

Former big men Moses Malone and Darryl Dawkins had jumped directly from high school to the NBA during the 1970s. Through the 1980s it seemed only teenagers with Malone's and Dawkins's massive bodies could hold up physically against the men of the NBA. Even players with the physical foundation to make it in the NBA, such as Patrick Ewing or Hakeem Olajuwon, followed the traditional route of spending two to four years in college. It was the safest way to guarantee a big NBA payoff at twenty-two.

In the era of Jordan, the equation shifted. Kevin Garnett, a six-foot, eleven-inch forward-center, jumped right to the NBA in 1995. The following year, Kobe Bryant, a swingman out of suburban Philadelphia, made the leap. New television contracts had allowed deals with new draft picks to skyrocket. Garnett earned a total of $5.2 million during his first three years. Kobe Bryant got $3.5 million during his.

Those numbers were just the start. Shaquille O'Neal, who entered the league after spending two years at Louisiana State University, received a $40 million guaranteed shoe contract from Reebok before he even stepped on an NBA court. Bryant and Garnett received similar deals. And it wasn't just the size of the deals; it was the marketing that went along with them. Overnight, Shaquille O'Neal became Superman. As Vaccaro put it, "The characters they played were bigger than the ones they actually were."

That was no accident. In 1992, Knight explained that for years Nike had thought of itself as "a production-oriented company, meaning we put all our emphasis on designing and manufacturing the product." But the Jordan boom helped Nike understand that the most important thing the company did was market the product. "We've come around to saying that Nike is a marketing-oriented company, and the product is our most important marketing tool."

In other words, Jordan didn't simply shift the market; he shifted the dominant psychology of his sport—and every sport. Pro basketball no longer existed as a quest for championships. David Stern created the modern NBA as a stage for the individual acrobatic exploits of a handful of outrageously gifted and very large athletes. The strategy proved wildly successful. Audiences for NBA playoff basketball began to demolish those for playoff baseball. The question no one seemed to be thinking about, however, was this: what happens when the focus becomes individual play and the financial rewards it can produce?

For the NBA, the greatest manifestation of teenage desperation for superstardom became the cavalcade of high school players who declared their intention to skip college and go directly into the pro ranks after Bryant did, and the need for these players to prove themselves as individuals. The league had no mechanism to prevent this. In 1971 it lost the so-called Spencer Haywood case, named for the collegiate All-American and NBA journeyman who sued for the right to leave college before he had exhausted his college eligibility. After that, the NBA adopted the "hardship rule," which essentially stated that players could apply to enter the draft if they could prove they needed the money. The league never rejected an application.

As salaries for star veterans rose, however, so, too, did the amount teams had to commit for signing the top draft picks. In 1985, center Patrick Ewing signed an unprecedented six-year, $17 million contract that set a new standard for rookies. Committing that amount of money isn't all that risky when it goes to a highly skilled seven-foot center who has carried his college team to four Final Fours, three championship games, and one championship. It's a much bigger risk when it goes to an eighteen-year-old who has done little more than crush the competition through high school. It's almost impossible for a bad team to get good in the NBA without getting a top draft pick. If a team blows that pick gambling on a teenager, the move can set the franchise back both competitively and financially for years.

To minimize that risk, in 1999 the NBA bargained with the Players Association for a rookie wage scale for draft picks. Drafted players had to sign a three-year contract at a predetermined salary on a sliding scale. The top pick earned the most, the next pick somewhat less, and so on. While the league's intention was to minimize risk for the franchises, the effect of the new agreement was to increase it. Sure, the wage scale limited the initial payout, but the three-year limit on the initial contract incentivized players to try to get into the league as quickly as possible regardless of their level of skill. Unintentionally, the league was telling players that the most important thing is to get to your second contract as quickly as possible, because that's where the real money would be. If the big payday is three years away, the idea is to start the clock ticking as soon as possible.

Soon a highly touted player might get a strike against him if he decided to go to college or, even more shockingly, stay in college for more than a single year, sparking rumors that something might be wrong. If you really thought you were good, you had to show it by going straight to the NBA whether you were ready or not, said Russ Granik, the league's deputy commissioner at the time. "Everyone was going to be pushed."

So a system that would produce LeBron James, the man-child who quickly became the planet's greatest basketball player and one of its most recognizable stars, and other teenage sensations such as Jermaine O'Neal, the forward who began at Portland and starred for the Indiana Pacers, and Toronto draftee and Houston star Tracy McGrady also ended up producing such underachievers as Kwame Brown, Sebastian Telfair, Al Harrington, and Tyson Chandler. All arrived raw but with guaranteed shoe contracts that may or may not have disincentivized them from working as hard as they could to maximize their talents. Telfair, a star high school guard out of Brooklyn, has said repeatedly that in retrospect he never would have signed a multimillion-dollar shoe contract. The guaranteed money made him feel like he could cut corners in his training.

Beyond the financial risks, the bum rush of teenagers created an image problem for the NBA. There was something unseemly about NBA scouts showing up at scholastic and AAU travel team games to evaluate fifteen-year-olds. The other big problem, however, was how these players and everyone else in the league began to play as they tried immediately to prove that they could live up to all the "next Michael Jordan" hype that smothered so many of them.

Let's set aside the societal questions involved in a high school player skipping college for the NBA, which can be—and have been—argued endlessly. The biggest problem for the league was that the height of the teen influx into the NBA, from the late 1990s until 2006, coincided with some of the most miserable basketball that has ever been played in a league that is supposed to represent the highest form of the sport. It was a time when so many players, especially the younger stars, fell victim to the ills of that "joy of shooting."

At its highest level, basketball is about motion and ball sharing. It's five players zigzagging and moving the ball up the court without it ever touching the floor, save for the artfully delivered bounce pass. It is a symbiotic, high-speed dance that carries the possibility of crushing physicality with every possession, whether it's two mammoth human beings battling for a rebound or one streaking in from the sideline for a climactic dunk. Basketball falls apart on an aesthetic level and becomes a cynical exercise when an offense becomes reliant on a single player, isolating him with the ball and sending his four floormates to the other side of the court to maximize the amount of room he has to maneuver.

Advanced analytics don't go back to the pre–Michael Jordan era, but estimates of the number of isolation plays teams ran then hover around 5 percent. In 2004 a company called Synergy Sports began tracking isolation plays. By 2005, teams were setting up an isolation-based attack at the rim nearly 15 percent of their trips up the floor. The Orlando Magic led the way, running isolation plays every fifth time up the floor. Assists plummeted, from nearly fifty per game in 1992–93, to just forty-one per game in 2005–2006. The thirteen lowest assists-per-game totals during the past thirty years have all occurred since 2000.

Beyond aesthetics, the results of isolation proved remarkably ineffective. Scoring collapsed. During the 1992–93 season, NBA teams combined for an average of 210.5 points per game. By the 2003–2004 season, they averaged 186.8 points per game, a thirty-year low for a full season, even though the league had changed the rules on how teams could play defense two years earlier to try to encourage more scoring.

The tendency to run isolation plays has been dropping since 2007, one year after the NBA enacted the rule prohibiting players from entering the NBA draft until one year after their high school graduation. This is the moment where any stat-head should raise his hand to point out that correlation does not necessarily imply causation. But is it purely happenstance that an era of professional basketball so heavily focused on individualism coincided so directly with a period when, almost overnight, there was so much money to be made from becoming an instant superstar?

At the center of this dynamic has always been an Oregon-based shoe company named Nike. Of course, Nike isn't the only company that uses advertising to turn celebrity endorsers into silly myths, but the company has long been at the core of the mythmaking revolution. Its mythmaking machine and its occasionally ruinous effects are hardly limited to basketball. Nike's annual revenue in 2013 was more than $24 billion. The company spends about $1 billion annually in endorsements.

The kings of mythmaking and its competitors have turned legend creation into an extremely profitable art form, even though it remains fraught with pitfalls, for basketball players and for all the other athletes who have volunteered for the kind of legend creation that has turned into a punch line so often lately. Somewhere between Arnold Palmer, the Quarterback Club, and Michael Jordan, too many athletes forgot that performance was supposed to serve as the foundation for their success both on and off the field, and that the object of sport is to win, not to become famous.

Where to start? Two words perfectly sum up all the absurdity: Lance Armstrong. Remember the commercials? "What am I on?" Armstrong asked in a voice-over to images of him pounding his pedals. "I'm on my bike, busting my ass six hours a day."

In 2012 the company dropped Lance Armstrong after doping authorities stripped him of his Tour de France titles. So much for those Nike commercials that helped Armstrong thumb his nose at accusations that he was cheating.

By the time of Armstrong's downfall, conversations like that one had become somewhat routine at Nike. Anyone who has had access to a newspaper knows this wasn't the first time some member of the company's stable of galactic sports figures has been a target of serious allegations. Among other Nike-sponsored athletes, NFL quarterback Michael Vick pleaded guilty in 2007 to federal dogfighting charges and served time in prison. Marion Jones went to jail after being convicted of lying to a grand jury about her use of performance-enhancing drugs. Tiger Woods apologized publicly for his involvement in a string of highly publicized extramarital affairs, even though his image crafters portrayed him as the ultimate family man. Former Penn State football coach Joe Paterno, the man Nike taught us to believe was the symbol of collegiate sports integrity, was fired by the school after reports emerged about the behavior of his former assistant coach, Jerry Sandusky, who was convicted of sexually abusing children for years while Paterno looked the other way.

Oscar Pistorius, the double-amputee runner from South Africa known as the "Blade Runner" for the prosthetic feet he wears in competition, appeared in multiple advertisements for Nike. He was hailed as track's leading human rights activist, an athlete with a disability who simply wanted to race with the fastest of the fast. The Nike myth machine had gotten so powerful that no one raised the obvious question of how Pistorius could help the company's biggest product. After all, he didn't wear shoes. That didn't seem to matter, though. One commercial showed him uncoiling from a start with the tag line, "I am the bullet in the chamber." Another contained images of the best of South Africa's athletes with a voiceover that pronounces, "My body is my weapon. . . . This is my weapon, this is how I fight."

In 2014, Pistorius was found guilty in the shooting death of his girlfriend, the fashion model Reeva Steenkamp. The shoe company's sponsorship deal with the athlete, and the unfortunate content of those ads, prompted a lot of uncomfortable questions for Nike. After Pistorius's arrest in 2013, his agent, Peet van Zyl, had to scramble to connect with Nike's top executives to figure out how to align the myth of Pistorius to the harsher reality that suddenly emerged: Oscar Pistorius is, after all, not such a great guy.

Through it all, the company has stayed a course centered on inspiration. Nike's $3.2 billion annual marketing budget carries massive cultural influence. Its endorsement commitments through the life of the current contracts are worth some $4 billion, or about 15 percent of its annual revenue. In the past it has been noted that when a Nike athlete falls to earth, the company's fortunes continue to soar. Nike's revenue more than doubled from 2003 to 2013. Nike maintains nearly 60 percent market share in running shoes and nearly 90 percent in basketball shoes.

After the Pistorius arrest, a Nike spokeswoman acknowledged, "Athletes are human and they do make mistakes but we still believe they inspire people and continue to do so every day."

Since 1984, when Nike boldly decided to offer nearly all of its basketball marketing budget to a single player and build a marketing campaign around Michael Jordan, the company has never wavered in that inspiration-heavy approach. But as major stars are unmasked, or the quality of play in a sport diminishes as its priorities shift, the time comes to reevaluate the strategy of mythmaking, no matter how irresistible it might be, and to acknowledge that the process Mark McCormack set in motion can go too far.

"This is the biggest lesson to learn: that there really aren't heroes," Jason Richardson, a hurdler who won a silver medal in London, said in the wake of the Pistorius arrest. "We're too quick to elevate people into these hero roles and they're not allowed to be human."

There is a sense that Nike somehow changed the rules of athletic success in a crass and craven way. Some accuse the company of commoditizing fame. The size of one's Nike contract—or, to be fair, contracts with other athletic apparel companies—has become another form of scorekeeping for the modern athlete, alongside things like the size of their playing contracts or the number of Twitter followers they have. This kind of scorekeeping often outstrips the one that is supposed to matter the most—the one that tracks the action on the field of play. The thing about Nike and so many other apparel companies that rarely gets acknowledged is that they don't sell shoes, or even athletes, as much as they buy and sell stories, narratives, fairy tales. They aren't shoe companies as much as they are dream factories—a condition of the aspirational mind.

Fans get most turned off when success isn't merely about winning and when sports aren't about the traditional forms of scorekeeping—things like trophies collected, points scored, bouts won, consecutive games played, or years of loyalty to a single team. Yet the hype machine rolls on. As Nike built the mythic cartoon character known as Michael Jordan, the ultimate measure of any competitor became something else entirely: how irresistible his story is. Jordan, the greatest basketball player ever, claims to have been cut from a high school team. Not really. He played junior varsity as a freshman and made varsity beginning in his sophomore year after he sprouted like a weed.

Nike doesn't make racing bikes. It signed Armstrong because he had survived cancer and come back to win the most grueling race in the world. Please check your brain at the door and don't ask how. It didn't sell golf clubs when it signed Tiger Woods. Nike brought him aboard because he was a potentially transformative star who had the ability to break down racial barriers in the world's most staid sport. (Worth noting: Tiger Woods won a lot of tournaments but had very little effect on minority golf participation.)

Stories are now the currency of the sports business. It's the world Roone Arledge created. In this world Oscar Pistorius can become the equivalent of a blank check. He's the kid who lost his lower legs before he could walk and was told he would never be able to play sports. He's the rare athlete who didn't just challenge our notions of fitness; he forced us to reconsider the definition of disability. There were undoubtedly moments when he, too, felt that joy of individual triumph that Bill Bradley couldn't resist. Yet if athletes don't want to let every ounce of power their predecessors fought for slip away in this post-McCormack world, here's what Pistorius and others desperately need to remember, whether they are juiced-up baseball players or the cleanest-cut young girls trying to make the US women's national soccer team: as the Nike lord Phil Knight himself once put it, "People will eventually find out if you try to sell them a dishonest product."

10

There They Go Again

In June of 2001, Leo Hindery entered a suite at the Loews Regency Hotel to see one of the kings of New York, George M. Steinbrenner III, the owner of the Yankees and the man known as "the Boss." Nearly everyone who worked with and for Steinbrenner during his nearly four-decade reign as the emperor of the most famous franchise in American sports addressed him as "Mr. Steinbrenner," especially in the early part of a relationship, and even when speaking about him. Hindery barely knew Steinbrenner. He was some twenty years younger than the Boss. He was a product of the West and had made his fortune in the pioneering days of the cable television industry, where honorifics didn't exist. Leo reached out his hand and said hello to "George."

If ever there was a time when Steinbrenner deserved to be happy, this was it. His Yankees had won three consecutive World Series and four of the previous five, the most sustained period of excellence the team had experienced in a half century. They had pulled this off in the era of free agency, when player movement was supposed to render dynasties impossible to sustain, even for a team like the Yankees that could outspend its rivals to buy the loyalties of the best players whenever they might become available. Steinbrenner had survived a suspension from baseball in the 1970s after he pleaded guilty to making illegal campaign contributions to Richard Nixon's reelection campaign. In 1991 he accepted a lifetime ban for paying a gambler to dig up dirt on his star outfielder Dave Winfield, only to have it lifted two years later, setting up a decadelong image rehabilitation campaign. Under the careful handling and guidance of the public relations wizard Howard J. Rubenstein, he morphed from an imperious tyrant into the ultimate competitor who would do and spend whatever it might take to win, all because that's what Yankees fans expected and supposedly deserved.

Yet when Hindery walked into Steinbrenner's suite at the Regency, the Boss was not happy at all. In fact he was pretty miserable, and he needed Hindery's help. Two years earlier, in 1999, Steinbrenner had joined forces with the owners of the New Jersey Nets, Raymond Chambers and Lewis Katz. Chambers, one of the creators of the leveraged buyout, had convinced Steinbrenner that he could unlock hidden value in his baseball team if he merged it with the Nets and created a sports empire. The idea was to control enough year-round television programming to launch a team-owned regional sports network that would air on cable. Like every other baseball team, the Yankees received a license fee each year for their local television rights. The annual payments from Cablevision's MSG Network were the largest in baseball, some $50 million, which gave the Yankees their huge spending advantage over the rest of the league. For years, Chambers and others had been explaining to Steinbrenner that if he launched his own network, his team could still collect an outsized rights fee and he could build equity in an asset whose value was sure to grow exponentially over the next decade as the cable business evolved. Cable channels with exclusive programming that could land on the basic platform every subscriber purchased had become the darlings of the media industry. The guaranteed monthly fees and long-term contracts that called for fee increases every year made these networks cash machines. Steinbrenner wouldn't even have to put up any cash. He could sell a part of the network to investors, who would fund the annual rights payments from the network to the teams in the first years until the money from the subscriber fees began to roll in. It all made plenty of sense. Chambers and Katz even promised to use their political connections in New Jersey to secure hundreds of millions of dollars in public funding for a fancy new arena for the Nets in downtown Newark, the city where Chambers had directed tens of millions of dollars in philanthropy. YankeeNets, as the combined company was known, hired Harvey Schiller, the former president of Turner Sports, as chief executive to make it all come to life. The Boss was going to be the king of an empire and a media mogul.

Two years after the merger, there was no arena and no network. Schiller, a former air force aviator, was failing miserably. Steinbrenner, notorious for keeping employees on the shortest of strings, had lost faith in him. YankeeNets needed adult supervision. Steinbrenner needed Leo Hindery.

Over coffee, Steinbrenner and Hindery shared stories of their respective upbringings. Steinbrenner, the product of a wealthy shipping and shipbuilding family, liked to make his childhood sound like a hardscrabble experience that included Culver Military Academy and the rough-and-tumble world of shipyards. In his view, he had pulled himself up by his bootstraps to land perhaps the most famous franchise in sports. The truth was he had a childhood of private education and privilege. He attended Williams College and enjoyed the kind of head start in business that can only come from inherited wealth. In 1973 he pulled together a group of investors to buy the Yankees for $8.8 million. Steinbrenner put up $100,000, enough to make him the managing general partner.

Hindery, meanwhile, really had experienced the kind of rough-and-tumble upbringing Steinbrenner could only fantasize about. Hindery grew up a loner in the Pacific Northwest. He wasn't dirt poor, but he wasn't comfortable, and he was taking odd jobs on farms near his home in the Seattle-Tacoma area when he was a young boy. He worked his way through high school, college at Seattle University, and business school at Stanford. Long before he became a cable executive, he was working in the merchant marine, handling sheet metal, and sorting packages for United Parcel. After business school, he spent a decade working for a mining company called Utah International. He started as the assistant to the CEO, did stints running mines in New Mexico, and eventually became the company's chief financial officer. In the 1980s he went to work for Chronicle, a book and newspaper publisher in San Francisco. Chronicle wanted to invest in the growing cable industry. That gave Hindery his entrée to cable titans like Bill Daniels and John Malone. These were Hindery's kind of people, risk takers who believed their work could change the world. He formed his own company, Inter-Media Partners, with $20,000 he had in the bank and Malone's support. Working with Malone, he helped launch a handful of regional sports networks, which he later sold to Rupert Murdoch's expanding News Corporation. He ended up running Malone's Tele-Communications, Inc., or TCI, one of the country's largest cable television distributors, from 1997 to 1999. In 1999 he sold it to AT&T for $52 billion—at the time, the largest deal in the history of the media industry. Hindery was fifty-two. His stock in the company allowed him to walk away with enough money to never work another day in his life. He could focus on his progressive political interests. He had an expensive hobby: racing his beloved Porsches. Now he could do that as often as he wanted as well.

He did both of those, pursuing a career as a professional race car driver and becoming one of the Democratic Party's top fund-raisers. But cable was the mistress he couldn't leave, not with Steinbrenner sitting across the coffee table from him, laying out what looked like a once-in-a-lifetime opportunity to rewrite the rules of the sports business.

Hindery liked Steinbrenner immediately. The feeling was mutual. Steinbrenner asked Hindery if he could help cure this network of its endless legal wrangling and get it off the ground. Hindery said he could. Could he figure out a way to persuade the cable companies to carry the channel? Yes, Hindery said, though he warned a tough fight lay ahead with Chuck and Jim Dolan, the father-son duo who controlled Cablevision and had a virtual monopoly on New York's regional sports networks. The Dolans owned the MSG Network and would fight the creation of a competitor at every turn. Eventually, they would have to give way, Hindery promised. Would Hindery back up his words with his wallet? Steinbrenner wanted to know. Hindery, who had created his fortune betting on himself two decades before, didn't want to do business any other way. He wanted skin in the game and would eventually cut a check for $15 million.

To Hindery, the story of sports during the past fifty years had really been a story about television and little else. The sports business thrived because the advertising industry figured out that sports are basically the only way to reach men between the ages of eighteen and fifty-four, who didn't watch prime-time television the way women did. If you wanted to reach the men, who bought beer and expensive cars and watches, you had to advertise during games.

As Hindery saw it, sports television had calendared the life of the country with events like the Olympic Games and annual behe-moths like Super Bowl Sunday. It created programming like *College GameDay, Sunday at the Masters, NCAA March Madness, Monday Night Football,* and *Breakfast at Wimbledon* (and later *Breakfast at Roland Garros*). Television had rescued entire leagues. Through the 1980s, British television broadcast just a single soccer game each year, the FA Cup final. Club owners feared that if their games were on television, especially the games between the best and most historic clubs, no one would buy a ticket to sit in the miserable British weather in what were then decrepit and dangerous British stadiums. It's possible they were right. As a child growing up in Liverpool in the 1970s, Roger Bennett, the British soccer commen-tator, went with his father to watch his beloved Everton Blues play at Goodison Park. Early in one game, as he stood on the ter-races, young Roger felt a warm trickle flowing down his back. A fan standing directly above him was urinating through a rolled-up magazine onto his neck—common behavior at an English soccer game at the time. Then, in 1992, Rupert Murdoch's money and the lords of the biggest clubs in English soccer created the English Premier League, now the top league of the world's most popu-lar sport, and cleaned up soccer in its birthplace. The television money, now about $7 billion a year, helped pay for stadium ren-ovations and foreign stars. By the first years of the twenty-first century, the wealthiest people in the world, such as the royal fam-ily of Abu Dhabi, Russian oligarch Roman Abramovich, and the developer and Walmart heir Stan Kroenke, were buying English soccer clubs.

Television had also funded the massive increases in the salaries of athletes. For nearly a century, ticket sales had been the main source of revenue in sports. As the millennium approached, televi-sion rights fees accounted for roughly half the money the world's biggest sports leagues collected. Today media money accounts for about 60 percent of the revenue in the NFL, which is roughly the same amount that owners spend on labor costs each year. Owners rode the rising tide of rights fee increases and saw the values of their teams improve over the decades. Now the question was whether an iconic sports team could help create and own a completely different asset: a cable network.

By the time Hindery left the Regency, he knew he had landed on his next project. He was going to completely upend and reshape the financial equation of the sports business, all with a little regional sports network that showed some baseball and basketball games. He also knew enough about the history of his business to understand how inevitable the process actually was, a confluence of a series of ideas an Arkansas appliance salesman had come up with some fifty-four years before.

Cable television has no Benjamin Franklin or Thomas Edison. No one knows exactly where it started or who first had the bright idea of capturing and distributing a difficult-to-receive television signal by building a very tall antenna, connecting a coaxial cable to it, then connecting that cable to a television set. The industry does, however, have a pretty sharp appliance store salesman named James Yates Davidson, who figured out that television held the keys to the kingdom of sports roughly forty years before anyone else did.

Davidson, the son of a Little Rock optometrist who managed to secure several radio patents in his spare time, served in the Navy's Signal Corps during World War II, then returned to Arkansas to run the appliance store in Tuckerman. In 1947 he learned that the Memphis radio station, WMC, had received a license to launch one of the first television stations in the South. Since he had served in the Signal Corps, he was smart enough to realize that Tuckerman residents didn't have a prayer of receiving a clear broadcast signal all the way from Memphis with a regular-sized rooftop antenna. Since Davidson wanted to sell television sets in the appliance store, this presented a problem. A television set wouldn't be worth anything if it couldn't receive a decent signal.

So Davidson built a one-hundred-foot antenna on top of a building next to his store. He then strung a cable from that antenna into his store and hooked it up to his television sets. Presto. When WMC began sending signals in the fall of 1948, perfectly clear pictures beaming from one hundred miles away appeared on the sets. Customers thought that was pretty cool, so Davidson ran another cable line from the antenna into the home of a gentleman named Carl Toler, who ran the local telegraph office. He hooked the cable up to Toler's television. Now Toler had a perfectly clear picture in his living room.

All of this caused quite a stir in Tuckerman, where residents flocked both to the Toler house and Davidson's appliance store to see cable television for the first time. They wanted it, too. The problem was how exactly to pay for all of this. Building the antenna, running the cables, and maintaining them required substantial capital expenditures. Davidson scratched out a business plan. He proposed a $150 installation fee and a monthly charge of $3 for maintenance and other expenses. In today's dollars, that calculates to nearly $1,500 for installation and $30 per month for upkeep. He needed to convince the citizens of a small, humble agricultural community in northeast Arkansas that such an investment would be worth their hard-earned money. His solution arrived on November 13, 1948, when Davidson ran a cable from the antenna to the local American Legion Hall for the broadcast of a football game between the University of Tennessee and the University of Mississippi. This was the masterstroke. Everyone wanted in. Before long, Davidson was building antennas and cable systems across Arkansas. Each time he built and sold subscriptions for a new system, he could use the revenue stream to pay for another one.

Davidson's foresight was astonishing. He got the business model right from the start and realized exclusive sports content was the magic bullet for selling it. His formula became the blueprint for building a pay television business. Sports didn't have the largest audiences. They were often a fraction of those for mainstream prime-time entertainment. But the passion sports evoked made the content extremely powerful. Sports could convince consumers they simply could not live without a certain product, whether that might be a color television set or a cable subscription.

In the 1950s, Irving Kahn, the chief executive of the TelePromTer Corporation, the company that produced screens that could scroll written text, wanted to expand into closed circuit television, so he signed a deal with the heavyweight champion Floyd Patterson to gain the television rights to his fights. In 1970, Cablevision founder Charles Dolan was looking to get traction for his fledgling cable television endeavor in Manhattan. Dolan couldn't get his product into more than 20 percent of homes. So he paid Madison Square Garden $24,000 for the rights to broadcast Knicks and Rangers home games and promised to pay for any empty seats the telecasts caused. That same year Ted Turner bought an Atlanta television station that became WTCG for $2.5 million. The investment looked dead in the water until 1973, when Turner gained the broadcast rights first to the Atlanta Braves and later to the Atlanta Hawks (he'd buy both teams eventually) and executed his plan to create a regional sports superstation for the South, which had no pro sports teams outside Atlanta.

In 1975, Jerry Levin was struggling to persuade cable systems to spend $100,000 to build the equipment they would need to receive satellite transmission of programming from a channel named Home Box Office. The cable operators were overrun with debt. The last thing they wanted to do was invest $100,000 in equipment for a premium channel they would then have to sell to subscribers for another $10 per month. So Levin bought the rights to Muhammad Ali and Joe Frazier's "Thrilla in Manila." Then Levin and his partners decided to install the equipment and deliver the signal to a system in Vero Beach, Florida, which had about ten thousand subscribers, a modern infrastructure, and no threats of bad weather that might cause any interference. They installed another link in Mississippi and a third in Atlanta, with plenty of press on hand to watch a signal beamed via satellites, landlines, and microwaves to produce a perfectly clear picture from the other side of the world. Three years later a Connecticut public relations guy named Bill Rasmussen plunked down $30,000 to reserve signal space on an RCA satellite to create a channel that would show lots of sports, especially Hartford Whalers and UConn Huskies games. He and his son argued back and forth about what to call it. Eventually they landed on the Entertainment and Sports Programming Network. We know it as ESPN.

Rasmussen's ESPN launched on September 7, 1979, and immediately began bleeding money. Cable was still a small-time business then, available in maybe 20 percent of US households, or about 15 million homes. Such a small pie meant ratings for any cable program would inevitably be minuscule. The audience certainly wasn't big enough to garner the level of advertising revenue necessary to cover the costs of a network like ESPN, which had to buy the rights to sports programming, then cover the costs of producing it. ESPN's controlling owners, at that time Getty Oil, could have made it a premium channel like HBO, which charged about $10 per month and split the revenues with the cable distributor. There was only one problem: ESPN's programming was anything but premium back then. It was a strange mix of boxing, tennis, and Australian rules football. Still, the network became an odd selling point for cable distributors on the hunt for subscribers. A twenty-four-hour sports channel was simple and appealing to a certain segment of consumers. Once they had it, they didn't want to lose it. Bored teenage boys could while away seventh-grade afternoons watching Australian rules football, and they did.

Bill Grimes, the company's chief executive, and Roger Werner, its chief operating officer, knew this. Grimes came to ESPN after a successful stint running CBS Radio. Werner was a former cable consultant for McKinsey & Company. They often rode the train together from New York to suburban Connecticut. Through those talks they concluded there was only one way for the network to survive. They needed to convince everyone who benefited from the network to take on a part of the responsibility for funding it. If cable distributors were using ESPN to sell subscriptions, then they needed to help pay ESPN's bills instead of the other way around, which is the way the business model essentially worked during the network's first years.

Werner and Grimes decided to start asking cable operators to commit to paying a few cents for each of their subscribers—four cents the first year, then six the next, and then eight, and so on. They worked off the assumption that ESPN would eventually become a successful and expensive channel filled with top-tier live events. At the time it seemed like a very optimistic, even goofy assumption. The network featured the leftover sports that broadcast channels had no interest in. They promised distributors that with time and money that would change, and ESPN would become the go-to place on television for sports. Here was a chance to lock in low rates for a few years, before prices went up.

Their sales campaign did not go well. Most cable distributors told them to get lost. Grimes flew west to see a top executive at United Cable Television. He even had an appointment. The United Cable executive refused to see him. In Denver at John Malone's TCI, they were told they would never receive a penny.

Finally, in late winter of 1981, Grimes and Werner got around to Long Island to try and get on the other side of the bargaining table from Charles Dolan and his deputies at Cablevision. Dolan was known as one of the toughest negotiators in the business. For months Dolan refused to meet with them. Werner met with Dolan's underlings and they all gave him the same message: there is no way Dolan is going to do this deal. Turner and the USA Network got fees, but they had quality programming, Werner was told. ESPN had quantity but little quality.

The deal between ESPN and Cablevision had expired. Grimes and Werner had their attorneys write a letter telling Dolan they planned to cut off the signal if Cablevision didn't agree to begin paying a nominal fee for each subscriber who received the network by Sunday, March 8. Grimes went to the Atlantic Coast Conference basketball tournament that Friday. When he landed in North Carolina he called the office. There was a message from Chuck Dolan asking him not to do anything until Monday, when they could meet at Cablevision headquarters. Grimes agreed.

Monday morning came and the meetings began. There was cursing and screaming and slammed doors, but no one left the table for good. That was a lot better than Grimes and Werner had fared elsewhere. The talks went on through an entire day. As the afternoon dragged on, it became clear that Dolan didn't want to give up ESPN. Dolan understood that sports could sell cable systems. He'd seen this up close twice already in his career, first with his Madison Square Garden investment, and then on Long Island in 1979 when the National Hockey League's Islanders cut a deal with a fledgling cable network called SportsChannel that moved nearly all Islanders home games to cable. There had been no shortage of outrage, but ultimately Long Island's densely packed communities of wealthy suburbanites signed up for cable in droves. Dolan knew his market. They loved sports and would pay for it.

Just before 6:00 p.m. Dolan, Grimes, and Werner reached a

deal. Cablevision agreed to include ESPN in its menu of basic cable channels and pay the network ten cents a month for each of its subscribers, a cost it could easily pass on as part of an annual fee increase. A precedent had been set. Sports cable channels now had something the broadcast channels didn't have: a dual revenue stream, one from advertising and one from subscriber fees. In the course of a day, ESPN and every other network that showed sports or planned to in the coming years became viable businesses. Grimes and Werner left and got into Werner's car. As they turned out of the parking lot a Mexican restaurant appeared. Grimes pointed to it. "We're going to Margaritaville," he said, and they did. ESPN's monthly fee for its suite of channels is now nearly $7 a month, which translates into about $8.4 billion in annual revenue before the network has sold a single Budweiser ad.

The windfall for ESPN and the regional sports networks that began popping up in the 1980s provided capital that was essential for sports. Free agency had come to baseball in 1975. Now it was spreading to basketball, hockey, and the NFL. A freer market was driving up salaries. Team owners needed to find more money. The new riches from cable sports networks desperate to sign up unique, premium programming they could point to when they wanted to raise their monthly bills created the obvious solution. Before long, deals to move top-tier sports from network television to cable began to snowball.

The first stunner arrived in 1987, when the NFL agreed to put eight Sunday night games on ESPN for $153 million over three years. Pete Rozelle had to go after ESPN's money to make up for the drop in rights fees from the broadcast networks. Collectively they had lost about $75 million from the previous deal. Importantly, though, the NFL never sold a playoff game to ESPN or any other cable network, a move that has probably cost the NFL hundreds of millions of dollars in the short term but has paid off in spades. (More on that in a bit.) Two years later, Major League Baseball moved to cable. ESPN agreed to pay $400 million over four years beginning in 1989 for weekly games. Also in 1989, the New York Yankees sold their local broadcast rights—the license to show games within the New York market—for the next twelve years to the Madison Square Garden Network for $500 million. The deal tripled the team's rights fees from what it had been receiving from the local broadcaster WPIX, which had been showing Yankees games for thirty-eight years. Over the next decade, every Major League Baseball team would move the majority of its games to cable. Beginning in 1996, baseball started putting its playoff games on cable.

The NBA and NBC rode Michael Jordan to unprecedented popularity from 1989 to 2002. During that time, NBC paid nearly $3 billion to air NBA basketball. The zenith came on a June night in 1998, when 72 million viewers watched Jordan clinch his sixth championship with a last-minute shot to beat the Utah Jazz. Then, in 2001, with the NBA's $1.6 billion deal with NBC set to expire in twelve months, NBA commissioner David Stern and NBC sports chairman Dick Ebersol took a long walk from Santa Monica to Venice one warm afternoon. Ebersol explained that his company had lost $300 million broadcasting NBA games. It could offer the league the most widely watched platform in the television business at the time, but not the dollars that cable and its dual revenue stream were going to throw at him. Within months Stern opted for two six-year deals with ESPN, ABC, and TNT worth $4.6 billion. That moved the vast majority of playoff games, even the conference finals, to cable television.

To Stern and every other owner of a sports team who moved the bulk of their teams' games to cable, the risk seemed negligible. Sports had helped build the cable industry. The lines between broadcast television and cable television were blurring as the percentage of households in the US with pay television surpassed 80 percent and headed toward 90 percent. Fans had shown this was the sort of entertainment they couldn't live without. They wouldn't dare try to. Would they?

Hindery and the Yankees formally announced the launch of the network they would call YES on September 10, 2001. Steinbrenner and the Nets owners took a 60 percent share of the network and divided that share 60–40. Hindery, Steinbrenner, and Chambers had raised $335 million from Goldman Sachs and Providence Equity Partners, who took a 40 percent stake in the network, which investors valued at $800 million. That provided the money to launch the channel and to cover the rights payments for the first years. It guaranteed that even if the network was a complete flop, the owners of the teams would break even. A $2 per month fee from cable operators projected about $190 million in annual subscriber revenue for YES. The network could likely collect another $25 million or so from advertising.

The next morning two planes flew into the World Trade Center, another crashed into the Pentagon, and a fourth crashed in a field in Pennsylvania. By midmorning, the world had become a completely different place. Baseball screeched to a halt for ten days in the heart of the pennant race. When it returned, the Yankees resumed their steady march toward the playoffs. In the divisional series, they magically came back from a 2–0 deficit against the Oakland A's, thanks in part to Derek Jeter's legendary shovel pass on a misguided throw from the outfield to catcher Jorge Posada that maintained a 1–0 lead in game three. In the American League Championship Series, they steamrolled the Seattle Mariners, who had won a record 116 games during the regular season. That brought the World Series to Yankee Stadium, a mere ten miles from Ground Zero, where the rubble still smoldered. In what was arguably the finest moment of his presidency, George

W. Bush donned a bulletproof vest, warmed up in the bowels of the House That Ruth Built, and fired a hard strike (for a president) over the middle of the plate for the ceremonial first pitch of game three. A crowd of 55,000 roared. A broken, mourning city was alive.

Down to their last out in games four and five, the Yankees got clutch home runs on consecutive nights. They would win those games in extra innings and take a 3–2 lead in the series before running out of magic in the desert in Arizona three nights later. A broken-bat single. A defensive misplay. And the great closer Mariano Rivera had somehow blown a ninth-inning lead in game seven. But the heartbreaking loss was in line with where New York was at that moment: down but never out, and more vital than ever. While those games were on Fox, their impact was felt across the franchise.

This was the hand Hindery played when he went to cable distributors the next winter to ask them to buy into his new network. One by one they all signed on, agreeing to pay roughly $2 per month for each subscriber during the next five years to show the games of the region's most important team. It seemed like the ultimate no-brainer to everyone involved. Well, almost everyone. As expected, Cablevision, led by Jim Dolan, refused, depriving roughly three million households in the New York market the chance to watch the Yankees.

While thousands of fans in Cablevision territory protested, Hindery spent most of the next year—the entire 2002 season—pulling every lever he could try to get the Dolans to relent. He held press conferences and charged them with utter hypocrisy, since the Dolans, who owned the sports cable network MSG, charged other cable operators nearly $2 per month for each subscriber to carry it. MSG had lost the network's highest-rated attraction, the Yankees, to YES, and they didn't feel like propping up their new competitor. Cablevision had about three million subscribers in the New York market, making it the region's biggest distributor, and Dolan really didn't want to have to pay Hindery and YES $6 million a month, a cost he would likely have to pass on to his customers.

Hindery appealed personally to Chuck Dolan, Jim's father and one of the fathers of the cable industry. Hindery had done business with him for fifteen years. Chuck didn't want to get involved. Cablevision was Jim's bailiwick now, he said. Hindery filed an antitrust lawsuit against Cablevision, charging discrimination, since Cablevision was refusing to distribute a network simply because it didn't own it. He lobbied the New Jersey State Assembly to pass a bill aimed at prohibiting a company like Cablevision from giving preferential treatment to its own sports channels to the exclusion of a potential competitor. He appealed to then New York State attorney general Eliot Spitzer and New York City mayor Michael Bloomberg, who pushed the two sides toward mediation and arbitration. Bloomberg even allowed them to negotiate in his Upper East Side mansion, giving them the run of his kitchen, including his chef.

With minutes to spare before the first pitch of the 2003 season, Spitzer went behind a microphone at his office in downtown Manhattan and announced the two sides had reached a deal to put the games on Cablevision immediately and pursue binding arbitration. Dolan barely participated in the arbitration, which took place later that year. He sent Tom Rutledge, his company's chief operating officer, in his stead. Rutledge didn't have much of a hand to play for the three-judge panel led by the retired federal judge Stanley Sporkin. The parameters of the arbitration had been set: the fair market value of Yankees programming in relation to the price that other sports networks and teams were receiving. The Yankees were by far the most popular team in the region. Their channel deserved as much as anyone else's. Rutledge suggested the Yankees might have some down seasons, and then the games wouldn't be worth much. It was a silly argument. By that time in 2004, the team had made the playoffs every year since 1995. The Yankees wouldn't miss the playoffs again until 2008. Sporkin didn't buy it. "He kept looking at Rutledge and saying, 'Come on, it's the Yankees,'" Hindery said.

The judges lowered the monthly fee for 2004 to $1.93 from $2.28, and they retroactively lowered the fee for 2003 from $2.12 to $1.85. The fees would steadily increase during the next five years. But the judges also said Cablevision had to distribute YES to all of its nearly three million subscribers, and the company had to pay YES as if it had done so for 2003 and 2002, since the company had clearly discriminated against a network it didn't own. The decision guaranteed YES nearly $200 million a year in subscriber fees. The network was suddenly worth more than $1 billion, since the market valued networks at roughly ten to fifteen times earnings at that time.

Making YES viable took two and a half years, but Hindery, Steinbrenner, and Chambers created something new and unique: a team-owned regional sports network that unlocked the real value of a sports team in a business increasingly driven by television. The increased television money could help finance the Yankees' massive payroll, but the implications were much larger than that. A guaranteed annual windfall from cable fees made the Yankees an exponentially more valuable franchise than it had ever been. Those fees and the value they produced had been landing largely in the pockets of network owners since the dawn of the modern cable business a quarter century before. Now the teams could capture it by owning their own networks. Finally, Hindery had gotten what he wanted—or at least he thought he had.

A rather predictable thing happened the day after the YES Network became a $1.5 billion asset, something far more valuable than any

US team. Every owner of a major-league sports team in the US read the headlines and thought, *I want one of those, too.*

Who could blame them? Owning a team had plenty of benefits. The losses could be written off. The teams mostly accrued value over time. It was a fun place to park cash. It was just about the only business that produced instant celebrity status within a community. It put an owner in an exclusive club with some of the wealthiest, most powerful businessmen and families in the US: Fords, Rooneys, Tisches, Waltons. Now it had allowed Steinbrenner to morph into a media titan. If he could do it, his fellow owners figured, they could, too.

To Hindery, that idea was absurd. A network for the Yankees was one thing. The Yankees were among the world's iconic sports entities. A few other teams had widespread appeal, especially within their regions, and could probably carry a network. MSG had its network, and the Red Sox owned 80 percent of the New England Sports Network, known as NESN, but those networks had been around for years before their owners acquired them. The idea that any run-of-the-mill franchise would have the nerve to try to launch an independent network built around its games, even if it partnered with another team so it had year-round programming, seemed like the ultimate hubris.

And yet, one by one, they began trying, each of them demanding a price in the neighborhood of what the Yankees had gotten from cable distributors in the New York area. Each of them made the same argument: their teams were vital programming to the community. To not pay them the fees they demanded and put the networks on the expanded basic cable system was to hold a public trust hostage.

During the next eight years, teams launched networks in Texas and Colorado, in Kansas City and Minneapolis. The Mets launched their own network in New York. The expansion NBA team, the

Charlotte Bobcats, launched one in North Carolina. The Washington Nationals, formerly known as the Montreal Expos, launched one in the mid-Atlantic states. The San Diego Padres tried one in San Diego. Several of them sold an equity stake to major cable providers, who in turn agreed to pay to carry the channels on their systems. For the cable providers this was akin to taking money out of one pocket and putting it in another.

The results were mixed: a major success in New York for the Mets, a major failure for the Altitude network in Denver, which was owned by Stan Kroenke, the owner of the Denver Nuggets of the NBA and the Colorado Avalanche of the NHL, and failed to gain widespread distribution. For the networks that failed, their teams had to go crawling back to places like Fox and Comcast, which already owned regional sports networks, and ask for new deals. For the fans, one effect was the same, no matter who owned the channels: someone was getting money from them for something that used to be free, or at least cost a lot less. During the ten years following the arbitrators' decision about the YES Network, the average monthly fees for regional sports networks climbed from a little more than a dollar to nearly $2.50, or about a 150 percent increase in the price of watching local sports, while ESPN's fee skyrocketed to roughly $7 per month for its suite of channels.

The overwhelming majority of cable providers buckled when teams and their fans put public pressure on them to put the networks on their systems, even though only a small fraction of their subscribers actually watched the games. One of the great illusions of the sports industry is mass fascination. Aside from the National Football League and the biggest games of the year in a handful of other sports, such as a World Cup final or Major League Baseball's All-Star Game, the TV audience for sports in the US is tiny, amounting to about 4 percent or less of households on average. Less than 3 percent of households with television in any given market, on average, will tune in to watch their hometown NBA teams play, and less than 2 percent will watch their NHL teams.

Occasionally the cable operators stood their ground and the independent networks failed. That's what happened to the Twins network in Minnesota, the Royals network in Kansas City, the Trailblazers network in Portland, and the Bobcats network in North Carolina. In these cases, the teams weren't very good or weren't particularly enmeshed in the culture of their cities, or both, and fans could easily live without them.

Still, by 2012, that didn't prevent the great sports media train from rolling on. Sports team owners were mostly getting even richer and their teams were becoming more valuable. Dozens of US sports teams not only collected rights fees but also owned a piece of a sports network, just as Steinbrenner had. Thanks largely to ESPN, the leagues were rolling in hundreds of millions of dollars in national television money as well. Meanwhile, the cable companies, which had invested heavily in regional sports networks, thought they had their magic bullet to keep their subscribers and attract new ones. After all, if you didn't subscribe to cable, you couldn't get the local regional sports network and couldn't watch your favorite team. No one had raised much fuss about the fact that even though fewer than 4 percent of subscribers were watching the sports networks on most nights, those networks were eating up nearly 20 percent of the average cable bill, much of it in payments for programming that used to be free. The purpose of a sports team had morphed from an entity that could provide joy and a sense of community to a city or a region to a commodity that could be used to create vast wealth, not merely by asking fans to pay more for tickets, but by charging everyone who paid for television—nearly 90 percent of the populace—a kind of tax on one of their utilities. The tax came in the extra $10 or $20 fans had to pay to watch sports each month. And that was on top of the more than $10 billion in subsidies citizens had to put out for stadium construction. In part, those fees were a natural outcome of the system the players had pushed for, a system that required the transformation of sports from mom-and-pop businesses into billion-dollar enterprises. But part of it was little more than a money grab by the new lords of the realm, driven by the same urges that motivated Wilson Sporting Goods to fool Arnold Palmer into signing an exploitative contract or to try to cheat Catfish Hunter out of his insurance policy. Why did the owners do it? Because they could. The fans would always be there for them.

Yet something else happened during those ten years after the launch of YES. While the sports industry and the cable business hitched their collective wagons to each other, the world changed. No one would have noticed it judging solely by the proliferation of sports coverage on television, in print, or on the Internet. To see the dynamic required a closer examination of how people were actually interacting with sports on television, or whether they wanted to at all.

In 2012, the Los Angeles Lakers, with their partner Time Warner Cable, launched their own regional sports network—actually two of them, one in English and one in Spanish—and decided to charge distributors more than $4 per month to carry the channels. All the major cable distributors in the Los Angeles market grudgingly accepted the terms, except for Dish Network, the satellite distributor, which counted 20 percent of the homes in the region as subscribers. Dish thought it was simply ridiculous to charge subscribers $4 a month for a channel that had worthwhile programming on just seventy-five nights, or about 20 percent of the year. When the season began in the fall, Dish watched closely to see if its decision cost the company subscribers or market share. It didn't. In fact, Dish actually gained subscribers during the next two years when it didn't have the Lakers channel.

In 2013, the Houston Astros partnered with the NBA's Rockets and Comcast to launch Comcast SportsNet (CSN) Houston. CSN Houston told distributors they would need to pay $3.40 each month per subscriber to carry the channel. Fox Sports Southwest had previously televised both teams' games, charging distributors about $2.50 for a channel that showed those games, as well as Texas Rangers baseball, Dallas Mavericks and San Antonio Spurs basketball, FC Dallas soccer, plus some regional college football. At the time, the Houston Astros were inarguably the worst team in Major League Baseball. By their own admission they were several years away from competing. From 2011 to 2013, the Astros lost 324 games. That's fifteen more games than the Yankees lost during the five seasons from 1998 to 2002. The Rockets, meanwhile, were wrapping up a season in which they finished a middling 45-37. Not bad, but hardly a team whose games can't be missed.

Every distributor but Comcast, an owner of the network, passed. Armed with data from state-of-the-art cable boxes, distributors knew how many games each subscriber watched, for how long, and whether they tuned in only for key games. The numbers were ugly. So was this one: only about a fifth of new households in 2012 even bothered to order cable. Until that level rose, whatever pressure the teams tried to bring to bear on the pay-television distributors through advertising or petitions could be ignored with near impunity, even in the tenth-largest television market in the country.

In 2014, the Los Angeles Dodgers, with Time Warner Cable as a partner, launched another regional sports network, an all-Dodgers-all-the-time venture the team and its partners declared fans absolutely needed. The price was more than $4 per month per subscriber in the first year with locked-in increases that would quickly send it above $5 a month. Just three years before, all Dodgers and Lakers games could be seen on free television or on Prime Ticket and a sister cable channel that also showed Los Angeles Angels, Clippers, and Kings games. It cost distributors about $2.50 a month. Now, including ESPN, Los Angeles fans (and non-fans) were looking at charges approaching $25 a month to watch sports.

Taking all this in from 2,500 miles away in New York, Leo Hindery could only shake his head. "You can try, but you can't abuse viewers in such an amazing way," he said.

Shifting the vast majority of sports to cable has made a fortune for team owners and players, who are guaranteed a share of league revenues in the NFL, the NBA, and the NHL. Major League Baseball is now an $8 billion business. The NBA isn't far behind. But that doesn't mean there haven't been costs to the money grab, especially for baseball and basketball. For all their popularity, they aren't creating enough new fans to replace the ones they are losing. Their cultural relevance started shrinking around the time the leagues began their stampede to cable in the 1990s, and the downward slide shows no sign of slowing.

Baseball celebrated in 2013 when an average of 15 million people watched the Boston Red Sox beat the St. Louis Cardinals in the World Series. But that's about two-thirds of the audience that tuned in in 1993 and half the number that watched in 1990, which was a four-game sweep by the Cincinnati Reds. In 2014, 13.8 million watched the San Francisco Giants' seven-game thriller over the Kansas City Royals. The next year, 900,000 more people tuned in on average, largely because New York had its Mets to watch. Since the NBA shifted the vast majority of its playoff games to cable, the biggest audience that has tuned in to an NBA Finals game was 28.2 million, but less than half that usually tunes in for the biggest games of the year. The LeBron James/Cleveland Cavaliers–Golden State Warriors 2015 finals were a hit, but nothing approaching what the audiences once were.

The most alarming numbers were the ones that showed the extent to which the next generation of sports fans was dwindling. Baseball fans were suddenly getting much older. The average viewer of postseason baseball in 2009 was 49.9 years old. In 2014 that viewer was 55. The average viewer of a regular season game in

2014 was 58. Kids under 18 were representing a smaller and smaller percentage of the audiences for the NBA and NHL playoffs as well.

The lords of sport attribute these declines to the fragmenting TV audience. It's true that many kids don't bother with television but engage with sports through tablets and smartphones. Yet participation rates are also continuing to decline, especially among casual players. Little League Baseball, which represented about two-thirds of the world's youth baseball, had 2.1 million players in 2012 compared with 2.6 million in 1997. Executives know that if kids attend games, stay up late to catch the last out of the World Series, and play baseball, they are much more likely to follow the game as adults and pass the habit on to their children. Fewer and fewer of them are following that scenario.

There is a fairly obvious pattern here. After the vast majority of the teams and leagues moved their most important games to pay television, audience sizes overall dropped. The decreases were most pronounced among young viewers. As those kids grew older, many of them seemed to decide sports weren't important enough to justify a $100-a-month cable bill.

There is one major US sports league that continued to put nearly all of its regular season games and all of its playoff games on network television. Of the 256 NFL games played each season, only 16 could be seen solely on cable channels. The rest were on the easiest-to-find, most available network channels on the dial. What were the results? The NFL was eons more popular than any other sport. The national telecasts of its games often averaged roughly 20 million viewers. The Super Bowl audience was roughly 100 million. NFL games usually account for twenty-nine of the top thirty shows on television each year. Usually, only the Oscars break the league's stranglehold on the top thirty.

Money in sports isn't, on its own, a bad thing. But when money becomes the motivating goal and main purpose in sports, that *is* a bad thing. It's bad for a player whose sneaker contract is more important than his team's win total, and it's bad for an owner or a league whose teams become little more than a commodity to be traded for a big-pay television contract. For fifty years television has been the golden goose for sports. It still is, but television was once used to expose the maximum number of casual fans to the best and biggest games to bring new fans into the fold. Then television kept those fans by letting them see most of the rest of the games without trying to take too much money out of their pockets. During the first years of the twenty-first century the sports television business began making people angry, and the lords of the realm everywhere except the NFL appeared to be cooking their own goose.

We've seen this type of behavior before. We know the tragic flaws among athletes are to overvalue their own identities compared with those of their teammates, or to cash in on their fame before their talents justify it, or to believe the legends their various handlers, enablers, and corporate sponsors create for them. The great flaw of team owners and nearly everyone else in a position of power in sports is to view everyone who is below them on the food chain as an entity that can be exploited. First, leagues and owners and tournament executives and federation chiefs overplayed their hand and tried to strong-arm the players into continuing what was ostensibly indentured servitude. After the players revolted, the object of their disrespect became the fans, the people they seem to believe have no other choice but to accede to their demands.

These fans, who have sustained the industry for a century and a half, don't want much—just the ability to enjoy the games they love and the athletes they admire without getting ripped off, lied to, or insulted, by either the athletes who play sports or the people who run them. It doesn't seem like a lot to ask. A fan's love of sports is a precious and unique thing. It isn't something to be trifled with, or used as a tool to prop up an overpriced media venture, or manipulated to sell a yellow rubber bracelet emblazoned with the lie "Livestrong." Fans don't like owners who try to fool them any more than they like athletes who do. The sports industry has never had to do that, and anytime the people who run it think about trying to pull another one over on a pretty sophisticated collection of consumers, they ought to run like hell in the other direction. We'll all be better off for it.

Epilogue

Glasgow. July 25, 2012. Just before 8:00 a.m.

A very good soccer player named Carli Lloyd walks into a gym in the basement of a hotel on the banks of the River Clyde.

The athletic competitions of the London Olympics will begin in a matter of hours, not with the big parade of athletes and the lighting of a grand torch—that won't happen for another two days—but with women's soccer. The US and France are on the schedule, a showdown between the world's most powerful team and its most technically skilled and sophisticated one. The US women are the sport's royalty, the two-time defending Olympic champions, a collection of athletes no nation can hope to match. The French, almost overnight, have become the envy of the world for the way they slide the ball across the field, connecting the perfectly played, bending ball with the perfectly timed diagonal run into space. Their coach, Bruno Bini, could blend with ease into the crowd at an avant-garde

Parisian café. He reads poetry to his players before games. His star striker, Gaëtane Thiney, can dance on a ball and dribble it through a crowd as though it is glued to her foot.

The US women have been waiting for this game and the start of this tournament for more than a year, since they somehow let a one-goal lead slip away with seconds to go in the World Cup final against Japan. Then came the most disastrous shoot-out in the history of a team that so often dominates when the pressure is highest. Lloyd, a midfielder who strikes the ball as well as any woman ever has, hit her shot so high it sailed deep into the crowd at Commerzbank-Arena in Frankfurt. It might have been the worst penalty shot Lloyd has taken since she was a child darting across fields in southern New Jersey.

More than a year has passed since that shot, and she hasn't recovered from it. She has basically stunk ever since. Her passes regularly miss her teammates. Long a pillar of boundless endurance and focus, she has of late disappeared in the middle of games, moving lethargically across the grass. Now she has been benched. She is a sturdy five feet eight inches and 140 pounds of muscle that no woman wants to battle with for a 50-50 ball in the middle of the field. She has crazy big brown eyes that are either sweet or fierce, depending on her mood. She scored the gold medal–winning goal against Brazil in Beijing in 2008. She has started nearly every big game for this team over the past six years. That is about to end.

Lloyd has come to the gym alone, and she heads over to a treadmill in the back corner. Headphones in her ears, she fiddles with her iPhone, searching for the right song. Another gym rat approaches. "You know you've got a game this afternoon, so you might not want to wear yourself out," he says.

"Yeah, like I'm gonna run a freaking marathon," she barks. She has just turned thirty but remains a girl with a chip on her shoulder from Jersey, where conversation is a form of combat, and she is always looking for an edge.

He laughs, asks her how she's feeling.

"I feel good," she says.

He asks if she is ready.

"Yeah," she says, "we're ready," and for a moment appears to be rolling her eyes.

He wishes her luck. She thanks him and hits the up arrow on the treadmill. She is on the move.

Five hours later she jogs onto the field for warm-ups at a strangely sun-splashed Hampden Park, Scotland's national stadium. Her teammates go through their usual routine of passing and shooting drills. She joins them for a few minutes, playing a game of keepaway, firing a few shots on net. Then she takes a ball and heads to the middle of the field alone. Her head down, she begins to juggle the ball with only her feet, keeping it airborne just above her laces, tap-tap-tap-tap-tap, up-up-up-up-up, with only the slightest effort for minutes on end. She thinks of everything that has happened since that penalty kick in the World Cup final, how she really has stunk, how her coach has just told her she will not start this game. She has lost everything she worked so hard for, everything she gave up boyfriends and a normal existence to experience. She is in the middle of a massive stadium with teammates all around. She is alone.

The whistle blows to start the match. She is on the bench. She watches her teammates fall behind by a goal in the first twelve minutes, and by two just minutes after that. For Carli Lloyd it is awful. It is awful to watch.

Then, in an instant, she no longer has to. Shannon Boxx, a defensive midfielder, injures her hamstring a dozen minutes in and struggles to run. Head coach Pia Sundhage calls Lloyd's name, then tells her to report to the sideline official and take out Boxx. A minute ago Carli Lloyd was dead. Suddenly she is alive. Then Lloyd begins to do what she hasn't done in a year. She controls the middle of the field. She sends perfect balls out to the wings, setting up a

US attack that cuts the score in half in the nineteenth minute, then ties up the match just after the half-hour mark. In the fifty-sixth minute, Lloyd collects a pass twenty-five yards from the French goal, takes a touch to her right into space, and rockets a shot into the left corner of the net. She turns, arms raised, and sprints to the bench, sliding across the slick grass on her knees when she gets close. At this moment, it feels like nothing can get better than this.

Only it does. Lloyd won't see the bench for the rest of the Olympics. There is a last-minute comeback win in the semifinal against Canada at Old Trafford, then the gold medal game, when Lloyd scores both goals for the US in a 2–1 win over Japan that goes a long way toward washing away the memory of the World Cup final of a year ago. It also makes Lloyd the first player to score the gold medal–winning goal in two consecutive Olympic tournaments.

"I think I just come up big in big moments," Lloyd said when it was over. She talked about working her butt off every day, all day, to prove wrong everyone who thought she didn't belong on the field. "I was on a mission."

Three years later, Lloyd was at it again. Instead of basking in Olympic glory, she heeded the words of her trainer and soccer whisperer back home in southern New Jersey, James Galanis, who told her she had become about 50 percent of the player she could be.

Six weeks before the 2015 Women's World Cup, Lloyd arrives at a town-owned gym in southern New Jersey, about a fifteen-minute drive from her home, just after 9:00 a.m. The building is a cinder block and steel structure with three basketball courts, devoid of modern accessories like machines to measure things like VO_2 max levels. Galanis and Lloyd work through a series of drills aimed at belatedly developing all the skills and creativity that come naturally to players who grow up playing pickup games all afternoon in Europe and Latin America. Even mediocre athletes in Brazil can play beach volleyball using only their feet. By contrast, children in the US rarely play soccer outside of a rigid, organized practice session. That leaves only one way to catch up as an adult—a seemingly endless series of repetitive drills that only increase in intensity with the World Cup a month away.

Like an eighth-grader at travel-soccer practice, Lloyd sprints up the gym floor dribbling only with her right foot, first the outside, then the inside. Then she does the same with her left. On one series, she fakes a kick before each touch, making sure to raise one arm in the exact motion. On another she dips her inside shoulder each time to accent a feint. She whacks the ball off the cinder block wall fifteen feet away, cradling the ricochets with her ankle the way a shortstop uses a glove to field a grounder. She takes a series of hard passes from Galanis at midcourt, turns with the ball, and sprints away with it. Then she pounds it against a wall, traps the rebound, and passes it back to Galanis, over and over. After a few minutes of one-touch, she hits a series of chips to Galanis, chasing the perfect arc. On and on it goes, basic drills that wouldn't seem necessary for the top midfielder on the world's top team. Forty-five minutes of strength training using tension cords are next. At night she will meet Galanis at a nearby track for ninety minutes of endurance training, everything from a series of fifty-yard sprints to three-mile tempo runs.

Two months later, on an early July afternoon in Vancouver, Lloyd becomes the first player to score a hat trick in a World Cup final, a performance that includes a fifty-five-yard wonder-strike from midfield. The US wins, 5–2, and America once again falls in love with its women's national soccer team.

It's become almost routine by now. A series of nail-biting wins from this group in the Olympics or the World Cup, and overnight a collection of women who are largely unknown every other week of the year are suddenly America's favorite athletes, making the rounds on the talks shows, selling out victory tours, getting accolades from and posing for pictures with the occupants of the White House.

They are not a perfect team, nor are they perfect people. It took a miracle goal in the waning moments against Brazil in the World Cup quarterfinal in 2011. They finished an ugly seventh at a tournament in 2014 and got their coach fired. Goalkeeper Hope Solo's personal life was a tabloid-worthy mess filled with combustible relationships. Yet they may very well be America's favorite team, perhaps because, in their own way, they remind us what sports were like before they seemed like they were all about money, media content, and automaton-like, specialized training. Many of the players owe their spots on the national team to an odd constellation of fortuitous circumstances and great performances when the right people happened to be watching.

I have spent the past fifteen years covering nearly every facet of the sports world. I have covered World Series and Super Bowls, Olympics and World Cups, the Masters and the US Open (both golf and tennis), interviewed modern legends like LeBron James and Masters of the Universe like Red Sox and Liverpool owner John Henry. Through all this, the US Women's National Soccer Team has always been my favorite, because it often seems to have so little connection to the modern sports economy. When I first began working on this book, I was stunned at how lowbrow the sports world was just a few decades ago. FIFA, world soccer's governing body and the owners of the World Cup, was run by a dozen people out of a house in Switzerland. Times change . . . for some. These women are Arnold Palmer grinding his own golf clubs in his Pennsylvania workshop. In 2015, when Meghan Klingenberg and Morgan Brian helped the team capture its third world championship, they were living with former NBA coach and television analyst Jeff Van Gundy in Houston. The arrangement wasn't about getting extra motivational tips. It came about because Klingenberg and Brian were earning about $30,000 to play for the Houston Dash of the National Women's Soccer League. The team asked local families if they could put up some of the players during the season to help make ends meet. The Van Gundys volunteered.

For Christie Rampone, soccer was a second sport until her senior year at Monmouth University, where she starred in basketball. But on a day when Monmouth happened to play a soccer match in the fall of 1997 against Central Connecticut State, Tony DiCicco, then the US head coach, happened to be in the stands. He'd driven down from his home in Massachusetts to see a buddy who coached at Central Connecticut. He had no idea who Rampone was, but then the girl from Point Pleasant who could run like a deer scored on consecutive breakaways. A few weeks later the Monmouth athletic department received a fax asking Rampone, the captain of the *basketball* team, to try out for the national *soccer* team at a camp in California. Rampone had heard of the star Mia Hamm but she couldn't name another national team player.

Rampone went to California. She was so clueless about what the camp might entail, she brought an entire suitcase filled with training gear and laundry detergent, not realizing she was going to be handed US Soccer clothes and cleats upon arrival. She'd never seen fields so lush. She hid her extra suitcase, the one with the training gear and the detergent, under her bed, pretending to have known the whole time she wouldn't have to worry about washing her clothes. She stayed for a week and was thoroughly outclassed, then returned home to wait for the phone to ring. Back at Monmouth she barely left her room, fearing she might miss the call. Finally it came. Other than the time required for her two pregnancies and surgery to repair a torn ACL, she has been on the team ever since. At forty, she still anchored the defense and was among the fastest players on the squad.

Midfielder Heather O'Reilly had her breakout game in a regional competition between the best under-sixteen girls from New Jersey against those from Virginia. O'Reilly was fifteen years old and knew next to nothing about strategy. She couldn't really kick the ball with her left foot, but she could beat anyone on the wing and get the ball in the back of the net. Down 2–0 midway through the game, she had the second half of her life and scored three times. US coach April Heinrichs was in the stands. Heinrichs told her to keep working hard and she'd land on the national team one day. The next year O'Reilly was touring the University of North Carolina, the mecca of college women's soccer and winners of sixteen national championships from 1982 to 2000. As she chatted with head coach Anson Dorrance, O'Reilly noticed space was getting tight for national championship banners. *Hey, Coach,* O'Reilly said to Dorrance, *if I come here, you're going to have to create space for four more banners.* "I was a bit of a dreamer," O'Reilly admitted later.

Soccer isn't their country's game. They lack the instinctiveness of the Germans, the technical skills of the Japanese, the artistry of the Brazilians. They learn the nuances of the game grudgingly, knowing that ultimately their speed, their strength, their athleticism, and their unshakable belief that they will prevail will see them through. More often than not, it does.

They make no claims on purity. They play for money and are proud of it. The team nearly went on strike ahead of the 1996 Olympics because they weren't receiving pay on par with the US men. The US Soccer Federation relented. The team rewarded the federation with a gold medal.

Offer them a hair care commercial or a few thousand bucks to show up at a clinic and they will jump at the chance. They are professionals, after all, with rent to pay and families to support, and they are the best in the world at what they do and deserve to be treated as such. Still, plenty of them show up at plenty of clinics every year for free because they feel a collective responsibility to grow their game and women's sports as a whole, to leave the existence of women's professional soccer in better condition than when they found it. Judging by the rosy-cheeked tweens and teens (and their parents) who swarm them after every match, they seem to be accomplishing their goal. At the end of the day, with their ponytails and headbands fashioned from athletic pre-wrap, they bear a striking resemblance to the daughters and sisters and friends that millions of people watch on park fields every weekend in America.

"People relate to us," Rampone said one afternoon on the Jersey Shore in 2013, when she was still figuring out whether she had another World Cup in her legs. (She did.) "They feel like they really know us. We're normal people, and they get that we started where they are. We fly in coach like everyone else. There's a realness to us and they want to see what we can do. In basketball you have to have the height and the size. Soccer is this game for normal-sized people. If you have some athletic talent there is no limit to what you can do."

That's about all we want from sports, isn't it? To believe that the people we are watching aren't all that different than we are, that they actually eat and breathe and care about what they are doing in the same way we do, even if it is their livelihood, and even if it is so much more commercialized, and so much more a business, than any of us imagined it would become. To be fair, the US women's soccer team does have certain advantages when it comes to winning our hearts. The kind of innocence and humility they exemplify is irresistible. As a professional endeavor, their sport is young; really, all women's sports are. They are so young that most aren't sustainable as stand-alone businesses. Women's pro soccer is propped up with funding from the US Soccer Federation. Two professional women's leagues in the US failed between 2001 and 2012. A third launched in 2013. Its existence figures to be tenuous for the foreseeable future. The players really are like the rest of us, whether they like it or not, although most of them seem to.

There are, of course, a handful of female athletes who star in individual sports, especially golf and tennis, and have amassed vast fortunes, both on the field of competition and off. They owe a heartfelt thank-you to the Hall of Fame tennis star Billie Jean King, who built the women's tennis tour in the 1970s and proved to the world that a viable business could be built around watching women battle and sweat. She deserves an entire volume to be written about her rather than a mention in the final pages of this book. I've had the pleasure of speaking with BJK on several occasions. She has a habit of coming up with those wise comments that remind you that she is and always has been a step or two ahead of the curve. In 2010, we sat together in Washington, DC, at a match of World Team Tennis, the coed pro league she started nearly forty years earlier. The outcome was going to be decided in the last game. The crowd and the players on each team were exploding and high-fiving each other after every point. "You see what we're trying to pull off here?" she said. "Men, women, playing together on the same team, pulling for each other. Pretty cool, right?" It was cool—very.

It's entirely possible that the women of the US national soccer team care so deeply about growing their game because they have to. If they don't, they will be unemployed. Perhaps if they didn't have to make all those appearances at clinics and stay late after matches to sign all those autographs, they wouldn't. Maybe if they could fly first class, or if their international matches and league games became high-value content that media companies could use to peddle cable subscriptions, they might fall victim to the same vanities that some of the stars in the most successful men's sports and the people who run them do. We don't know that yet. With any luck, for their sake, before too long we'll have the chance to find out. All we know is that when these women take the stage, we can't stop watching, nor should we.

Within that dynamic are so many lessons for a sports world that becomes more obsessed with financial scorekeeping every year. The lessons aren't complicated. Most are so simple, they are almost cliché: be genuine. Be a good teammate. Don't act like a jerk. Lead and manage the way you would want to be managed, with fairness and respect. Celebrate the joy of shooting and the glory it brings, but remember that someone passed you the ball or taught you how to shoot, so share credit and the financial windfalls that success breeds with everyone who deserves it. Even in individual sports, it takes a team to win a championship. Following those credos doesn't keep any of the people who make a living in sports—athletes, owners, federations, media executives—from having a chance to make a pile of money.

Most of us are even happy to cheer for them when they do.

Acknowledgments

I once heard a woman describe the man who eventually became her husband like this: "When I met him, he was at least a $100,000 renovation."

The same can be said of my attempts to make a career as a writer. Against all better judgment, a very large group of people put their faith in me over the years and have made both this book and my professional life possible.

Foremost in that group is my wife, the brilliant and beautiful Amy Einhorn. Amy met me when I was a twenty-three-year-old editorial assistant working in a neighboring cubicle. She put up with my nagging attempts at conversation for reasons I still don't quite understand. Three children and more than two decades later, I still work in a cubicle. She has a large, bright office, and she took apart the roughest draft of *Players* and put it back together again. This book is dedicated to her because she has made everything possible.

The brain trust of the *Wall Street Journal*, notably Robert

Thomson, Gerry Baker, and Mike Miller, gave me the green light to pursue this project, and I am forever grateful to them for that and for the trust they have put in me to represent the world's most trusted news organization. Sam Walker, the *Journal*'s mad genius of a sports editor, has given me every opportunity I could ask for, taught me endless lessons about writing, and helped guide this book from the start through crossing the finish line. Several other *Journal* editors, including Eben Shapiro and Rich Turner, have also been vital.

I got my first lessons in how to be a respectable and decent sportswriter at the *Star-Ledger*, the great New Jersey daily. Jim Willse, Kevin Whitmer, Chris D'Amico, George Jordan, and Kevin Shinkle all guided my career for the better part of eleven years when it needed daily—if not hourly—guidance.

The good fortune of my life began at childbirth, when I was lucky enough to be born to Stanley and Linda Futterman. They filled their house with books and told their children to pursue their dreams. Their support is unending. My brothers, David and Daniel, made fun of me for a long time (and still often do), but I would not trade them for anyone.

Jofie Ferrari-Adler, my editor at Simon & Schuster, bought into a vague concept in 2012 when he acquired a project then called "Untitled on Sports by Matthew Futterman." It was quite a roll of the dice. I hope he feels it paid off. I certainly do, largely because of Jofie's never-ending support and Zen-like ability to fix entire chapters with a single sentence of sage advice. I am also grateful for the support from the rest of the team at S&S, including Jon Karp, Richard Rhorer, Cary Goldstein, Stephen Bedford, Benjamin Holmes, Leah Johanson, Jackie Seow, and Julianna Haubner.

Suzanne Gluck, my agent at WME Entertainment, has stuck with me through lows and highs. She is wise and honest, and, most important, charming company. Cara Stein was once also an agent at WME, but for me she is more of a life guru, and she came up with the title for this book. My friends Steve Warner and Barry Rosenfeld read early drafts and helped immensely with their refinement.

David Carter, director of the sports program at the University of Southern California's Marshall School of Business, has long been a guidepost in the industry. He read an earlier version of *Players* and provided essential criticism. Jean Morrissey did a brilliant job of fact-checking, allowing me to rediscover restful sleep. Kirsten Kay, chief archivist of Mark McCormack's papers at the University of Massachusetts, was endlessly patient and facilitated much of the research for the first third of the book. Todd McCormack offered invaluable help. Jim Gallagher vouched for me early and often. Steve Horowitz seemingly knows everyone in the sports business and has provided an introduction to countless people over the years.

I would also like to thank a long list of teachers who taught me to love reading and writing a long time ago and to aspire to do both well. They include Kay Kobbe, the late Barbara Brownell, Allen Falber, Rose Scotch, Michael DiGennaro, Brenda Wineapple, Jordan Smith, and Skip Hays.

To my children, Ashley, Tess, and Jolie, I am sorry my work takes me away from you so often and for such long stretches. Thanks for putting up with it, and for making coming home from the road such a joy. You are all that matters.

Source Notes

The blessing and the curse of writing about sports is the terrific work that so many have done long before I embarked on this project. It is a blessing because it makes research far easier, and it is a curse because the challenge of producing something original that can measure up to such high standards is incredibly daunting. Scores of interviews form the foundation of this book. I conducted many during the time I was actively working on it, but a lot of those discussions have taken place during my sixteen-year career as a sportswriter, first at the *Star-Ledger* of New Jersey and since 2008 at the *Wall Street Journal*. However, I am deeply indebted to a number of other writers whose valuable work contributed to my knowledge and understanding of the evolution of modern sport. Works that provided direct information that appears in this book are listed below.

CHAPTERS 1–3

I relied heavily on *Arnie: The Evolution of a Legend* by Mark H. McCormack (New York: Simon & Schuster, 1967), which was in fact written by Dan Jenkins and edited by Ray Cave. Both men were generous enough to share their rich experiences of working with McCormack in the 1960s. *The Match: The Day the Game of Golf Changed Forever* by Mark Frost (New York: Hyperion, 2007) is an exemplary work about the transformation of professional golf in the 1950s that proved very helpful.

The McCormack archive at the University of Massachusetts, under the direction of the irreplaceable Kirstin Kay, includes roughly five million documents from McCormack's forty-five-year career. Kay helped recover numerous fascinating documents about McCormack's business affairs, including the transcript of an interview with the documentarian Stewart Binns, as well as scores of correspondence that McCormack collected over the years. The archive includes thousands of boxes of documents, which provide insight into McCormack's mind at work, especially in the early years when even he didn't really know what he was creating. Those documents are the backbone of the first three chapters of this book.

Sports Illustrated is an invaluable asset that I have been reading weekly since I was eight years old. The magazine covered Palmer exhaustively, including "The Battle for the Amateur" in September 1954, and a 1960 feature on Palmer's string of tournament wins ahead of the Masters. It also served as an excellent resource for the Superteams competition in Hawaii in 1975. That competition would never have occurred had it not been for David Martin's story in *Life* magazine in June 1969 on Edward Villella. The Harvard Business School produced a case study on IMG in 2001. Material from that study by Bharat Anand and Kate Attea appears in this book.

CHAPTER 4

There is no better tennis book than the 1971 treatise *The Education of a Tennis Player* by Rod Laver with Bud Collins (New York: New Chapter Press, 2010). Collins was also helpful in sharing his

near-encyclopedic knowledge of pro tennis. Additional information and insight have been culled from John McPhee's *Levels of the
Game* (New York: Farrar, Straus and Giroux, 1969), another brilliant
tennis meditation; Michael MacCambridge's *Lamar Hunt: A Life in
Sports* (Kansas City, MO: Andrews McMeel, 2012); and Jimmy Connors's *The Outsider: A Memoir* (New York: HarperCollins, 2013).

CHAPTER 5

Charles P. Korr wrote the definitive history of the Major League Baseball Players Association, *The End of Baseball as We Knew It: The Players Union, 1960–81* (Champaign: University of Illinois Press, 2012).
Korr's insights, his research, and his personal support and friendship
helped this chapter immeasurably. John Thorn's *Baseball in the Garden of Eden: The Secret History of the Early Game* (New York: Simon &
Schuster, 2011) was also helpful, as was his patience during countless
interviews. Marty Appel is the preeminent resource on the New York
Yankees in the Steinbrenner era. His *Pinstripe Empire: The New York
Yankees from Before the Babe to After the Boss* (New York: Bloomsbury,
2012) served as a reference, as did *Catfish: My Life in Baseball* by Jim
"Catfish" Hunter with Armen Keteyian (New York: Berkley, 1989).

The MLBPA provided me with a series of interviews it taped
with Marvin Miller in his final years. Michael Weiner, may he rest
in peace, was a guidepost. I can't remember life before the advent
of Baseball-Reference.com, nor do I want to. (There was a great
book called *The Baseball Encyclopedia*. It was heavy and expensive and didn't update after every game the way Baseball-Reference
.com magically does.)

CHAPTER 6

This chapter is largely the product of extensive interviews with all
the principals, including Nick Bollettieri, Brian Gottfried, Jimmy

Arias, and Monica Seles. There are several key details about Sandy Koufax, including that he attended college classes the night the Brooklyn Dodgers won the World Series in 1955. Many of them come from Jane Leavy's *Sandy Koufax: A Lefty's Legacy* (New York: HarperPerennial, 2010).

CHAPTER 7

I defy anyone to write about the Olympics without David Wallechinsky and Jaime Loucky's *Complete Book of the Olympics: 2012 Edition* (London: Aurum Press, 2012) and the database that Dr. Bill Mallon, an orthopedic surgeon in North Carolina, keeps on his computer in North Carolina. They are the authorities on all things Olympic, and their work was a tent pole for this chapter. Edwin Moses, an amazing and humble person, is one of the most overlooked legends of American sport. I am immensely appreciative for the time he gave me.

CHAPTER 8

The Game That Was: The Early Days of Pro Football by Myron Cope (New York: World, 1970) served as an outstanding reference for the early years of the NFL. *Finding the Winning Edge* by Bill Walsh, Brian Billick, and James Peterson (Champaign, IL: Sports Publishing, 1997) is the ultimate guidebook to management, coaching, Bill Walsh's mind, and the transformation of pro football from a running game to a passing game. Discussions with Brian Billick helped, too. Several details of the 1978 Bluebonnet Bowl appeared in *Stanford* magazine's coverage of the game. (I was nine years old at the time and somehow missed that one.) *Those Guys Have All the Fun: Inside the World of ESPN* by James Andrew Miller and Tom Shales (New York: Back Bay, 2011) was a valuable resource that provided details both in this chapter and chapter 10.

CHAPTER 9

During a lengthy interview, Bill Bradley suggested I read his *Life on the Run* (New York: Vintage, 1995). I did. It is an extraordinary work, and several details about life in the NBA in the 1970s that appear in that book are also in this one. John McPhee's *A Sense of Where You Are* (New York: Farrar, Straus and Giroux, 1999) is an amazing portrait of Bradley's senior year at Princeton, and I relied on it. *Wheelmen: Lance Armstrong, the Tour de France and the Greatest Sports Conspiracy Ever* by my colleagues Reed Albergotti and Vanessa O'Connell (New York: Dutton, 2013) is the definitive work on the corruption of the modern celebrity athlete. *Just Do It: The Nike Spirit in the Corporate World* by Donald Katz (New York: Random House, 1994) is the closest anyone will get to understanding the mind of Nike founder Phil Knight. Knight doesn't grant interviews much, so Katz's work and the thoughts Knight shared with the *Harvard Business Review* in 1992 were what I worked with. *Playing for Keeps: Michael Jordan and the World He Made* by David Halberstam (New York: Broadway, 2000) served as an excellent resource. And, thankfully, Sonny Vaccaro loves to talk.

CHAPTER 10

Distant Signals: How Cable TV Changed the World of Telecommunications by Thomas P. Southwick (Overland Park, KS: Primedia, 1999) is the best resource out there about the evolution of cable television and its takeover of the US media industry. There may be no better portrait of a company from birth to middle age than *Those Guys Have All the Fun: Inside the World of ESPN* by James Andrew Miller and Tom Shales (New York: Back Bay, 2011). It is an invaluable reference for details about the so-called Worldwide Leader in Sports. People like me will be pulling information from it for decades. Leo Hindery has long been a remarkable resource on the past, present, and weirdly, the future.

Index

About the Author

Matthew Futterman is a senior special writer for sports with the *Wall Street Journal*. He has previously worked for the *Philadelphia Inquirer* and the *Star-Ledger* of New Jersey, where he was part of the team that won the Pulitzer Prize for Breaking News Reporting in 2005. He is married to the book publisher Amy Einhorn. They have three daughters and live on Manhattan's Upper West Side. He grew up in Larchmont, New York, attended Mamaroneck High School, Union College, the University of Arkansas, and Columbia University's Graduate School of Journalism. Like a lot of sportswriters, he is something of a frustrated athlete and is still trying to figure out how he went 0-8 in singles during his senior season on the Union College tennis team. He runs marathons in his spare time. He is not sure why.